Nordic Criminal Justice in a Global Context

This book critically investigates Nordic criminal justice as a global role model.

Not taking this role for granted, the chapters of the book analyze how Nordic approaches to criminal justice were folded into global contexts, and how patterns of promotion were built around perceptions that these approaches also had a particular value for other criminal justice systems. Specific actors, both internal and external to the region itself, have branded Nordic criminal justice as a form of 'penal exceptionalism' associated with human rights, universalistic welfare, and social cohesion. The book shows how building and using the brand of Nordic criminal justice allowed stakeholders to champion specific forms of crime control across a variety of criminal justice areas in both domestic and international settings.

The book will be of interest to scholars and students of criminal justice, international law and justice, Nordic and Scandinavian studies, and more widely to the social sciences and humanities.

Mikkel Jarle Christensen is Professor with special responsibilities at iCourts, Faculty of Law, University of Copenhagen, Denmark.

Kjersti Lohne is Professor of Criminology at the Department of Criminology and Sociology of Law at the University of Oslo, Norway.

Magnus Hörnqvist is Professor of Criminology in the Department of Criminology at Stockholm University, Sweden.

Nordic Studies in a Global Context

This new book series aims to open up more empirical, critical and reflective perspectives on the Nordic cultures, institutions, legal frameworks and "models" in a global and comparative context and to create a bridge between humanistic Nordic studies and the comparative and IR-oriented social sciences and law programmes. It looks to encourage methodologically driven and critical reflection on the nature, construction and use of Nordic traditions, models, institutions, laws, discourses and images. The series welcomes submissions from a broad range of disciplines across the social sciences, law and humanities.
Series editors: Haldor Byrkjeflot, University of Oslo, Norway; Eirinn Larsen, University of Oslo, Norway; and Cathie Jo Martin, Boston University, USA

The Making and Circulation of Nordic Models, Ideas and Images
Edited by Haldor Byrkjeflot, Lars Mjøset, Mads Mordhorst and Klaus Petersen

Nordic Criminal Justice in a Global Context
Practices and Promotion of Exceptionalism
Edited by Mikkel Jarle Christensen, Kjersti Lohne and Magnus Hörnqvist

Nordic Criminal Justice in a Global Context

Practices and Promotion of Exceptionalism

Edited by Mikkel Jarle Christensen, Kjersti Lohne and Magnus Hörnqvist

Routledge
Taylor & Francis Group
LONDON AND NEW YORK

First published 2023
by Routledge
4 Park Square, Milton Park, Abingdon, Oxon OX14 4RN

and by Routledge
605 Third Avenue, New York, NY 10158

Routledge is an imprint of the Taylor & Francis Group, an informa business

British Library Cataloguing in Publication Data
A catalogue record for this book is available from the British Library

ISBN: 978-1-032-04979-3 (hbk)
ISBN: 978-1-032-04993-9 (pbk)
ISBN: 978-1-003-19550-4 (ebk)

DOI: 10.4324/9781003195504

Typeset in Times New Roman
by Deanta Global Publishing Services, Chennai, India

Contents

Contributors

Mikkel Jarle Christensen is Professor with Special Responsibilities at iCourts, Faculty of Law, University of Copenhagen. Christensen's work investigates how criminal justice ideas and practices have been pushed beyond the borders of the state. He is particularly interested in the structural power dynamics behind such developments and the role it gives criminal justice in a globalized world. Christensen is Principal Investigator of the *JustSites* project funded by the European Research Council (ERC Starting Grant 802053) and serves as Action Chair for the COST Action Justice360.

Isabel Crowhurst is Reader in Sociology at the University of Essex, UK. Through the conceptual lens of intimate and sexual citizenship, her work explores how social norms operate as mechanisms of exclusion. Recent publications include *Third Sector Organizations in Sex Work and Prostitution* (Routledge 2021) co-authored with Susan Dewey and Chima Izugbara, and *The Tenacity of the Couple Norm* (UCL 2020) co-authored with Sasha Roseneil, Tone Hellesund, Ana Cristina Santos, and Mariya Stoilova.

Johan Edman is Professor in Criminology and Associate Professor in History at the Department of Criminology at Stockholm University. He has mainly conducted research on social exclusion, alcohol and drug policy, and the treatment substance misusers and vagrants from the nineteenth century onwards. His publications include 'A medical challenge: The alcohol disease in Sweden 1946–1955', *Social History of Medicine* (2020) and 'A century of dissonance and harmony in Swedish intoxication policy', in: Henrik Tham (ed.), *Retreat or Entrenchment. Drug Policies in the Nordic Countries at a Crossroads*, Stockholm UP 2021.

Peter Fransen holds a Ph.D. in History and is Senior Researcher at the Danish National Archives in Copenhagen since 2013. He worked 1990–2013 at the Provincial Archives of Funen. He has written about the Danish Prison and Probation Service and the prisons in Nyborg and Horserød.

Steve Hall is Professor Emeritus of Criminology at Teesside University. He is co-founder of the ultra-realist school of criminology and author of many books and articles, including *Theorizing Crime and Deviance: A New Perspective* (Sage, 2012).

Keith Hayward is Professor of Criminology at the Faculty of Law, University of Copenhagen, Denmark. He has published widely in the areas of criminological theory, cultural criminology, crime and technological culture, and terrorism and extremism.

Magnus Hörnqvist is Professor of Criminology at Stockholm University. His recent work deals with punishment, power and recognition in the intersection of philosophy and social science. The author of *The Pleasure of Punishment* (Routledge 2021). Other publications include *Risk, Power and the State* (Routledge 2010) and articles in journals such as *Regulation & Governance*, *Philosophy & Social Criticism*, and *Punishment & Society*.

Mark Klamberg is a Professor in Public International Law at Stockholm University. He is the author of several publications on international criminal law, surveillance, privacy and other fields of international law, including the monographs *Evidence in International Criminal Trials* (Martinus Nijhoff Publishers, 2013), *Power and Law in the International Society* (Routledge, 2015) and as a scientific coordinator for the volume 'Investigation and Prosecution in Scandinavia of International Crimes' (Scandinavian Studies in Law, 2020).

Kjersti Lohne is Professor of Criminology at the University of Oslo. Her primary research interest lies in the sociology of punishment beyond the nation state, which is the topic of publications such as *Advocates of Humanity: Human Rights NGOs in International Criminal Justice* (OUP 2019) as well as the research project *Promoting Justice in a Time of Friction: Scandinavian Penal Exports (JustExports)*, funded by the Norwegian Research Council.

David Sausdal is an Associate Professor at Lund University's Department of Sociology. Based on extensive police ethnography, Sausdal has researched and published widely on issues of (transnational) policing in and beyond Denmark. This includes among other things publications in top criminological journals such as *Theoretical Criminology*, *European Journal of Criminology* and *Policing and Society*.

Johan Karlsson Schaffer is an Associate Professor at the School of Global Studies, University of Gothenburg. His research interests include the politics of human rights, judicial politics, and legal mobilization, especially in the Nordic region. He has also published on democratic theory, the philosophy of human rights and legitimacy and authority in global governance.

Peter Scharff Smith is Professor in the Sociology of Law at the University in Oslo, Norway. He has studied history and social science, holds a Ph.D. from the University of Copenhagen and has also done research at the University of Cambridge and at the Danish Institute of Human Rights. Peter has published books and articles in Danish, English and German on prisons, punishment and human rights, including works on prison history, prisoner's children and the use and effects of solitary confinement in prisons. He has also published books and articles on the history of the Waffen-SS and the Nazi war of extermination at the Eastern Front. He is the author or co-author of nine monographs and co-editor of several edited collections. His latest books in English are Jules Lobel and Peter Scharff Smith (eds.): *Solitary Confinement: Effects, Practices, and Pathways toward Reform* Oxford University Press 2020, and Rachel Condry and Peter Scharff Smith (eds.): *Prisons, Punishment, and the Family: Towards a New Sociology of Punishment?* Oxford University Press 2018.

May-Len Skilbrei is a Professor of Criminology at the University of Oslo. Her recent and ongoing work is on the legal regulation of prostitution and sexual violence and policy debates thereof. She recently published the book *Sexual Politics in Contemporary Europe* (Palgrave, 2022) with Sharron FitzGerald, and edited the book *Reconfiguring Stigma in Studies of Sex for Sale* (Routledge, 2021) with Jeanett Bjønness and Lorraine Nencel. She also publishes on dilemmas in disseminating research in controversial fields, e.g., the article 'Taking on the categories, terms and worldviews of the powerful: The pitfalls of trying to be relevant' in the journal *Identities* (2021).

Axel Tengwall is an MA student in Global Studies at the University of Gothenburg.

Henrik Tham is former Professor of Criminology at Stockholm University and is now emeritus. His main field of research is the development and determinants of criminal policy. His latest book in English is editorship of *Retreat or Entrenchment. Drug Policies in the Nordic Countries at a Crossroads*.

Preface

This book was conceptualized as a collective endeavour supported by the NOS-HS Workshop grant *Nordic Exceptionalism in International Criminal Justice: Myth and Reality* (2016–00227/NOS-HS) and the research project Nordic Branding at the University of Oslo. We held three workshops and conferences in Stockholm (2017), Copenhagen (2018), and Oslo (2019). The collective work that took place at these sessions identified a selection of themes that became the focal point of individual chapters. The aim of this concerted selection of themes was to contribute a comprehensive investigation of Nordic criminal justice in a global context.

Introduction

Nordic criminal justice in a global context

Mikkel Jarle Christensen, Kjersti Lohne, and Magnus Hörnqvist

Nordic criminal justice has 'gone global' in at least two ways. On the one hand, and as part of the wider globalization of crime control ideas and practices, Nordic criminal justice agents and institutions are now active across borders. On the other hand, the idea that Nordic criminal justice is somehow inherently Nordic and unambiguously linked to a positive valuation has itself gone global. In the midst of the globalization of crime control that followed the end of the Cold War, Nordic criminal justice has been framed as an exceptional role model by local, national, and international stakeholders in specific contexts. It is in the meeting between these two developments, between practical and symbolic patterns of globalization, that this book contributes original research. The book's chapters critically investigate the historical, political, and legal contexts of Nordic criminal justice gone global, highlighting how specific stakeholders have developed ideas of Nordic exceptionalism and/or promoted Nordic criminal justice ideas and practices in a global context.

The book follows three different analytical trajectories that intersect in and across its chapters. Taking different conceptual and methodological routes, the first trajectory investigates when and how Nordic criminal justice practices and ideas became folded into larger globalized contexts. This line of questioning allows the book to highlight temporal baselines for Nordic criminal justice going global, and to contribute to critical studies of how and why agents, discourses, and practices invested in Nordic symbolism gained particular ground at particular times and what practices this symbolism was used to legitimize. The second trajectory challenges established perspectives on 'Nordic exceptionalism' as a thesis that unifies the region's take on crime control to show how Nordic criminal justice, also in its embeddedness in the global, is multifaceted and at times rooted in internal regional and national differences and distinctions. This perspective allows the book to analyze at which point in time the symbolism of exceptionalism became powerful and how it has been used by specific stakeholders in different contexts, both inside and outside of the Nordics, to legitimize or reproduce certain practices. The third trajectory studies how, often on the basis of vague ideas of Nordic exceptionalism, Nordic criminal justice has been promoted in particular contexts by different stakeholders. These stakeholders were, typically, engaged in or around global crime control characterized by intensified

DOI: 10.4324/9781003195504-1

interactions across borders, including the contest to define what characterises 'good' criminal justice. As such, the book rests on a conceptual differentiation between ideas of exceptionalism formulated outside of the Nordics and direct attempts at promoting Nordic criminal justice to different stakeholders. This perspective allows its chapters to analyse how criminal justice, unmoored from its traditionally perceived role as part of the internal affairs of the state, has become a fixture in Nordic foreign policy. Across these three trajectories (Nordic criminal justice being folded into a global world, ideas of exceptionalism and practices of promotion), the book contributes original studies of how, precisely, Nordic criminal justice is perceived and practiced as part of transnational patterns of cooperation and policy building and what effects this has had on the ways in which both Nordic and globalized criminal justice are imagined and practiced.

As evidenced in the book's chapters, Nordic criminal justice has been influenced by, as well as actively promoted within, a global world at specific historical periods. From the 1990s, branches of national criminal justice systems, such as the police, increasingly became involved in transnational interactions.[1] In addition to transnational cooperation, coordination and, at times, competition, new international and regional criminal justice institutions were built during this period.[2] Such international organizations include the International Criminal Court (ICC) as well as, in different regional contexts, more collaborative institutions such as Europol or Afripol used to coordinate transnational efforts. These coexisting, and at times overlapping, transnational and international developments have created new challenges and opportunities for crime control professionals working in national or international criminal justice institutions as well as stakeholders involved in policy and knowledge building around law enforcement and security.

The globalization of crime control have paved new ground on which stakeholders compare criminal justice systems, prioritize some choices over others, and offer new opportunities and audiences for promoting specific solutions. As criminal justice initiatives have globalized, so have parts of the contest to define the ideals and the norms that drive it and legitimate its materiality. Crime control professionals and other stakeholders often have different perspectives on criminal justice and compete to define its direction, reach and, ultimately, its effects and impact. As evidenced in this competition, criminal justice is infused with and built around specific ideals and norms, and there is a constant search for standards and role-models on the international arena. Whereas national criminal justice systems have long adopted innovations from each other, going back to the remarkable spread of the cell prison across the globe in the 19th century, new transnational and international cooperation coexist with new patterns of globalized import/export, branding and promotion of specific ideals and solutions.

It is in this global context that Nordic countries have been promoted and perceived as role models. This perception may be linked to a positive valuation of the welfare systems of these countries, developed by a reform-minded social democracy from the 1950s through to the 1970s. It may also be linked to the Nordic countries' relatively high levels of social cohesion and trust in public institutions. With the further acceleration of globalization after the end of the Cold War, a period in which prison populations and private security were also on the rise, and the global War on Drugs was supplemented by the global War on Terror, the Nordic model appeared to stakeholders in different settings as an alternative to more repressive models of crime control. Referring to such arrangements or developments, a range of political and legal stakeholders from around the world called upon the Nordics as examples to follow. Such stakeholders include agents as different as the president of the French republic and small NGOs working to ban the purchase of sexual services.[3]

The construction of Nordic criminal justice as a role model has often been conceptualized as a form of Nordic exceptionalism—a general thesis that argues that criminal justice systems in this region are both different from and better than the norm in other global north countries.[4] While the perception that Nordic criminal justice models offer a less punitive and more welfare oriented system is not new,[5] the rapid globalization of other criminal justice initiatives seems to have reinvigorated attempts to both learn from and promote this form of regional crime control.[6] Importantly, and as analysed in this volume, the (re)production of Nordic criminal justice as a role model is multi-directional and driven both by stakeholders external to this region and, especially, by agents within it that can, under the right circumstances, act as perceived spokespersons for this role model and promote specific ideas and practices—often using ideas of exceptionalism as a background for doing so, even if implicitly.

The book and it chapters locate and analyze how, in different settings and ways, Nordic criminal justice systems were folded into a global world and how this embeddedness was related to stakeholders developing and using positive normative valuations of these systems. As part of its collective perspective, the chapters of the book also show how global crime control is characterized by practices and ideals that coexist and at times collide. Seen through the perspective of the construction and the promotion of Nordic role models, globalized crime control also becomes a playing field in which soft diplomatic power can, potentially, yield benefits for both Nordic and non-Nordic stakeholders. As such, the perspectives in the book engage with scholarship of and debates about the globalization of crime control and how it is linked to wider diplomatic and political processes and imaginaries. In this context, critically studying Nordic criminal justice in a global context becomes a window into how 'the global' is constituted and reshaped by different perspectives on what role crime control ought to play within it.

Analytical framework

Taking three different paths to Nordic criminal justice in a global context, as identified above, the book engages with at least three different literatures. The engagement with these three literatures runs through the different chapters of the book, each of them taking their own approach. The first literature focuses broadly on the globalization of crime control and has often been produced by social science researchers to understand the emergence of new international institutions and patterns of criminal justice that accelerated from the 1990s. The second literature is focused explicitly on the presumed exceptionalism of Nordic criminal justice, a debate that has remained alive in criminological scholarship as well as among crime control professionals and other stakeholders despite criticism. Finally, the third literature takes nation branding and the promotion of (perceived) national ideas and practices as its object. This literature links to wider international relations (IR) scholarship, as well as to research on the promotion of the 'Nordic model' in a foreign policy context.

The first literature has contributed important insights into how crime control has been globalized. Some of this scholarship has focused on transnational policing[7] and how crime control in different forms have been crafted at the borders of the state, for instance in the context of the European Union.[8] Another scholarship has focused on the field of international criminal justice that targets atrocity crimes such as war crimes, crimes against humanity and genocide.[9] Whereas some research has cut across developments of transnational security and international criminal justice,[10] scholarship has often specialized in one of the two. In the context of atrocity crimes, social scientists have highlighted how elites within the international criminal courts have helped define and drive their establishment and further development.[11] Other research has shown how stakeholders in this wider field, including academics, NGOs and other stakeholders,[12] have shaped efforts to adjudicate criminal responsibility for atrocity crimes as part of a new form of 'penal humanitarianism'.[13] Nordic crime control agents and institutions have been active in both transnational police and security and the field of international criminal justice, and some chapters in this book investigate the specific ways in which regional stakeholders both responded to and engaged with new global developments. Some of these engagements coexisted with and activated perceptions that Nordic criminal justice was exceptional in a wider global context.

The second literature is built around the idea that Nordic criminal justice stood for tolerance and other values, conceptualized in comparative criminology as Nordic penal exceptionalism. John Pratt, in particular, helped establish a notion of a 'Nordic Exceptionalism',[14] as a counterpoint to the discussion on the presumed 'American Exceptionalism' built around mass incarceration and retention of the death penalty.[15] The rapid globalization of other criminal justice initiatives seems to have reinvigorated attempts to both learn from and promote this form of regional crime control.[16] The Nordic criminal justice systems were considered beacons of light in an otherwise overly repressive context. The notion of exceptionalism posited that punishment in the Nordic countries was relatively humane, exemplified by lower imprisonment rates and more lenient prison conditions as compared to those found in other liberal democracies in the global north. The exceptionalism thesis frequently focuses specifically on penal practice, at times even more narrowly on prisons. The root causes were seen to lie in the region's political economy, the welfare state and its presumed culture of equality.[17]

The idea of Nordic exceptionalism has sustained massive scholarly criticism over the course of the last decade. The perspective has been characterized as narrowly Anglocentric.[18] It was the view from afar. As such, it may have obfuscated rather than shed light on the complexities and the contradictions of Nordic policy promotions, not to speak of the day-to-day practices of criminal justice. The exceptionalism thesis has moreover been criticized for romanticizing the Nordic condition,[19] for ignoring human rights violations associated with pre-trial segregation,[20] or the harsh interventions against drug users.[21] In addition, scholars have highlighted how the focus on Nordic criminal justice as an exception overlooks the 'pains of freedom'[22] and ignores the 'benevolent violence' of the welfare state, its regressive border control politics,[23] and the recent invention of prison islands and immigrant prisons.[24]

Taking its cue from other critics of exceptionalism, this volume displaces the thesis from its assumed ontology as linked to Nordic welfare states and high levels of social cohesion to instead analyse it as part of wider transnational processes driven by specific agents with the goal of having specific effects. To our knowledge, this is the first attempt to systematically and collectively displace the penal exceptionalism thesis from its implicit association with the Nordic welfare state to consider how it fares both at the borders and outside of the national frame of criminal justice. This allows a critical perspective on how and why, despite strong scholarly pushback, the idea of Nordic exceptionalism in criminal justice seems to prosper. As shown in some of the chapters, the utility of the idea seems linked to the global import and export of criminal justice ideas and technologies that takes place between different national and international institutions and organizations. It has exchange-value for stakeholders, both inside and outside of the Nordics, which appear to sustain perceptions of exceptionalism notwithstanding scholarly criticism.

The third literature that chapters in this book enter into dialogue with is the scholarship focused on international relations and specifically branding practices in diplomacy and foreign policy. In this wider context, this book zooms in on the apparent promotional value of the particular brand of Nordic crime control. To do so, the volume connects with constructivist IR theory that focuses on foreign policy promotion of the 'Nordic model', and of nation-branding more generally—meaning here also outside of the specific domain of crime control.[25] In this larger setting, the notions of 'exceptionalism' and the 'Nordic model' have gained prominent status in international affairs.[26] Perceived as 'a particular Nordic way of doing things',[27] the notion of the Nordic model is based on two assumptions: First, that it is 'better' than other models, standing for progressive values and socio-economic organization; and second, that it can be copied and implemented in other places. Much of this literature treats the Nordic model 'as an asset, or even a brand—a resource that can be—and routinely is—put to strategic use to achieve specific purposes'.[28] While much has been written about branding the Nordic model across the pursuit of world peace,[29] human rights,[30] development[31] and humanitarianism,[32] none of this literature has engaged with criminal justice—something that reflects the division of labour between criminology and international relations in studying the internal and external dimensions of the state.[33] In this context, chapters in the book also enter into dialogue with scholarship on 'norm entrepreneurs'—in this case what could be called the entrepreneurs of Nordicity. In international politics, the Nordics—as a region of small states—are often considered to be norm entrepreneurs on issues of environment, gender, human rights, human security, and peace-building.[34] Our book investigates specifically whether ideas about Nordic criminal justice gives agents from these countries a certain status and allows for the creation of branding strategies that link penal practices and ideas with national foreign policy interest,[35] both at the level of official diplomacy and in more tacit sub-political processes. As such, the volume bridges literature on norm entrepreneurship in international relations with the criminological focus on crime control and penal policy-making, thus contributing to the emerging work on transnational, or global, moral entrepreneurs on issues of transnational criminal justice.

Contribution of the book

Following the overall trajectory of the edited volume, the book brings together Nordic scholars with expertise on different fields of criminal justice, including on the Nordic systems themselves, transnational crime control, transnational policing, prisons, and international criminal law. Across these thematic areas, the book offers multidisciplinary perspectives on Nordic criminal justice in a global context and brings together legal scholars, criminologists, political scientists, historians, and sociologists around a common research agenda. On this basis, the book contributes new theoretical perspectives and original empirical findings. These perspectives cut across the three trajectories identified above: It takes Nordic engagements in the global, ideas of Nordic exceptionalism and branding practices as its objects. The three thematic threads are woven into the chapters in different ways; most deal explicitly with two of them, a few with them all.

At a conceptual level, the book combines thinking tools from different research disciplines to identify and analyse how the perception of good norms and practices were produced and promoted. With regard to new conceptual perspectives, the book's different chapters underline how the globalization of crime control is partly driven by implicit and explicit valuations of some forms of criminal justice rather than others. More precisely, using the Nordics as exemplars, the book shows how specific narratives and imaginaries help structure how crime control is structured at the borders to the state. This raises larger questions as to the role of the Nordic countries in the global space of criminal justice and international affairs. In this global legal and political space, the perception (or even mythology) of Nordic exceptionalism offers specific opportunities, regardless of whether or not it fits the empirical reality of criminal justice in the region. Often assumed to have a connection to regional—historical, cultural, linguistic—affinities, the symbolism of exceptionalism continues to give access to a certain soft power—the power of the good example—that distinct stakeholders in the global space of criminal justice mobilise at different junctures.

Outside of the scope of this edited volume, this opens up larger questions about the soft power of good examples in the global space of criminal justice, and its borders to international affairs more generally, including hard power in global governance. Such questions link to wider debates about moral power in international affairs, including how it is linked to patterns of global inequality that cut across large global powers as well as north/global south divides often originally defined by, but still not rid of, colonial patterns of rule and dominance. As such, and rather than producing a unified theoretical framework, the book opens new conceptual trajectories to studying how nations, political unions, geographic regions, or different types of other groupings have coordinated reactions or contributions to global crime control. Such entities could include formal political unions such as the African Union and European Union, as well as the Commonwealth or other organizations of countries tied together by history and language—often linked to old empires, including those organized around big global powers that include such as the US, China, and Russia. Playing out across different national engagements, transnational patterns of cooperation and international institutions, the relationship between material (here both in relation to physical force and financial influence) and symbolic power (hard and soft power) in globalized criminal justice, and its relation to outcomes for law enforcement as well as those subjected to crime control, needs further research. In this context, the story of the good examples of the Nordics also opens for more difficult, but likely just as important, questions about the obstacles and opportunities structured by the reproduction of bad examples tied to ideas and practices seen as iterations of counterproductive or repressive crime control, including how they affect the strategies of the agents in perceived reverse role model countries or contexts.

At a more empirical level, the contributions of the chapters fall in two broad categories that also structure the book. The chapters either focus on practices or promotions of Nordic criminal justice. By *practices*, the book refers to the patterns of coordination of criminal justice that underpin Nordic criminal justice debates or practices that have come to be associated with the Nordics. These chapters look into the complexities and the contradictions of Nordic approaches, how they came to be established, their underlying ideas and norms, modes of political cooperation and debate, and to what extent particular practices actually distinguish themselves in international perspective. This category of chapters highlights the ways in which Nordic criminal justice was written into larger transnational and/or international developments, both responding and contributing to them. By *promotion*, the book refers to explicit acts of importing or exporting Nordic criminal justice systems as role models—at times, but not always, utilising ideas of exceptionalism. These patterns of promotion have both an internal Nordic dimension, as Nordic criminal justice stakeholders branded themselves with respect to the outside world, and an external dimension, as Nordic systems are mobilized as role models in other countries and regions. These two categories indicate the main focus of the individual chapters, while perspectives, themes and patterns also cut across them.

The chapters' empirical contributions particularly stress the importance of temporality and context. In different ways, the contributions of the book underline the importance of understanding Nordic criminal justice as linked to different temporal periods. Generally, the chapters identify and analyse three different periods. The first is that of the construction of Nordic criminal justice, meaning here intra-Nordic debates about criminal justice and coordination across countries in the region. This period is rooted in the solidification of bureaucratic states with extensive criminal justice apparatuses in the region during the early to mid-20th century. The second follows the golden age of the Nordic welfare states—the heyday of Scandinavian international solidarity and a continuation of intra-Nordic criminal justice debate and coordination. Finally, the chapters analyse a third period characterized by the rise of the regulatory state and neoliberal welfare state reform,[36] as well as intensified globalization that put internal regional coordination and thinking of criminal justice under pressure. At this crossroads between a Nordic region in which regional cooperation and welfare states were weakening, agents within the Nordic states were able to refashion themselves as proponents of human rights, the rule of law and gender equality on the world scene. The internationally established position then boosted their symbolic and moral value, which radiated back to domestic audiences.

As is evident from this book, criminal justice was one of the domains for the Nordic states to fashion themselves into brands that could be promoted abroad—both at the official diplomatic level of foreign policy and in more informal lines of collaboration outside of the public eye. As several chapters highlight, the invocation of the Nordics as particularly 'moral' has played a central role in branding practices of various criminal justice policies. This may mean that Nordic welfare state logics in the area of criminal justice take on the language of morality when they are exported out of the nation-state. Moreover—as demonstrated by the book's temporal perspective—it appears that the Nordic export of criminal justice policies are increasingly legitimated through claims to morality, tolerance, and human rights, as the promotional value of the Nordic welfare state on the international arena seemed to dwindle.

An overview of the volume

Part 1: Practices of Nordic criminal justice

Defending the North and exporting its criminal justice: the reproduction of Nordic criminal justice cohesion in a global world

Mikkel Jarle Christensen's chapter sets the scene for the edited volume by analyzing an important site of scholarly and practical debate on Nordic criminal justice. The chapter analyses articles published in the *Nordisk Tidsskrift for Kriminalvidenskab* (NTfK) to trace the origins and transformations of cross-Nordic debates about criminal justice. Analyzing the NTfK across half a century, the chapter provides a unique insight in the making and breaking of a welfarist Nordic coordination and thinking about crime control. After WWII, the journal embodied the close link between academia and practice, which was foundational for the journal and Nordic criminal justice and criminology. It was a privileged site for discussing social engineering through crime control seen as instrumental in the endeavour of building a better society. During the 1970s, however, the intimate relationship between academics, practitioners, and policy makers, previously represented on the pages of the NTfK, was dismantled. The change meant that the journal lost its former centrality for policy debates as well as for academic career-making. In the 1990s, debates in the journal were also challenged by the parallel internationalization of criminal justice and scholarly production. This development, especially evident within the context of the European Union, made former debates about Nordic coordination and regional unity less topical at the same time as scholarly careers increasingly relied on publishing in international rather than Nordic journals. During the same time period, articles emerged on Nordic exceptionalism, discussing how Nordic crime control could be exported, drawing on its tacitly assumed privileged status. In this way, debates in the journal mirrored how Nordic criminal justice was imagined and promoted as an exceptional good in a context where this exceptionality seemed to refer to a world of yesterday and was increasingly called into question in scholarship, a scholarship that was itself moving away from the Nordic.

Shaping Nordic punishment: penal exceptionalism and the correctional revolution at Ringe Prison in the 1970s

Peter Fransen and Peter Scharff Smith likewise pursue an empirical historical approach in their fascinating account of Nordic punishment as shaped by the 'correctional revolution' at one Danish prison in the 1970s. The chapter documents the twists and turns of the historical evolution of the Ringe prison project, which came to include self-catering, prison officers without professional training, mixed sexes on prison wings and other practices considered radical at the time. Intriguingly, rather than reading the development of such 'exceptional' practices as a product of the dominant rehabilitative ideal of the social democratic welfare state, Fransen and Smith's innovative argument is that the penal reforms at Ringe prison was part of an international rights revolution, which among other things helped set up the principle of normalization as a guiding principle for reform. The principle of normalization stressed the civil rights of prisoners and mobilized local health care, education, and employment services to improve living conditions within correction facilities. Although there is nothing specifically Nordic about the principle of normalization and the so-called right revolution was international in scope, Fransen and Scharff Smith consider the Nordic welfare state as an important backdrop and fertile ground for its development and traction in shaping Nordic punishment. They raise important questions about the embeddedness of Nordic exceptionalism in the global, and how particular practices and ideas were shaped around larger globalized trends rather than particular national distinctions. At the same time, they demonstrate the importance of specific actors—here, individual leadership in the Danish prison service—who were willing to break with the Danish penal tradition and implement novel practices in a highly localized setting. As such, their chapter provides a much needed empirical analysis of Nordic punishment in international and local perspective, where the association between Nordic penal exceptionalism and the Nordic welfare state is called into question.

Nordic perspectives on international criminal law and international humanitarian law

In the following chapter, Mark Klamberg provides an analysis of Nordic legal practices in relation to the globalization of international crime control. Alongside their reputation as penal role models, Nordic criminal justice is also increasingly influenced by new forms of international and transnational crime control, including legal institutions and legislation. Klamberg offers a detailed account of how the respective Nordic governments have imported and implemented two bodies of law regulating and criminalizing individual acts in war and conflict: international humanitarian law (IHL) and international criminal law (ICL). Through a country-by-country comparison, the chapter provides a detailed overview of Denmark, Finland, Norway and Sweden's implementation of IHL and ICL, of prosecutorial discretion, jurisdiction, and government involvement in investigations and prosecutions, and of cases being investigated and adjudicated by courts on so-called atrocity crimes in the Nordic countries. While finding important differences and legal characteristics among the countries, including at what time they adopted international legislation in their domestic statues, Klamberg finds an overarching common Nordic approach to IHL and ICL. This is explained by a common historical and cultural heritage as well as by conscious and close Nordic co-operation in the field of legislation, positioned in between the continental European law tradition and the Anglophone common law tradition. Demonstrating how the Nordics have responded to and engaged with new global developments, Klamberg suggests that, in a global comparison, the 'Nordic approach' shows how domestic investigation and prosecution of international crimes have been successively imported and integrated into existing structures of criminal justice. The chapter thus illustrates one of the ways in which Nordic criminal justice practices merges with global developments, importing legal practices while at the same time showcasing their support and engagement with international and transnational criminal justice.

Part 2: Promoting Nordic criminal justice

To be both in the world and yet not of it: Swedish drug policy and the international context

Henrik Tham and Johan Edman's contribution deals with the official Swedish stance on drugs in international context. Sweden has, also in comparison to other Nordic countries, maintained a particularly high profile internationally, as the 'Swedish model' came to signify a restrictive zero-tolerance approach to drugs. As the authors document the rise and fall of this particular 'brand' on the international arena, they provide unique insight into the strategic nation-branding of criminal justice policy abroad and its relationship to domestic logics and policy effects 'at home'. Although Sweden during the 1990s was 'the self-proclaimed star of international drug policy', its influence on the policies of other countries was negligible. But the effects within Sweden was however considerable, as the international status made it possible to portray the distinctive Swedish drug policy as a success, despite adverse policy outcomes in terms of drug use and drug-related deaths. Their analysis shows that nation-branding in foreign policy—also of criminal justice policy—may simultaneously speak just as much to national as to international audiences. This though-provoking finding is not the only insight offered by this rich text. Two additional points are worth mentioning. First, and as indicated by several of the other contributions in this book too, Sweden's comparative success in branding itself as a role model internationally follows a distinctive temporal curve. Sweden, arguably alongside the other Nordic countries, seem to have 'peaked' in terms of international standing in the 1990s only to adapt a more defensive line in the following decades. When the promised success of the harsh drug policies failed to arrive, the official Swedish stance on the international arena increasingly resorted to more loosely defined goals backed by a rhetoric based on morality and human rights. This is a trend observable in the past two decades (see in particular the contribution by Karlsson Schaffer and Tengwall) which intersects with the self-portrayal of the Nordic countries as moral superpowers after the demise of the welfare state and its redistributive ambition. While Tham and Edman are not first to show the domestic orientation of foreign policy, their contribution is an original and fascinating account of the multi-layered meaning of Nordic criminal justice policy going global.

Swedish, Nordic, European: the journey of a 'model' to abolish prostitution

Isabel Crowhurst and May-Len Skilbrei trace another key Nordic criminal justice export, namely the international export of prostitution policy from the Nordics. By focusing on the 'Swedish model'—the approach whereby the buyers as opposed to the sellers of sexual services are criminalized—the chapter discloses the complexity of actors, discourses, and logics at play in the policy transfer of the model originally conceptualized as first Swedish, then Nordic, later as pan-European and ultimately as the 'end-demand' or 'gender equality' model. While the approach was further removed from its origins, the symbolic capital of the 'Swedish model' remained. Demonstrating the progressive internationalization of the Swedish model and its subsequent transformations, the chapter offers crucial insights into how this particular export of criminal justice policy takes on a life of its own, as it travels between countries and is adopted by new political actors. Rather than a uniform set of regulatory interventions, the politics of promoting the 'Swedish model' was centred around a highly normative discourse of gender equality, which was utilized as a competitive advantage along with the Nordic flair. At the same time, the model was increasingly 'out of touch' with the political realities in the contemporary Swedish society, often in the name of gender equality. It was questioned by sex worker advocacy groups, and the detrimental consequences on foreign nationals and its heterosexual normativity appeared no longer tenable. Crowhurst's and Skilbrei's chapter raises several critical questions about the political economy of criminal justice policy exports, including, notably, about 'what' is really promoted by and as Nordic criminal justice: criminal justice practices and policies, or discursive imaginaries of Nordic approaches?

A cult(ure) of intelligence-led policing: on the international campaigning and convictions of Danish policing

David Brehm Sausdal's chapter delves into imaginaries of Nordic policing, as he pertinently probes the 'content' of branding in a domestic institutional context. His contribution focuses on the Danish police' branding of themselves as at the international forefront of intelligence-led policing, and the embeddedness of such branding practices in the everyday work of the police. The call for intelligence-led policing originated in the US and the UK in the early 1990' and has echoed across the globe ever since, also finding its way into Danish police. While high-ranking police officers project an image of the Danish police as being at the frontier of intelligence-based policing, Sausdal' ethnographic research among rank and file police officers tell a different story—one in which the police do their work 'as usual', decoupled from the top-down policy focus on 'intelligence-led policing'. His analysis highlights the complexity of representation in Nordic criminal justice, demonstrating above all gaps and inconsistencies of images projected at international conferences, as well as within the organization. In this case, Sausdal finds, the branding of the Danish police as exceptionally modern and efficient, at the forefront of intelligence-led policing, appear inevitably as 'without content'. The Danish police operate as moral entrepreneurs involved in the business of imposing policies and worldviews on themselves and on international others. They believe in ILP and brand themselves as ILP vanguards, although they do not seem to know what it is that they believe in. His chapter thus provides a new empirical dimension to the critical literature on nation branding that view brands predominantly as 'simulacra'—copies without originals, which nonetheless materialize in transnational commercial landscapes designed to extract profit.[37]

Nordic penal humanitarianism: status-building, brand-alignment, and penal power

Concerned with moral authority as 'profit', Kjersti Lohne's chapter offers an analysis of how Nordic penal exceptionalism fares outside the national welfare frame of criminal justice. By analyzing Norway's engagement in international criminal justice, she argues that the notion of Nordic penal exceptionalism has become part of a politics of branding the Nordics as particularly 'good punishers' at the international level, representing both competence and 'humanity' in penal policy. Through these branding practices, she suggests, Norway's 'penal aid'[38] and other forms of penal engagement gains particular value for international export and engagements in international politics. The analysis is based on a conceptual framework that merges criminology with international relations theory. First, she emphasizes the role of 'status' as a differentiating feature in international society, and one that middle-size powers, such as Norway, can claim through moral authority. Second, she asserts that such moral authority is incrementally claimed through practices of branding, and specifically, by aligning brands of Nordic exceptionalism in foreign policy engagements such as human rights policy, peace-building, development aid, women's rights, and humanitarian policy. Lastly, she builds on the notion of 'penal humanitarianism'[39] as an explanatory concept for understanding how humanitarian logics facilitates the travel and expansion of penal policy beyond the national frame of justice. Lohne presents an analysis of Nordic criminal justice as a form of penal humanitarianism, whereby Nordic penal power is put to use as a form of soft power and positioning at the international level. By doing so, her contribution raises interesting questions of how punitive approaches can emerge and expand from and beyond the Nordic welfare state.

From model to problem: the demise of Sweden's anti-torture brand

Similarly, Johan Karlsson Schaffer and Axel Tengwall probes into some of the paradoxical features embedded in Sweden's brand as a 'penal do-gooder', both domestically and internationally. Specifically, the chapter offers important insights into both practices and promotion of Nordic exceptionalism by focusing on the demise of Sweden's anti-torture brand in an international legal context. As the authors point out, in the late 1980s, Swedish authorities and political elites took pride in Sweden being the first state to ratify the United Nations Conventions against Torture (CAT) and one of the states whose ratification brought the Committee for the Prevention of Torture and Inhuman or Degrading Treatment or Punishment (CPT) into force. However, based on an empirical analysis of CAT and CPR's reports and official government responses from the late 1980s through the 2010s, the authors show how Sweden's anti-torture practices are initially put forward by the committees as models for other countries to follow, yet incrementally come to be seen as conducive of problematic practices. The contribution provides insight into the normative discrepancy between international promotion and domestic practices of human rights in Sweden. Moreover, the chapter's detailed temporal reading of committee reports discloses both shifting understandings and problematizations of torture, but also of Sweden's criminal justice system and penal practices as seen from the outside. Despite a notable shift in the early 2000s, as the criticism of CAT and CPR toward Swedish practices increased, following certain key events such as police brutality at the 2001 EU summit in Gothenburg and the Swedish government's participation in the CIA-organized rendition flights of alleged terrorists, the Swedish 'do-gooder' brand remains surprisingly sticky. While the demise of Sweden's anti-torture brand can be seen to signify an end to the previous 'politics of international virtue', the stickiness of Sweden's 'good state' brand indicates the affective influence of such brands and its embeddedness in what Chris Browning has analyzed as a 'fantasized notion of Nordic identity' (2021: xx).

Through Scandinavia, darkly: a criminological critique of Nordic noir

Keith Hayward and Steve Hall close our book by probing further into the affective, fantasized realm of the Nordic. Theirs is a cultural criminological critique of the

Nordic noir genre—a Nordic brand with remarkable commercial success internationally—and of the imaginaries of Nordic society, ultimately revealing troubled political and social conditions. From its 'lofty cultural perch', Nordic noir challenges the image of the Scandinavian welfare state and of their criminal justice systems as role models, exposing the systems' flaws and repressive tendencies. Alongside its bleak spatial aesthetics, gloomy atmosphere, and psychologically troubled lead characters (personified by Lisbeth Salander in Stieg Larsson's *Millennium* trilogy), a critique of the Scandinavian welfare state model is a characteristic feature of the genre, 'allow[ing] consumers to glimpse the "gritty reality" of Scandinavian society'. However, bridging cultural criminology with an ultra-realist approach, the critique of Hayward and Hall moves on to consider Nordic noir's contemporary representations as reflections of a legitimacy crisis of the welfare state model. Today, the genre has retreated into sensationalism and nostalgia, existing more in the realm of fantasy than in reality. Hayward and Hall see this as a reflection of a form of political impotence, 'a psycho-cultural cul-de-sac', where sensationalist fantasy becomes deflection rather than critique. As such, we can only hope that this chapter, alongside the rest of this book, succeeds in its attempt to scrutinize whether a specifically Nordic form of criminal justice still has a distinct meaning in a broader global context, who might be advocating this meaning and for what purpose.

Notes

1 Andrew John Goldsmith and J. W. E. Sheptycki, *Crafting transnational policing : police capacity-building and global policing reform*, Oñati international series in law and society, (Oxford: Hart Pub., 2007). Table of contents only http://www.loc.gov/catdir/toc/fy0803/2008273098.html; J. W. E. Sheptycki, ed., *Issues in transnational policing* (London: London : Routledge, 2000). Goldsmith and Sheptycki, *Crafting transnational policing : police capacity-building and global policing reform*; Sheptycki, *Issues in transnational policing*.

2 John Hagan, *Justice in the Balkans: Prosecuting War Crimes in the Hague Tribunal* (Chicago: University of Chicago Press, 2003); Mikkel Jarle Christensen, 'From symbolic surge to closing courts: The transformation of international criminal justice and its professional practices', *International Journal of Law, Crime and Justice* 43, no. 4 (2015); Didier Bigo, *Mapping the Field of EU Internal Security Agencies* (Paris: L'Harmattan, 2007).

3 Nathalie Blanc-Noël, 'A recurring mantra in French political debate: reference to the Nordic model', *French Politics* 16, no. 2 (2018). See, for instance, the NGO Nordic Model Now! (https://nordicmodelnow.org/)

4 See generally Browning, Christopher S. 'Branding Nordicity: Models, identity and the decline of exceptionalism'. *Cooperation and conflict* 42.1 (2007): 27–51; Pratt, John, and Anna Eriksson. *Contrasts in punishment: An explanation of Anglophone excess and Nordic exceptionalism*. Routledge, 2014.

5 Vanessa Barker, 'Nordic Exceptionalism revisited: Explaining the paradox of a Janus-faced penal regime', *Theoretical Criminology* (2012); Tapio Lappi-Seppälä, 'Penal Policies in the Nordic Countries 1960–2010', *Journal of Scandinavian Studies in Criminology and Crime Prevention* 13 (2012), https://doi.org/10.1080/14043858.2012.740858; John Pratt, 'Scandinavian Exceptionalism in an Era of Penal ExcessPart I: The Nature and Roots of Scandinavian Exceptionalism', *The British Journal of Criminology* 48, no. 2 (2008), https://doi.org/10.1093/bjc/azm072, http://dx.doi.org/10.1093/bjc/

azm072; John Pratt and Anna Eriksson, *Contrasts in punishment: An explanation of Anglophone excess and Nordic exceptionalism*, vol. 7 (Routledge, 2014); Thomas Ugelvik, *Penal exceptionalism?, Nordic prison policy and practice* (Abingdon, Oxon: Routledge, 2012); Joachim Savelsberg, 'Knowledge, Domination, and Criminal Punishment', *American Journal of Sociology* 99, no. 4 (1994).

6 Hyatt, Jordan M., et al. 'We Can Actually Do This': Adapting Scandinavian Correctional Culture in Pennsylvania'. Am. Crim. L. Rev. 58 (2021): 1715.

7 Goldsmith and Sheptycki, *Crafting transnational policing : police capacity-building and global policing reform*; Sheptycki, *Issues in transnational policing*.

8 Bigo, *Mapping the Field of EU Internal Security Agencies*.

9 Robert Cryer, Darryl Robinson, and Sergey Vasiliev, *An introduction to international criminal law and procedure* (Cambridge University Press, 2019).

10 Prabha Kotiswaran and Nicola Palmer, 'Rethinking the 'international law of crime': provocations from transnational legal studies', *Transnational Legal Theory* 6, no. 1 (2015); Mikkel Jarle Christensen and Ron Levi, 'Introduction: An Internationalized Criminal Justice: Paths of Law and Paths of Police', in *International Practices of Criminal Law: Social and Legal Perspectives*, ed. Mikkel Jarle Christensen and Ron Levi (London: Routledge, 2017); Mikkel Jarle Christensen, 'Why lawyers internationalize and police transnationalize: disjointed criminal justice at the border of the state', *Crime, Law and Social Change* 77, no. 1 (2022).

11 John Hagan and Ron Levi, 'Social Skill, the Milosevic Indictment, and the Rebirth of International Criminal Justice', *European Journal of Criminology* 1, no. 4 (October 1, 2004 2004), https://doi.org/10.1177/1477370804045693, http://euc.sagepub.com/content/1/4/445.abstract

http://euc.sagepub.com/content/1/4/445.full.pdf; John Hagan and Ron Levi, 'Crimes of War and the Force of Law,' *Social Forces* 83, no. 4 (2005); Mikkel Jarle Christensen, 'The Judiciary of International Criminal Law: Double Decline and Practical Turn', *Journal of International Criminal Justice* 17 (2019); Mikkel Jarle Christensen, 'The Professional Market of International Criminal Justice: Divisions of Labour and Patterns of Elite Reproduction', *Journal of International Criminal Justice* 19, no. 4 (2021), https://doi.org/10.1093/jicj/mqab062, https://doi.org/10.1093/jicj/mqab062.

12 Kjersti Lohne, *Advocates of Humanity: Human Rights NGOs and International Criminal Justice* (Oxford: Oxford University Press, 2019); Marlies Glasius, *The International Criminal Court: A Global Civil Society Achievement* (New York: Routledge, 2006); Karen Engle, 'Anti-impunity and the turn to criminal law in human rights', *Cornell L. Rev.* 100 (2014); Mikkel Jarle Christensen, 'Preaching, Practicing and Publishing International Criminal Justice: Academic Expertise and the Development of an International Field of Law', *International Criminal Law Review* (2016); Mikkel Jarle Christensen, 'International Prosecution and National Bureaucracy: The Contest to Define International Practices within the Danish Prosecution Service', *Law & Social Inquiry* (2018); Mikkel Jarle Christensen, 'Transnationalt dansk politi: Mellem internationalt samarbejde og nationalt modarbejde', in *Politi, magt og historie*, ed. Peter Blume, Helle Vogt, and Mette Volquartzen (Copenhagen: DJØF, 2018).

13 Kjersti Lohne, 'Penal humanitarianism beyond the nation state: An analysis of international criminal justice', *Theoretical Criminology* (2018), https://doi.org/10.1177/1362480618806917, https://doi.org/10.1177/1362480618806917.

14 Pratt, John. 'Scandinavian exceptionalism in an era of penal excess Part I: The nature and roots of Scandinavian exceptionalism'. *The British Journal of Criminology* 48.2 (2008): 119–137; Pratt, John. 'Scandinavian exceptionalism in an era of penal excess: Part II: Does Scandinavian exceptionalism have a future?' *The British Journal of Criminology* 48.3 (2008): 275–292; Pratt, John, and Anna Eriksson. *Contrasts in punishment: An explanation of Anglophone excess and Nordic exceptionalism*. Routledge, 2014.

15 James Whitman, *Harsh justice: criminal punishment and the widening divide between America and Europe*. (New York: Oxford University Press, 2003); Kevin Reitz, 'Introduction American Exceptionalism in Crime and Punishment: Broadly Defined', in: Reitz K, (ed.) *American exceptionalism in crime and punishment*, (New York: Oxford University Press; 2017).
16 Hyatt, Jordan M., et al. 'We Can Actually Do This': Adapting Scandinavian Correctional Culture in Pennsylvania.' Am. Crim. L. Rev. 58 (2021): 1715.
17 Barker, 'Nordic Exceptionalism revisited: Explaining the paradox of a Janus-faced penal regime.'; Lappi-Seppälä, 'Penal Policies in the Nordic Countries 1960–2010.'; Pratt, 'Scandinavian Exceptionalism in an Era of Penal ExcessPart I: The Nature and Roots of Scandinavian Exceptionalism.'; Pratt and Eriksson, *Contrasts in punishment: An explanation of Anglophone excess and Nordic exceptionalism*, 7; Ugelvik, *Penal exceptionalism?, Nordic prison policy and practice*; Savelsberg, 'Knowledge, Domination, and Criminal Punishment'.
18 Louise Brangan (2020), 'Exceptional states: The political geography of comparative penology'. *Punishment & Society*. 22(5): 596–616.
19 Thomas Mathiesen (2012) 'Scandinavian Exceptionalism in Penal Matters: Reality or Wishful Thinking?', in T. Ugelvik, and J. Dullum, eds., *Penal Exceptionalism? Nordic Prison Policy and Practice*. London: Routledge; Roddy Nilsson, (2012). 'The Most Progressive, Effective Correctional System in the World', *Nordic Prison Practice and Policy-Exceptional Or Not?: Nordic Prison Policy and Practice*. in T. Ugelvik, and J. Dullum, eds., *Penal Exceptionalism? Nordic Prison Policy and Practice*. London: Routledge.
20 Smith, P. S. (2017), 'Punishment Without Conviction? Scandinavian Pre-Trial Practices and the Power of the 'Benevolent' State', in P. Scharff Smith and T. Ugelvik, eds., *Scandinavian Penal History, Culture and Prison Practice*, 129–155. London: Palgrave Macmillan.
21 Heini Kainulainen and Pekka Hakkarainen, 'Drug Control as an Exception in a Humane and Rational Criminal Policy in Finland' in: Tham, H (ed.) 2021. *Retreat or Entrenchment?: Drug Policies in the Nordic Countries at a Crossroads*. Stockholm: Stockholm University Press.
22 Keramet Reiter, Lori Sexton and Jennifer Sumner (2018), 'Theoretical and Empirical Limits of Scandinavian Exceptionalism: Isolation and Normalization in Danish prisons', *Punishment & Society*, 20(1): 92–112; Viktor Lund Shammas (2014), 'The Pains of Freedom: Assessing the Ambiguity of Scandinavian Penal Exceptionalism on Norway's Prison Island', *Punishment & Society*, 16(1): 104–123.
23 Vanessa Barker (2013), 'Nordic Exceptionalism Revisited: Explaining the Paradox of a Janus-faced Penal Regime', *Theoretical Criminology*, 17(1): 5–25; Vanessa Barker, *Nordic nationalism and penal order: walling the welfare state*. Abingdon: Routledge; 2018.
24 Vanessa Barker and Peter Scharff Smith (2021) 'This is Denmark: Prison Islands and the Detention of Immigrants', *The British Journal of Criminology*, Vol 61(6): 1540–1556.
25 Geoffrey Roberts, 'History, theory and the narrative turn in IR', *Review of International Studies* 32, no. 4 (2006). Louis Clerc, *Histories of Public Diplomacy and Nation Branding in the Nordic and Baltic Countries, Representing the Periphery*, ed. Louis Clerc, Nikolas Glover, and Paul Jordan (Leiden: BRILL, 2015); Johannes Magnus, 'International branding of the Nordic region', *Place Branding and Public Diplomacy* 12, no. 2–3 (2016), https://doi.org/10.1057/s41254-016-0015-9; Nordic Council of Ministers, *Strategy for international branding of the Nordic Region, 2015–2018*, Nordic Council of Ministers (2015).
26 Marklund, C. (2016). 'The Nordic Model on the Global Market of Ideas: The Welfare State as Scandinavia's Best Brand'. *Geopolitics*: 1–17; Mouritzen, H. (1995). 'The Nordic model as a foreign policy instrument: its rise and fall'. *Journal of Peace*

Research, 32(1): 9–21; Kettunen, P., U. Lundberg, M. Östberg and K. Petersen 82016), 'The Nordic model and the rise and fall of Nordic cooperation', in J. Strang (ed.), *Nordic Cooperation. A European Region in Transition*, London Routledge: 87–88.

27 Browning, Christopher S. 'Branding Nordicity Models, Identity and the Decline of Exceptionalism.' *Cooperation and Conflict* 42, no. 1 (2007): 27–51.

28 de Bengy Puyvallée, A. and K. Bjørkdahl (2021). *Do-gooders at the End of Aid: Scandinavian Humanitarianism in the Twenty-first Century*, Cambridge University Press.

29 Jakobsen, P. V. (2006). 'The Nordic peacekeeping model: Rise, fall, resurgence?' *International Peacekeeping, 13*(3): 381–395.

30 Langford, Malcolm, and Johan Karlsson Schaffer. 'The Nordic human rights paradox: Moving beyond exceptionalism.' *University of Oslo Faculty of Law Research Paper* 2013–25 (2015); Bailliet, C. (2016), 'A Nordic Approach to Promoting Women's Rights within International Law: Internal v. External Perspectives', forthcoming *Nordic Journal of International Law* 2016; Christoffersen, J. & Madsen, M. R., 2011. 'The End of Virtue? Denmark and the Internationalisation of Human Rights'. *Nordic Journal of International Law*, 80(3), pp. 257–277; Makko, A. (2012). 'Traditions, Values and Political Realities: The Nordic Countries and Human Rights at the CSCE'. *The Nordic Human Rights Paradox, Workshop*. University of Oslo, 10–11 December.

31 Elgström, O., & Delputte, S. (2016). 'An end to Nordic exceptionalism? Europeanisation and Nordic development policies'. *European Politics and Society, 17*(1): 28-41.

32 de Bengy Puyvallée, A. and K. Bjørkdahl (2021). *Do-gooders at the End of Aid: Scandinavian Humanitarianism in the Twenty-first Century*, Cambridge University Press.

33 Scholarship on Nordic branding, itself linked to the narrative turn in constructivist international relations theory, has proliferated in recent years, not least due to intense funding to initiatives such as the Nordic Branding project at the University of Oslo and a range of new initiatives that cut across the Nordic countries.

34 Ingebritsen, C. (2002). 'Norm Entrepreneurs: Scandinavia's Role in World Politics', Cooperation and Conflict 37(1): 11–23

35 Wohlforth, William C., et al. 'Moral authority and status in International Relations: Good states and the social dimension of status seeking.' *Review of International Studies* (2017): 1–21.

36 Hörnqvist M. (2020) 'Neoliberal security provision: Between state practices and individual experience'. *Punishment & Society* 22(2): 227–246.

37 Kaneva, Nadia. 'Simulation nations: Nation brands and Baudrillard's theory of media.' *European Journal of Cultural Studies* 21.5 (2018): 631–648.

38 Brisson-Boivin, Kara, and Daniel O'Connor. "The rule of law, security-development and penal aid: The case of detention in Haiti." *Punishment & Society* 15.5 (2013): 515–533.

39 Bosworth, Mary. "Penal humanitarianism? Sovereign power in an era of mass migration." *New Criminal Law Review* 20.1 (2017): 39–65; Lohne, Kjersti. "Penal humanitarianism beyond the nation state: An analysis of international criminal justice." *Theoretical Criminology* 24.2 (2020): 145–162.

Bibliography

Barker, Vanessa. "Nordic Exceptionalism Revisited: Explaining the Paradox of a Janus-Faced Penal Regime." *Theoretical Criminology* 17, no. 1 (2013): 5–25.

Becker, Howard. *Outsiders: Studies in the Sociology of Deviance*. New York: The Free Press, 1991 [1963].

Bigo, Didier. *Mapping the Field of Eu Internal Security Agencies*. Paris: L'Harmattan, 2007.

Blanc-Noël, Nathalie. "A Recurring Mantra in French Political Debate: Reference to the Nordic Model." *French Politics* 16, no. 2 (2018): 213–30.

Browning, Christopher S. "Branding Nordicity Models, Identity and the Decline of Exceptionalism." *Cooperation and Conflict* 42, no. 1 (2007): 27–51.

Christensen, Mikkel Jarle. "From Symbolic Surge to Closing Courts: The Transformation of International Criminal Justice and Its Professional Practices." *International Journal of Law, Crime and Justice* 43, no. 4 (2015): 609–25.

———. "International Prosecution and National Bureaucracy: The Contest to Define International Practices within the Danish Prosecution Service." *Law & Social Inquiry* 43, no. 1 (2018): 152–81.

———. "The Judiciary of International Criminal Law: Double Decline and Practical Turn." *Journal of International Criminal Justice* 17 (2019): 537–55.

———. "Preaching, Practicing and Publishing International Criminal Justice: Academic Expertise and the Development of an International Field of Law." *International Criminal Law Review* 17, no. 2 (2017): 239–58.

———. "The Professional Market of International Criminal Justice: Divisions of Labour and Patterns of Elite Reproduction." *Journal of International Criminal Justice* 19, no. 4 (2021): 783–802. https://doi.org/10.1093/jicj/mqab062. https://doi.org/10.1093/jicj/mqab062.

———. "Transnationalt Dansk Politi: Mellem Internationalt Samarbejde Og Nationalt Modarbejde." In *Politi, Magt Og Historie*, edited by Peter Blume, Helle Vogt, and Mette Volquartzen, 167–89. Copenhagen: DJØF, 2018.

———. "Why Lawyers Internationalize and Police Transnationalize: Disjointed Criminal Justice at the Border of the State." *Crime, Law and Social Change* 77, no. 1 (2022): 27–46.

Christensen, Mikkel Jarle, and Ron Levi. "Introduction: An Internationalized Criminal Justice: Paths of Law and Paths of Police." In *International Practices of Criminal Law: Social and Legal Perspectives*, edited by Mikkel Jarle Christensen and Ron Levi, 1–14. London: Routledge, 2017.

Clerc, Louis. *Histories of Public Diplomacy and Nation Branding in the Nordic and Baltic Countries, Representing the Periphery*. Edited by Louis Clerc, Nikolas Glover, and Paul Jordan. Leiden: BRILL, 2015.

Cryer, Robert, Darryl Robinson, and Sergey Vasiliev. *An Introduction to International Criminal Law and Procedure*. Cambridge: Cambridge University Press, 2019.

de Bengy Puyvallée, Antoine, and Kristian Bjørkdahl. *Do-Gooders at the End of Aid: Scandinavian Humanitarianism in the Twenty-First Century*. Cambridge: Cambridge University Press, 2021.

Engle, Karen. "Anti-Impunity and the Turn to Criminal Law in Human Rights." *Cornell Law Review* 100 (2014): 1069.

Finnemore, M., and K. Sikkink. "International Norm Dynamics and Political Change." *International organization* 52, no. 4 (1998): 887–917.

Glasius, Marlies *The International Criminal Court: A Global Civil Society Achievement*. New York: Routledge, 2006.

Goldsmith, Andrew John, and J. W. E. Sheptycki. *Crafting Transnational Policing: Police Capacity-Building and Global Policing Reform*. OñAti International Series in Law and Society. Oxford: Hart Pub., 2007. Table of contents only http://www.loc.gov/catdir/toc/fy0803/2008273098.html.

Hagan, John. *Justice in the Balkans: Prosecuting War Crimes in the Hague Tribunal.* Chicago, IL: University of Chicago Press, 2003.
Hagan, John, and Ron Levi. "Crimes of War and the Force of Law." *Social Forces* 83, no. 4 (2005): 1499–534.
———. "Social Skill, the Milosevic Indictment, and the Rebirth of International Criminal Justice." *European Journal of Criminology* 1, no. 4 (October 1, 2004): 445–75. https://doi.org/10.1177/1477370804045693; http://euc.sagepub.com/content/1/4/445.abstract.
http://euc.sagepub.com/content/1/4/445.full.pdf.
Kotiswaran, Prabha, and Nicola Palmer. "Rethinking the 'International Law of Crime': Provocations from Transnational Legal Studies." *Transnational Legal Theory* 6, no. 1 (2015): 55–88.
Lappi-Seppälä, Tapio. "Penal Policies in the Nordic Countries 1960–2010." *Journal of Scandinavian Studies in Criminology and Crime Prevention* 13 (2012): 85–111. https://doi.org/10.1080/14043858.2012.740858.
Lohne, Kjersti. *Advocates of Humanity: Human Rights NGOs and International Criminal Justice.* Oxford: Oxford University Press, 2019.
———. "Introduction: On the Resilience of the Scandinavian Humanitarian Brand." In *Advocates of Humanity: Human Rights NGOs in International Criminal Justice.* Clarendon Studies in Criminology, 2. Oxford: Oxford University Press, 2019.
———. "Penal Humanitarianism Beyond the Nation State: An Analysis of International Criminal Justice." *Theoretical Criminology* (2018): 1362480618806917. https://doi.org/10.1177/1362480618806917.
Magnus, Johannes. "International Branding of the Nordic Region." *Place Branding and Public Diplomacy* 12, no. 2–3 (2016): 195. https://doi.org/10.1057/s41254-016-0015-9.
Nordic Council of Ministers. *Strategy for International Branding of the Nordic Region, 2015–2018.* Copenhagen: Nordic Council of Ministers, 2015.
Nadelmann, Ethan A. "Global Prohibition Regimes: The Evolution of Norms in International Society." *International organization* 44, no. 4 (1990): 479–526. http://dx.doi.org/10.1017/S0020818300035384.
Pratt, John. "Scandinavian Exceptionalism in an Era of Penal Excess, part I: The Nature and Roots of Scandinavian Exceptionalism." *The British Journal of Criminology* 48, no. 2 (2008): 119–37. https://doi.org/10.1093/bjc/azm072.
Pratt, John, and Anna Eriksson. *Contrasts in Punishment: An Explanation of Anglophone Excess and Nordic Exceptionalism.* London: Routledge, 2014a.
Roberts, Geoffrey. "History, Theory and the Narrative Turn in Ir." *Review of International Studies* 32, no. 4 (2006): 703–14.
Savelsberg, Joachim. "Knowledge, Domination, and Criminal Punishment." *American Journal of Sociology* 99, no. 4 (1994): 911–43.
Sheptycki, J. W. E., ed. *Issues in Transnational Policing.* London: Routledge, 2000.
Smith, Peter Scharff. "A Critical Look at Scandinavian Exceptionalism: Welfare State Theories, Penal Populism and Prison Conditions in Denmark and Scandinavia." In *Penal Exceptionalism?*, edited by Thomas Ugelvik, and Jane Dullum, 50–69: Routledge, 2012.
Ugelvik, Thomas. *Penal Exceptionalism?, Nordic Prison Policy and Practice.* Abingdon, Oxon: Routledge, 2012.

Part 1

Practices of Nordic criminal justice

1 Defending the North and exporting its criminal justice

The reproduction of Nordic criminal justice cohesion in a global world

Mikkel Jarle Christensen

Introduction

Most perspectives on Nordic exceptionalism were produced outside of the Nordic countries themselves.[1] Ideas of exceptionalism focus on the similarities between Nordic criminal justice when compared to other crime control and penal systems. Relatedly, but not necessarily building on comparative ideas of exceptionalism, specific Nordic debates and practices within Nordic countries have helped stimulate perceptions of cohesion between national criminal justice systems in the region. Such discussions were produced as part of linked academic, political, and practical initiatives, networks, and patterns of collaboration. As such, internal Nordic perceptions of regional criminal justice cohesion are historical products that were created and reproduced in specific political and professional contexts. The production of ideas of Nordic cohesion was often linked to formalized forms of cooperation and coordination or to distinct venues or outlets. One important outlet has been the academic journal *Nordisk Tidsskrift for Kriminalvidenskab* (the *Nordic Journal of Criminal Science* or *NTfK*). Historically, this journal has hosted important debates about Nordic criminal justice that cut across professional groups and perspectives.

Nordic debates and collaboration also took place outside of academic publishing. In relation to political initiatives, a prominent example of Nordic coordination is article 5 of the 1962 Helsinki Treaty. The article created a framework for harmonizing criminal offences and their punishment, as well as the ability to investigate and prosecute crimes across Nordic boundaries.[2] Outside of formal, legal regional coordination and cooperation initiatives, national political debates about the justice sector in the region often, and almost automatically, reference other Nordic systems and their solutions to specific challenges.[3] Nordic criminal justice practitioners also work together to enforce criminal laws. This happens in the investigation and prosecution of concrete cases that have cross-border dimensions as well as at the top of the systems. For instance, the heads of the Nordic prosecution services meet annually. There are also collaborative networks in Nordic academia. The Meeting of Nordic Jurists, focused on general law issues including criminal law, has existed since 1872 and the *Scandinavian Research Council for Criminology* (*NSfK*) was established in 1962 by the ministries of justice of

DOI: 10.4324/9781003195504-3

Denmark, Finland, Iceland, Norway, and Sweden. The mission of *NSfK* is to conduct and support criminological research and advise governments in Nordic countries. Collectively, these patterns of cooperation and supporting discourses cut across politics, practice, and academia. In a larger context, ideas about regional criminal justice cohesion are likely linked to wider perceptions and practices of the Nordic welfare states, their culture, and history.

This chapter investigates debates on Nordic criminal justice in the centrally placed *NTfK* between 1949 and 2017. Situated at the professional crossroads between academia, practice, and policy building, the *NTfK* was emblematic of the development of Nordic perceptions about regional criminal justice and the cohesion between national criminal justice systems as they have played out since the post-WWII era. Analyzing the articles published in the *NTfK*, this chapter contributes a critical analysis of the changing role and status of the journal over the studied period. In this period, the journal went from the central site of Nordic criminal justice debates to become a more marginal outlet that came under pressure from international journals and the broader value attributed to international publications in the academic system. This change was linked to ideas of Nordic criminal justice increasingly being contrasted to European and international criminal justice perspectives and initiatives that accelerated from the 1990s. Debates in the *NTfK* reflected these changes and at times explicitly pushed back against them. As such, debates in the *NTfK* helped co-construct and reproduce perceptions about Nordic criminal justice, including its place in an increasingly globalized world where it could be marketized and promoted, despite being weakened due to globalization itself.

This chapter comprises four sections. The first section briefly outlines the theoretical framework of the chapter, its methods, and data. The second section zooms in on the disciplinary battles that characterized the *NTfK* and how they played out over the four different temporal periods into which data was coded. The third section investigates, again following the four time periods, the contest to define Nordic research objects and perspectives and to defend the Nordic perspective in an increasingly globalized world. Finally, the chapter concludes by situating the debates of the *NTfK* in the wider context of Nordic cooperation, competition, and nation branding.

Theory, method, and data

Theoretically, the study is inspired by sociological tools developed around ideas of conceptual frames[4] combined with ideas about how such frames are connected to the position of the agents that use and develop them in a given social space.[5] Scholarship on the use of frames has been used to highlight the existence of specific conceptual frameworks,[6] and how such frameworks help set the agenda on specific social (or legal) issues. Inspired by the sociology of Pierre Bourdieu and others, the article links such conceptual frames to the agents that produce and reproduce them. In this case, these agents have particular, often professional, stakes in Nordic criminal justice, whatever this might mean to them. While the analysis will stop short of investigating in detail how individual positions and position-takings visible in publications in the *NTfK* were tied to power balances in national fields, the analysis contributes insights into the different professional profiles that publish in the journal and how they change over time.

At a collective level, analyzing differences in the representation of specific professional groups, including different types of practitioners and academics as well as policymakers, allow the chapter to analyze how the *NTfK* changed over time and how this is reflected in debates in the journal. The journal publishes articles in the different Nordic languages, some of which are similar or at least readable by natives of other countries. This is not the case, however, for Finnish. Publications from Finland were often written in Swedish, or later in English, to be readable by a broader Nordic audience. English articles began to appear in the journal in the 1990s. As part of these developments, as well as in the debate about Nordic criminal justice systems generally, discussions in the journal addressed questions of Nordic cohesion directly and indirectly. Debates helped stimulate conversations about national criminal justice systems, and the similarities and differences between them. Publishing in the journal, professionals (importantly both academics and practitioners as well as, to a lesser extent, politicians) produced ideas about criminal justice that targeted a Nordic audience and, at times, explicitly distanced themselves from more international conceptions of how criminal justice ought to be practised and studied. In other words, the journal is analyzed as a site of production, reproduction, and transformation of conceptual schemes of what constitutes Nordic criminal justice, its cohesive dynamics, and who is seen as legitimate professional participants in its discourses and practices.

The dataset analyzed in the chapter consists of all digitally available articles published in the *NTfK* between 1949 and 2017. The articles were collected from the website of the journal.[7] Although the overall data quality is good, several early years are incomplete (typically lacking one issue—in a few cases more). In total, the material includes 1.123 articles. Other types of texts such as book reviews, editorials, and comments were excluded. To analyze temporal developments, the articles were grouped into four different periods that cover approximately the same number of years. These periods cover 1949–1966 (a total of 229 articles), 1967–1983 (285 articles), 1984–2000 (313 articles), and finally 2001–2017 (296 articles). The slightly lower number of articles in the first period reflects the poorer data quality (the years 1954–1957, for instance, are missing). The first layer of coding covers these four periods. The articles were coded in two additional layers. The first coded the professional perspective of authors publishing in the *NTfK*. This coding enables the article to analyze changing representation of professionals publishing in the *NTfK* and how it affected perspectives on criminal justice in the journal. The categories of this layer of coding were *legal scholarship* (this category being disaggregated into *academics* and *practitioners*), *criminology and sociology*, *medicine*, *psychology and psychiatry*, contributions from *humanities and political science*, and a final one that dealt with *political* contributions. The second layer coded the perspective of the article, more precisely the kind of topic it addressed. Five categories were created covering articles that dealt with *national or Nordic* problems communicated in the *NTfK* to a Nordic audience. Two other categories coded for *European* or *international* topics. The fourth category includes *comparative articles* or articles that imported ideas and concepts and deployed them on a Nordic phenomenon. The fifth category coded for articles whose main topic was related to *theoretical discussions*.

To ensure the quality of the coding, inter-coder reliability tests were conducted on samples of articles. Using these tests, as well as having two researchers construct the original coding scheme, the categories were adapted in several iterations until they stabilized. Early versions of the coding and analysis were also workshopped in the group of scholars that contributed to this edited volume. In addition to the coding, a number of texts were read manually to support the analysis of the article. The coding and qualitative reading allow for a diachronic analysis of who published in the *NTfK* and what their object was. In other words, the perspectives of these authors and their texts serve as the point of entry for analyzing how Nordic perspectives were co-created through the social and collective process of scholarly publishing. The journal was a hub for professional exchanges on Nordic criminal justice and for calibrating exactly what this meant.

Before *Nordisk Tidsskrift for Kriminalvidenskab*

The *Nordisk Tidsskrift for Kriminalvidenskab* was established in 1949 by the Nordic associations for criminal science, the oldest being the Danish one established in 1889. A similar association was created in Norway in 1892, the Swedish association was formed in 1911, the Finnish in 1934, and the Icelandic in 1949 (following independence from Denmark in 1944).[8] The *NTfK* itself was a revamped version of the *Nordisk Tidsskrift for Strafferet* that had been published since 1913 under the aegis of the same associations. This journal had links to a previous initiative, *Nordisk Tidsskrift for Fængselsvæsen, og øvrige penitentiære institutioner, organ för den nordiske Penitentiærforening* published from 1889.

Professionally, early contributors to the creation of a new criminal science were mainly lawyers and medical doctors—including psychiatrists—the latter inspired by a larger international movement that aimed to explain criminal behaviour through emergent scientific studies of body and mind, a movement that went back to early phrenology whose most celebrated proponent in the late 1800s was Lombroso. The creation of Nordic associations of criminal justice research were in dialogue with wider international currents that included the 1889 creation of the *Union internationale de Droit pénal* formed by the Franz von Liszt, Adolphe Prins, and Gerard van Hamel and continued in 1934 as the *L'Association Internationale de Droit Pénal* (AIDP). In addition to international professionalization, early Nordic exchanges on criminal justice partly built on other initiatives, including the Meetings of Nordic Jurists that began in 1872 and are still ongoing.[9] Inspired by similar initiatives in Germany and England, the meetings aimed to create stronger coordination and approximation between laws passed in Denmark, Sweden, and Norway (in union with Sweden until 1905). Finland joined after independence in 1918. The meetings between lawyers counted both practitioners and academics and were connected ideologically to a wider political idea of a union between Scandinavian countries that was briefly in vogue in the 1840s and 1850s, but was effectively ended with the second Prussian war of 1864 which Denmark fought alone and lost.[10] None the less, the impetus from this initiative continued at the level of legal coordination and led to a range of different topics, especially in commercial, but also in criminal, law.

The period in which Nordic cooperation became a political and professional priority was also characterized by justice sector reforms in countries either transitioning from absolutism or developing new forms of independence and governance. In the second half of the 19th century, the 1849 Danish constitution began a slow reform process that would culminate with new criminal laws in 1866 and 1930, and a new administration of justice bill in 1919. Finland and Iceland were transitioning into independence when their unions of criminalists were formed, and Norway and Sweden peacefully dissolved their union in 1905. Alongside these larger political and societal changes, criminal justice became the object of scientific study, and new academic disciplines arose around the study of crime, its causes, and the effects of the criminal justice system itself. Social science pioneers often belonged to either the legal or the medical field, as was the case, for instance, with the criminological perspectives spearheaded by the Danish prison doctor, Christian Geill.[11] These professional dynamics—in which legal academia, legal practitioners, and medicine were dominant—remained active as the revamped *NTfK* began publication in 1949.

Disciplinary battles in the *NTfK*

Over the span of the 68 years of publications studied for this article, a range of different professionals published in the *NTfK*. The professional representation of different types of criminalists is important for understanding what types of topics and debates characterized the journal at different times. In general, the temporal development of the journal has two different dynamics. One was related to legal scholarship. Articles written by legal professionals were and remained the largest category throughout the four time periods, but the balance between articles written by legal practitioners and professional academics changed considerably towards the dominance of the latter. In addition to this development, the medical sciences moved into the background as other disciplines, especially criminology, gained traction. The analysis will begin by studying the latter dynamics to debunk how the balance between professionals changed and how it reflected and impacted the role of the journal in the larger context of contributing scholarship relevant to the welfare state.

The early issues of the *NTfK* featured a significant number of articles written by the emerging disciplines of psychiatry or psychology, the latter building on a longer institutional tradition than the former. These articles were especially prevalent in the first studied periods (57 were published between 1949 and 1966 and 54 were published between 1967 and 1983). Early medical and psychiatric articles aimed to be scientific, but also reflected contemporary attempts to explain complex phenomena through nascent methods. These articles mirrored debates on how to perceive the criminal that reverberated in European criminology and criminal science at least since Lombroso.[12] Depending on whether the criminal or criminal behaviour was seen as an innate or social problem (the answer for medical sciences often landing somewhere in the middle of these two positions), the proposed remedy varied. In this context, the medical sciences generally focused on how to treat the criminal and on deploying legal and medical technologies to curb new crime. In this process, publications were not always particularly worried about the rights of the individuals seen as criminals or outcasts.

One emblematic article is a 1950 piece on the tattooing of women[13] written by Chief Physician, MD, Max Schmidt. In the paper, Schmidt argued for the criminalization of tattooing of women and children on the grounds that 'The vast majority of the population finds tattooing of women as being clearly hideous and repugnant, and this is the case even far into the ranks of the prostitutes'. The ban was 'naturally' not to include men, but was portrayed as a way to ensure the resocialization of women who had fallen outside of civilized society into crime and prostitution. Another text from the same period, written by Niels Pape of the Danish Ministry of Justice's (MoJ) psychiatric clinic analyzed what was identified as the pernicious urge to steal among women going through the climacteric.[14] Whereas these examples were admittedly outliers in terms of the problems they addressed, they were typical for the wider ambition of the medical sciences in this period and its aim of changing behaviour on the basis of clinical and medical tools.

The 1950s and 1960s also saw the emergence of new thinking on resocialization and at times medicalization of different criminal groups, including prostitutes, typical of the emergent welfare state. A 1965 article, written again by employees in the Danish MoJ psychiatric clinic (this time a co-authored piece with a male and a female author), argued against the criminalization of prostitution and presented alternatives in the form of internment in institutions. This would enable psychiatric monitoring of the progress of young women who were the object of the study as an alternative to criminalization.[15] However, while there was a close relationship between legal and medical science in the early years of the welfare state, an exchange in which early criminology was tested, medicine would become a less frequent contributor in the later *NTfK*. In the two later periods, only 36 and 17 medical articles were published. This decline was likely linked partly to the delegitimization of medical and etiological explanations of crime and criminal behaviour, and partly to the emergence of criminology as an independent academic and practical discipline that helped establish a wider intellectual shift toward the perception of crime as a social problem (Figure 1.1).

The decline in medical and psychiatric texts corresponds with the institutionalization of criminology and the effects of the anti-psychiatric movement of the 1960s and 1970s.[16] The pushback against medicine and psychiatry mirrored a larger professional rebalancing in which the discipline of criminology, oriented around social explanations of crime, became increasingly influential and the medical discipline to a large extent retreated from the criminal justice

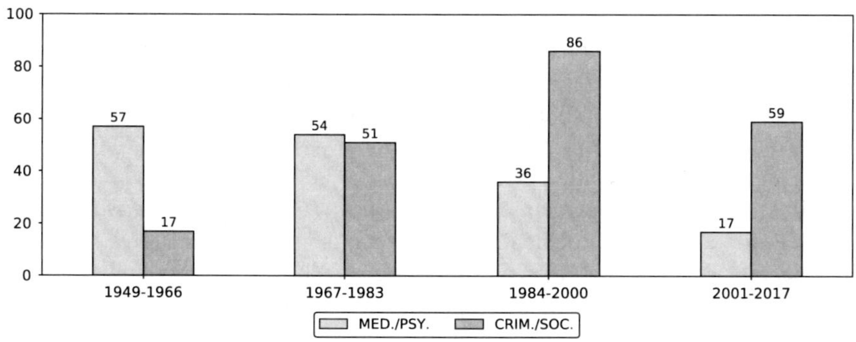

Figure 1.1 Medical v. criminological publications in the four time periods.

field. Anti-psychiatry also allowed the new discipline of criminology to distance itself from what was partly its own history, having been pioneered in jails and psychiatric wards by medical professionals as well as legal scholars. The surge of criminology was linked to the perception of the translatability of its research results into policy, something that was again part of a larger conjuncture of social engineering that was strong in this period, as was also written into the purpose of the Scandinavian Research Council for Criminology founded in 1962. Due to the shared idea of the type of knowledge criminology, at least some forms of criminology, ought to produce as tailored to the needs of the system it studied, criminologists were employed also in the criminal justice system. In a Danish context, the links between criminological knowledge produced in academia and in practice led to the creation of a particular research unit under the Ministry of Justice in 1997/1998. This office was built on a proximity between mainly criminological scholarship and the production of institutional knowledge on which to base criminal policy. As a result, this unit focused on identifying and analyzing national problems. As such, the criminologists publishing in the *NTfK* pushed back against the medical sciences, but also partly inherited a research focus that serviced the criminal justice system of the welfare state. This gave the discipline an important strength, but also led to criticism from within the discipline itself.

As criminology grew, important fault lines were visible in theoretical and methodological struggles. As criminology became institutionalized, some scholars fought back against the dominance of perspectives aimed at measuring the effects of crime and criminal justice that typically had a close link to policy building. Shortly after the creation of main chairs in criminology in the Nordic countries, an article set out to locate 'The Missing Sociology' in Nordic criminology. The 1976 article investigates in particular American criminology and its influence on its Scandinavian parallel as it was built after the Second World War, criticizing the latter's dependence on the former for leading to 'theoretical paralysis' (*teoretisk handlingsförlamade*).[17] According to Persson, himself a criminologist and successful writer of crime novels, instead of crafting and testing new ideas,

Nordic criminology was merely testing American concepts and theories and thus ignoring the classics of sociology and the questions they might bring researchers to asking. Such questions would involve seeing crime as a product of the society in which it emerged. Here in particular the materialist tools developed in Durkheimian or Marxist thinking were overlooked. In opposition to the theoretical contribution of these thinkers, that had originally also been part of the study of crime, criminology was being performed with the 'left hand',[18] lacked reflexivity and built on a 'positivistic perception of individuals' (*positivistiska individsynen*)[19] that foregrounded criminal behaviour rather than the societal structures in which crime occurs. While some Nordic criminologists, such as Aubert and Christie, were highlighted as offering some important conceptual elements, they still did not contribute an empirically based investigation of how societal structures structured crime and vice versa.

Alongside the movement away from medical sciences and increased influence of criminology, the representation of legal academic scholars—on the one hand, legal practitioners; on the other, those that published in the journal—was recalibrated. In the first period coded for this chapter, articles written by practitioners often from the criminal justice system itself outnumbered those published by academics. In later periods, legal practitioners, who had been influential in the first periods of the journal's life, became less active compared to academics, something that demonstrates an increasing specialization in the legal field and an increased distance between scholars and practitioners. Although the two remained in dialogue, a closer analysis of the authors of articles shows how their dialogue was also transformed (Figure 1.2).

Alongside the wider move towards social sciences, the academization of the roster of legal authors in the *NTfK* is a testament to the growth of universities and law faculties that expanded their student populations between five and seven times as the welfare state was entrenched.[20] This also weakened the direct linkages between criminal justice practice and academia and is visible in a decline of practical and policy influence of the *NTfK*. In the first period covered by the coding, for instance, practitioners included a range of high-ranking profiles who

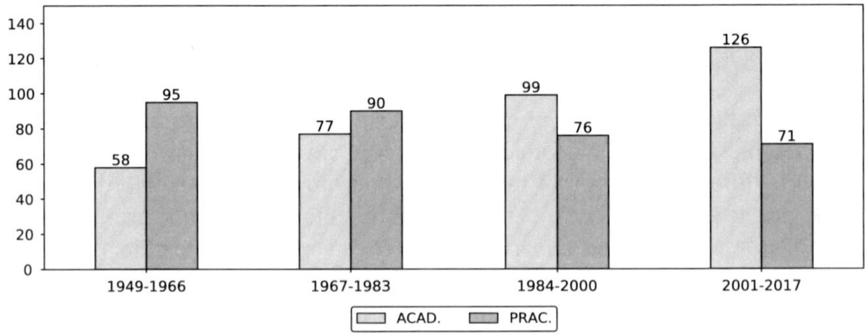

Figure 1.2 Academic v. practical publications in the four time periods.

held some of the most influential positions in their respective systems, including Supreme Court judges, directors of public prosecution, attorney generals, directors of police, directors of prisons and prison services, etc. In other words, there was a strong link between the elite of the Nordic criminal justice systems (and the justice systems as such) and the authors publishing *NTfK*. Through this homology that tied the legal elites of the Nordic welfare states to the intellectual debate about how to perceive and respond to crime and criminals, many of the core debates about criminal justice that characterized this period took place in the *NTfK*.

In the latest period (2001–2017), examples of practitioners publishing in the *NTfK* can also be found, but their presence was far less pervasive and fewer of them were in leadership positions. The practitioners with active publication profiles in this period were characterized, in particular, by the emergence of a different group of authors whose career was tied to the research branches of different justice institutions. Such institutions count, for instance, research units in ministries, in other government agencies, or in more independent organizations dedicated to working with the prevention of crime such as the Swedish *Brottsförebyggande rådet* (The Swedish National Council for Crime Prevention). This development mirrors the growth of academic staff in the engine room of the welfare state where legally trained staff was joined by other types of professionals trained, for instance in the police that increasingly employed academic staff in positions related to crime analysis and organizational management.[21] While this recalibrated professional balance was visible in the professional profiles that published in the *NTfK*, many articles still focused on contributing perspectives relevant to Nordic criminal justice institutions in which (or in the vicinity of which) they worked. As such, many contributions depended on conceptual schemes that were linked to criminal justice institutions of the welfare state and focused on having at least potential practical or policy interest, for instance by supporting the move towards knowledge-based crime policy that built on research results.[22] This line of thinking originated outside of the Nordic systems, but were imported into them and tied to the academization of the welfare state.

As part of this development, criminologists were perceived and to a certain extent perceived themselves as tasked with contributing knowledge that had direct value for society. It was in this context that Nils Christie underlined, on the pages of the *NTfK*,[23] that remaining critical toward the system and the role of the law remained pivotal for criminology. Maintenance of a critical stance was particularly important because the proximity to this system exerted a constant material and symbolic pull on the discipline of criminology evidenced through funding opportunities, or the less tangible expectations for criminological research coming from its practical audience. However, this proximity was also being recalibrated in the same period. Parallel to the process of professional diversification and specialization that characterized Nordic welfare states, the close link that had existed between the higher echelons of practitioners and academics regarding how to organize, manage, and reform the criminal justice sector was slowly dismantled. A similar point is made by Henrik Tham when he refers to the fall and rise of the interventionalist alliance.[24] The *NTfK* was no longer the natural outlet for dominant debates about the state and direction of Nordic criminal justice systems. Instead, the journal was dominated by academic practitioners, employed both within the criminal justice system, in research units related to it, or in the university sector, for whom the NTfK functioned as a scholarly outlet that allowed them to publish within their field or subfield. As such, while many authors in the journal shared with previous generations a pragmatic perspective on the role of research as a tool that could generate knowledge about criminal justice systems and thus help improve concrete aspects of their functioning and performance, their contributions were increasingly tied to specific academic and disciplinary submarkets, in particular legal scholarship and criminology.

Defending the North in a global world

Through the four time periods coded for this chapter, publications that took European or international topics were few and far between when compared to articles that focused on Nordic criminal justice systems, as seen in the figure below (Figure 1.3).

Generally, three types of international texts can be identified in the data. The first focused on crime and punishment in other parts of the world and on introducing other criminal justice systems to a Nordic readership.[25] The second assessed international developments, for instance at the UN level or reporting from international conferences, or the efforts to create new international institutions of criminal law and justice.[26] The third type of text dealt with more abstract questions of internationalised law.[27] Articles taking on international and European topics saw a slight rise over the course of the four periods. However, articles on international issues declined after a brief peak between 1984 and 2000. On the European and international stage, this period was characterized by a proliferation of new criminal justice initiatives.[28] This is only partially reflected in the *NTfK*, where publications on these developments remained marginal. Considering the readership and traditional focus of the *NSfK* as a scientific and policy-oriented journal closely

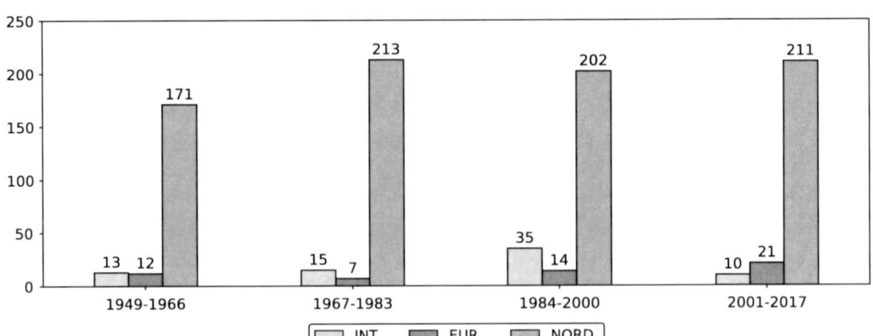

Figure 1.3 International, European, and Nordic perspectives in the four time periods.

related to practices in and around Nordic criminal justice systems, the lack of international texts is perhaps unsurprising. However, from another perspective the relative absence of international and European criminal justice perspectives in a period where these spaces saw intense institution building is striking. In the same period as international criminal law institutions were being built, universities began attributing more value to international publications as part of successful career paths. This would put the *NTfK* and its traditional focus on Nordic criminal justice under pressure.

While there was an increase in the number of articles that concerned international matters in the 1990s, some of which was driven by a 1994 special issue the internationalization of crime and police/judicial cooperation beyond borders,[29] publications on international topics in the *NTfK* remained rare. This is likely because scholarship on international issues is more likely to target outlets that fit a more international publication profile in demand in the higher education sector. Some such outlets were organized around Nordic networks. For instance, outlets such as the *Nordic Journal of International Law* or the *Nordic Journal of Criminology* (formerly the *Journal of Scandinavian Studies in Criminology and Crime Prevention*) are likely to give access to a wider international audience.[30] The latter was created from a specific Nordic organization, the *NSfK*, mentioned also in the introduction. Some authors publishing in the *NTfK* can also be found on the pages of these Nordic journals and in more international outlets. This shows how scholars often diversified their profiles to adapt to the increased demand to publish internationally. While such strategies of diversification could explain some of the lack of internationalized perspectives in the *NTfK*, initiatives around the journal were set in motion to counter this development. In 1991, the Danish association of criminalists established a sub-grouping for international and European criminal law and EU law with the explicit goal of publishing articles in the *NTfK*. This group counts both legal scholars and practitioners.[31] The creation of this group clearly mirrors wider conjunctures of internationalization. However, this group does not seem to have made a permanent dent in the dearth of internationalized perspectives in the journal.

The lack of international perspectives was likely also linked to the traditional role of the *NTfK* as a meeting place between scholarship, practice, and policy building. From this perspective, international and European criminal justice can easily be seen as a marginal affair with little potential effect on national or regional affairs, a perspective that can be found also in the criminal justice systems themselves.[32] A reason for the lack of European perspectives specifically could also be the very different relations between the Nordic countries and the EU. Finland and Sweden are full partners in Europol and Eurojust. Denmark has seen its relation to these institutions change somewhat after a 2016 national referendum that formally pulled Denmark out of the two,[33] although a new cooperation agreement fell into place in 2019.[34] Norway and Iceland are not part of the EU, but both have cooperation agreements with Eurojust and Europol. Reflecting this heterogeneous state of affairs, few practitioners wrote about European criminal justice affairs, and scholars focused on EU criminal justice affairs often used other publication venues. The few scholars that did publish on European criminal justice in the *NTfK* were usually employed in the university sector and also published on more national and Nordic aspects of criminal justice as well as on international law.

Although the internationalization of academia was not reflected in the topics written about in the *NTfK*, it did affect the journal. In the early 1990s, the *NTfK* began publishing English summaries and, later, English abstracts for all articles. However, despite this opening towards internationalization, many perspectives remained focused on national affairs and actively defended this choice, pointing to potential decreases in knowledge that could follow from intensified internationalization. In 1994, Flemming Balvig, then docent (later professor) of criminology at the University of Copenhagen, Faculty of Law, published an article entitled 'Criminology as National Counteraction' (*Nationalt modarbejde*).[35] Balvig was an active contributor to the *NTfK* and member of the *NSfK* where he served as chair from 1998–2000, and also published also in other Nordic and international journals, for instance in the *Journal of Scandinavian Studies in Criminology and Crime Prevention* and the *European Journal of Criminology*. The short piece in the *NTfK*, while not opposed to international cooperation, sets forward two dogmas for criminology. First, criminology ought mainly to collect its data from national sources. Second, criminology ought to target national audiences with research formulated as questions rather than solutions. As such, Balvig underlines that criminology needs to build a deep understanding of national and local society. In addition, a lack of knowledge of crime in the national society criminologists themselves belong to is attributed, at least partly, to the increasing demand for internationalization as an element in academic trajectories. In Balvig's perspective, the existence of professional pressures to publish in English or demands that researchers spend part of their training abroad, thus not engaging with local society, also entailed risks that scholars become 'dumber and dumber' and, in fact, build less knowledge that could be shared with international colleagues.[36] As such, Balvig pointed to an important potential danger of internationalisation and cautioned that criminology risked losing part of its value for national, and likely also regional, societies as new globalised topics and career routes were developed.

Such warnings and pushbacks against internationalization were rare, even in a journal focused on Nordic criminal justice. Despite their rarity, such pushbacks underline the distance between Nordic and international/European topics and professional perspectives. This distance and the emergence of new regional and international institutions also led to calls for increased Nordic criminal justice cooperation. A 2007 article by Gustav Möller, then judge at the Swedish Supreme Court (*Justitierådet*), outlined the acceleration of criminal justice initiatives in the EU and put forward the Nordics as an alternative. Specifically, Möller underlined how more intensified Nordic cooperation could entail that any criminal case could be handled in the same way across Nordic countries, a level of ambition that was not possible in the EU.[37] A similar perspective is found in a 2014 article with the title: 'The Golden Age of Nordic Cooperation'. While its author, Per Ole Träskman, professor of criminal law at the University of Lund and frequent contributor to the journal, pointed to a decrease in Nordic criminal justice initiatives due to the intensification of other forms of regional cooperation (in particular in the EU).[38] He also highlighted the particularities of the closely knit countries in the North. The cohesiveness of the Nordic countries ought not only to be appreciated, but should also be marketed to international stakeholders: 'We have to value these (positive traits) and would do well to market them in the context of international cooperation'.[39] These traits included 'rationality, humanity, and general value awareness (*värdemedvetenhet*), the quest to reduce the societal costs of crime and to distribute them justly'. Träskman also noted that, if promoted abroad, these values might provide a bulwark against nationalistic and populist currents and other emotional calls for more repressive policies against crime and criminals.

Through such perspectives, mainly put forward by scholars and practitioners who had been in the Nordic criminal justice space for decades, conceptual frames organized around ideas of the North as a region characterized by a specific form of cohesion were reproduced and defended. The fact that scholars who had invested a lot in Nordic criminal justice were also at the frontline of its defence points to homology between the position of these agents and their position-taking on Nordic cohesion and its potential. However, this reproduction also extended to other agents and stakeholders. The reproduction of ideas of Nordic criminal justice cohesion took place in a period that was characterized by increasing internationalization as well as the weakening of the alliance between scholarship, practice, and policy building that has been central to the historic importance of the journal. In this new context, ideas of Nordic cohesion were crafted into a potential export rather than something that was more implicit to the stakeholders that published the *NTfK*. As exemplified by the perspective of Träskman, when situated in a global context, the value and potential of Nordic cohesion could also be turned into a political tool that could be marketed internationally. As such, Träskman's article can be seen as an early example of what would later become Nordic branding projects, some of which are explored in this edited volume. Such forms of branding infused Nordic criminal justice with a refreshed political importance at the very moment when the linkage between politics, practice and academia had weakened within the region.

Conclusion

Historically, the *NTfK* had an important role as an intellectual site in which ideas and perceptions of Nordic criminal justice systems were built and developed. With threads to previous regional journals and forms of cooperation, as well as to other international networks, the journal was used by practitioners, academics and, to a lesser extent, policymakers, to analyze problems and challenges for criminal justice in the different Nordic countries and to propose solutions for these problems. Reflecting larger societal restructurings, the history of the *NTfK* was characterized by a dual development that affected the articles published in the journal and the representation of scholarly perspectives of its authors.

The first development was a rebalancing of professional groups publishing in the journal. In the early periods of the journal, between 1949–1966 and

1967–1983, medical publications were numerous and exerted a strong influence on debates, and legal perspectives were characterized by a tacit alliance between practitioners and scholars that was dominated by the former. Both of these categories demonstrate the close link between the journal and the criminal justice systems of the Nordic countries at a time when their welfare states were being created and solidified. In the last two periods, 1984–2000 and 2001–2017, the role previously played by medical sciences had been taken over by criminology and other social, political, and human sciences had weaker links to the criminal justice system. Publications written by the leaders of these systems in the *NTfK* also became less numerous. Over the same period, the balance between legal practitioners and academics turned in favour of the latter, a development that helped erode the access to practical and policy influence previously associated with publishing in the *NTfK*.

In addition to the academization of perspectives published in the *NTfK*, itself related to a similar development in parts of the welfare and criminal justice systems, internationalization challenged the Nordic perception of criminal justice that had been developed on the pages of the journal as well as around other cooperative organizations and networks. The internationalization of criminal justice initiatives and patterns of collaboration made Nordic attempts at coordinating and cooperating less valuable. The transformation of the wider international and transnational context in which criminal justice plays out had significant effects on professional practices linked to ideas of Nordic cohesion and unity. From being a practical and ideological force in the region as well as on the pages of the *NTfK*, perceptions of Nordic cohesiveness in criminal justice affairs were pushed to the side, as were the professional investments of some of the agents that had helped reproduce it. This led to pushback that pointed out how, especially seen from a specific Nordic perspective, some important forms of national and regional professional knowledge might be weakened or even lost with globalisation. However, parallel to this relative weakening of Nordic perspectives and resulting criticism of the international, Nordic criminal justice was reconfigured as a normative set of ideals that could be marketed precisely to the global space that had been created around new law enforcement networks, organisations, and practices. This marketing of Nordic criminal justice was able to play on ideas of Nordic exceptionalism originally built outside of the region. In a new global context, these external perceptions helped support ideas about the value and specificity of Nordic criminal justice crafted by internal stakeholders as they developed new symbolic and practical exports. Through such exports, ideas of Nordic criminal justice went on the global offensive, resuscitating in the process waning perceptions of its value inside of the region.

Notes

1 John Pratt, 'Scandinavian Exceptionalism in an Era of Penal Excesspart I: The Nature and Roots of Scandinavian Exceptionalism', *The British Journal of Criminology* 48, no. 2 (2008); John Pratt and Anna Eriksson, *Contrasts in Punishment: An Explanation of Anglophone Excess and Nordic Exceptionalism*, vol. 7 (London: Routledge, 2014).

2 *The Helsinki Treaty: Treaty of Co-Operation between Denmark, Finland, Iceland, Norway and Sweden.*

3 Mikkel Jarle Christensen, 'Skabelsen Af Det Moderne Skandinaviske Politi: Udkast Til En Komparativ Historisk Sociologi', in *Motmæle: En Antologi Til Kjersti Erichsson, Cecilie Høigård Og Guri Larsen*, ed. Liv Finstad and Heidi Mørk Lomell (Oslo: Novus Forlag, 2014).

4 Erving Goffman, *Frame Analysis: An Essay on the Organization of Experience* (Cambridge, MA: Harvard University Press, 1974).

5 Pierre Bourdieu, *Le Sens Pratique* (Paris: Editions de minuit, 1980), 112.

6 David A. Snow and Robert D. Benford, 'Ideology, Frame Resonance, and Participant Mobilization', *International Social Movement Research* 1, no. 1 (1988); David A. Snow and Robert D. Benford, 'Clarifying the Relationship between Framing and Ideology',in *Frames of Protest: Social Movements and the Framing Perspective* edited by Hank Johnston and John A. Noakes (Oxford: Rowman and Littlefield Publishers, 2005).

7 https://tidsskrift.dk/NTfK, last visited 1 October 2021.

8 Peter Garde, *Dansk Kriminalistforening 1899–1999* (Special issue of *Nordisk Tidsskrift for Kriminalvidenskab*, November 1999).

9 Henrik Tamm, *De Nordiske Juristmøder 1872–1972, Nordisk Retssamvirke Gennem 100 År* (Kbh.: Arnold Busck, 1972).

10 Ditlev Tamm, *Retshistorie*, 2. udgave ed. (Kbh.: Jurist- og Økonomforbundet, 2005), 375–378.

11 Christian Geill, *Kriminal-Antropologiske Studier over Danske Forbrydere* (Copenhagen: 1906); Christian Geill, *Statens Sindssygehospital I Viborg Gennem 50 Aar (1877–1927)* (Copenhagen: 1930); Christian Geill, *Nogle Bemærkninger Angaaende Den Moderne Sindssygebehandling* (Copenhagen: 1895).

12 Klas Lither, 'Lombroso Och Marnamorden I Sverige', *Nordisk Tidsskrift for Kriminalvidenskab* 48, no. 2 (1961).

13 Max Schmidt, 'Tatovering Af Kvinder', *Nordisk Tidsskrift for Kriminalvidenskab* 37, no. 4 (1950).

14 Niels Pape, 'Sygelig Stjæletrang Hos Klimakterielle Kvinder', *Nordisk Tidsskrift for Kriminalvidenskab* 46, no. 3 (1959).

15 Gunnar Mortensen and Emma Vestergaard, 'Efterundersøgelse Af 300 Unge Prostituerede Kvinder', *Nordisk Tidsskrift for Kriminalvidenskab* 52 (1965).

16 Jacob Hilden Winsløw, *Narreskibet: En Rejse I Stofmisbrugerens Selskab Fra Centrum Til Periferi Af Det Danske Samfund* (Holte: Social- og Sundhedspolitisk Gruppe, 1984).

17 Leif G. W. Persson, 'Sociologin Som Försvann', *Nordisk Tidsskrift for Kriminalvidenskab* 63, no. 1 (1976): 117.

18 Ibid., 123.

19 Ibid.

20 Ari Antikainen, 'In Search of the Nordic Model in Education', *Scandinavian Journal of Educational Research* 50, no. 3 (2006).

21 Mikkel Jarle Christensen, *Fra Det Evige Politi Til Projektpolitiet, En Kamp Om Position Og Ideologi* (København: Jurist- og Økonomforbundet, 2012), 175–222.

22 Agneta Bäcklund, 'Kundskapsgrundad Kriminalpolitik', *Nordisk Tidsskrift for Kriminalvidenskab* 94, no. 3 (2007).

23 Nils Christie, 'Fagets Fiender', *Nordisk Tidsskrift for Kriminalvidenskab* 74, no. 4 (1987).

24 Henrik Tham, *Kriminalpolitik: Brott Och Straff I Sverige Sedan 1965* (Stockholm: Norstedts Juridik, 2018).

25 See for instance Ulrik Borch, 'Litt Om Behandlingen Av Juvenile Delinquency I U. S. A.', *Nordisk Tidsskrift for Kriminalvidenskab* 40, no. 3 (1952); Carl-Johan Cosmo, 'Västtyskland Begränser Användingen Av Frihetsstraffet', *Nordisk Tidsskrift for*

Kriminalvidenskab 56 (1969); Natalya B. Khutorskaya, 'Alternatives to Custody in Russia: Today and Tomorrow', *Nordisk Tidsskrift for Kriminalvidenskab* 83, no. 2 (1996).

26 See for instance Philip Jessup, 'En International Kriminaldomstol', *Nordisk Tidsskrift for Kriminalvidenskab* 40, no. 4 (1953); Matti Joutsen, 'Elaboration of a United Nations Convention against Transnational Organized Crime', *Nordisk Tidsskrift for Kriminalvidenskab* 86, no. 3 (1999).

27 See for instance Stephan Hurwitz, 'Ernest Delaquis', *Nordisk Tidsskrift for Kriminalvidenskab* 36, no. 1 (1949); Linda Gröning, 'Towards a Theory of the Criminal Justice System', *Nordisk Tidsskrift for Kriminalvidenskab* 99 (2012).

28 Didier Bigo, 'Sociology of Transnational Guilds', *International Political Sociology* 10, no. 4 (2016); Mikkel Jarle Christensen and Ron Levi, 'Introduction: An Internationalized Criminal Justice: Paths of Law and Paths of Police', in *International Practices of Criminal Law: Social and Legal Perspectives*, ed. Mikkel Jarle Christensen and Ron Levi (London: Routledge, 2017); James Sheptycki, ed. *Issues in Transnational Policing* (London: Routledge, 2000).

29 Lars Oftedal Broch, 'Kriminalitetens Internationalisering', *Nordisk Tidsskrift for Kriminalvidenskab* 81, no. 2 (1994); Stein Ulrich, 'Internationalt Politisamarbejde', *Nordisk Tidsskrift for Kriminalvidenskab* 91.

30 In addition to these outlets, the *Nordic Journal of European Law* published its first issue in 2019.

31 www.kriminalistforeningen.dk, last visited 11 November 2021.

32 Mikkel Jarle Christensen, 'International Prosecution and National Bureaucracy: The Contest to Define International Practices within the Danish Prosecution Service', *Law & Social Inquiry* 43, no. 1 (2018).

33 'Anklagemyndigheden Og Det Internationale Arbejde', *Retfærd* 1, no. 156 (2017).

34 Danmark og Eurojust, 'Aftale Om Det Strafferetlige Samarbejde Mellem Eurojust Og Kongeriget Danmark' (2019).

35 Flemming Balvig, 'Kriminologien Som Nationalt Modarbejde', *Nordisk Tidsskrift for Kriminalvidenskab* 81, no. 3 (1994).

36 Ibid., 276.

37 Gustav Möller, 'Den Ökade Rååttsliga Internationaliseringen: Norden Et Alternativ?', *Nordisk Tidsskrift for Kriminalvidenskab* 94 (2007).

38 Per Ole Träskman, 'The Golden Age of Nordic Cooperation'. Har De Nordiska Kronjvelerna Kommit På Museum?—Den Nordiske Brottskontrollen: Nutid, Datid Och Framtid', *Nordisk Tidsskrift for Kriminalvidenskab* 100 (2013).

39 Ibid., 353.

2 Shaping Nordic punishment

Penal exceptionalism and the correctional revolution at Ringe Prison in the 1970s

Peter Fransen and Peter Scharff Smith

Introduction

In 1974 the planning of a new Danish high-security prison outside of Ringe, on the island Funen, was well underway and the construction committee pulling the strings authored an internal note on the process and the future plans. Under the heading 'Basic principles' the committee declared that the coming prison 'should be run with the greatest possible co-influence from officers as well as prisoners'.[1] In this spirit the already appointed governor, Erik Andersen, planned to use his prison staff in a novel manner in order to create a new kind of relational work between officers and prisoners. To achieve this Andersen chose, and was granted the authority to proceed with, a radical approach in the sense that he wanted to staff his prison primarily with officers who had no previous experience working in prisons (Andersen, 1977, p. 125.). A clear and conscious attempt to break with the *path dependency* (as coined by Douglas North) of an otherwise very historically rooted Danish prison estate (Smith, 2003).

Just by looking back at these few facts around half a century later, it immediately becomes clear that something novel in the penal realm was taking form in Ringe in the middle of the 1970s. At the time, four decades had passed since the last new closed prison in the form of Herstedvester had opened in Denmark. Herstedvester Prison had sported a new and comprehensive psychiatric treatment model, and the ambition was to create something completely new and very different this time around. Whereas Herstedvester and its (for a while) widely acclaimed psychiatric methods marked the heyday of the rehabilitative model, Ringe State Prison took a rather different approach where the rights and the autonomy of the individual prisoner played a much more important role. Among the other revolutionary novelties in Ringe was the construction of numerous kitchens where prisoners could cook their own meals, access to a private grocery store inside the facility, as well as the decision to mix sexes on the prison wings. The mixing of genders especially took the world's press by storm when the prison opened in 1976. Taken together, several of the elements in the regime at Ringe State Prison came to lay the foundation for important contemporary Scandinavian prison practices.

DOI: 10.4324/9781003195504-4

In this chapter, we will, through a case study of Ringe State Prison, examine the history of some of the key components of what has later been termed Nordic penal exceptionalism (Pratt, 2008a, 2008b). We will also briefly discuss the degree to which these can be associated, especially with a social democratic welfare state as claimed by several scholars. Finally, we will look at the subsequent rise of penal populism in Denmark, which has shaped the more recent history of Ringe State Prison and left the original elements of exceptionalism in disarray.

Importing Nordic punishment practices?

Recent years have witnessed an intensive international interest in Nordic, and especially Norwegian, penal practice. The Nordic countries are typically lauded for their humane and rehabilitating practices and often the story goes that we have the best prisons in the world. For example, *Time Magazine* has described Halden Prison in Norway as the 'the world's most humane prison' and *The Atlantic* hails Scandinavian prisons as 'a model for the rest of the world to follow' (Smith and Ugelvik, 2017, p. 4). We find these representations not only in international media but also in popular culture. In Michael Moore's movie *Where to Invade Next*, for example, he goes to Bastøy Prison in Norway to bring their practices back to the US. More recently, world famous musician David Byrne described the Norwegian prison system and the country's low rates of recidivism (the latter he ascribes to the rehabilitative power of the prisons) as one of the world's current 'reasons to be cheerful'.[2]

Interestingly, the image from media and popular culture is to a significant extent backed by academic research. The traditional example is criminologist John Pratt's two articles about 'Scandinavian Exceptionalism in an Era of Penal Excess' where the main thrust of the argument was that the Nordic countries have low rates of imprisonment and humane prison conditions and that these could be explained by looking at the Nordic welfare state and their 'cultures of equality' (Pratt, 2008a, p. 119). In fact, Cavadino and Dignan, among others, had previously argued that the Nordic welfare states produced less punitive penal regimes than their conservative (Germany, for example) and especially their liberal counterparts (US, UK etc.) (Cavadino and Dignan, 2006). Several others have, in various ways, made more or less similar arguments although with different empirical and theoretical focal points (Wacquant, 2008; Lappi-Seppälä and Tonry, 2011). The same year as Pratt published his work on Scandinavian prisons, Lappi-Seppälä did a thorough review of 'differences in penal severity in industrialized countries' and concluded that: 'The most powerful predictors of moderation in policy and practices are high levels of confidence in fellow citizens and in government, strong welfare states, and consensus compared with conflict political systems' (Lappi-Seppälä, 2008, p. 314 and 313).

In this chapter, we will initially address the relative lack of empirical historical research that deals directly with the history of those prison practices that are normally associated with penal exceptionalism. Thereafter we will turn to our case study of Ringe State Prison which is split into two sections about what happened before and after the prison opened. The latter section will include a thorough discussion of the most novel elements in the Ringe Prison regime. As we shall see Ringe State Prison helped shape important elements of what is today considered Nordic penal exceptionalism by putting the principle of normalization into practice in hitherto unseen ways. Interestingly, the penal revolution in Ringe was apparently not primarily a product of a social democratic welfare approach (as it is often claimed in the literature) but was rather part of an international rights revolution that helped create the principle of normalization. Finally, we will briefly follow the history of Ringe Prison up until today, which prompts us to ask the question of the fate and possible downfall of Nordic penal exceptionalism.

Nordic penal exceptionalism and its uncovered history

According to Pratt and Eriksson, the Nordic countries feature much better prison conditions than the Anglophone world which, they argue, include more respectful officer/inmate relations, more out of cell time, better food, and better material conditions along with superior access to work and education (Pratt and Eriksson, 2013, pp. 8–21). However, some of the work on Nordic penal exceptionalism has been criticized quite extensively by several scholars for ignoring or downplaying problematic aspects of Nordic practices (Barker, 2012; Mathiesen, 2012; Smith, 2012). And indeed, there is good reason to argue that the theory of Nordic penal exceptionalism cannot stand alone if we want to understand Nordic penal culture and practice (Barker and Smith, 2021). However, this is not a discussion we will engage in here (we have done so in other places: Smith, 2012; Smith and Ugelvik, 2017; Barker and Smith, 2021) and as stated previously by one of the present authors, regardless of the problematic aspects of the exceptionalism theory 'there is no doubt that several examples of Danish penal practice' can 'be drawn forward in order to support the notion of Scandinavia as carrier of a humane penal culture' (Smith, 2012). It is these practices and their history that we will focus on in this chapter. In that sense, we want to study and thereby understand how and why core elements of Nordic prison practice (often associated with penal exceptionalism) have actually come about and developed.

For example, the extensive use of open prisons and their relatively liberal regimes, as well the policy of self-catering, are, along with the principle of normalization, often highlighted as examples of Nordic penal exceptionalism (Smith, 2012; Pratt and Eriksson, 2013). However, despite the many attempts to explain these practices as being grounded in the Nordic welfare state model and its (more or less) egalitarian values (Cavadino and Dignan, 2006; Pratt, 2008a; 2008b; Pratt and Eriksson, 2013; Wacquant, 2008) there has been a peculiar lack of interest in actually documenting this empirically by looking at how and why Nordic prison practices came to be the way they are. A study of the rise of open prisons in Denmark indicate that the breakthrough of this important 'exceptional' Nordic prison practice had little to do with the rise of Nordic welfare state values (Fransen, 2017b). And as we shall see in the following, the practice of self-catering originated in Ringe State Prison in a climate that had more to do with prisoner rights than with social democratic societal engineering based on treatment, rehabilitation, and social control.

Hence, it is our belief that we need empirical historical research that will actually demonstrate how the Scandinavian prison practices that have received so much attention were actually created and for what reason. With a Foucauldian term we are interested in the genealogy of Nordic penal exceptionalism and not just speculations about whether or not such exceptionalism coincides with specific welfare state values. This, we think, will provide a better understanding of Nordic prison practices, their rationale, purpose, and the culture they are based on.

Ringe State Prison – a case study

The prison in Ringe was devised in the 1950s, designed in 1960, but was not realised until the mid-1970s. The prison is situated on the island of Funen in central Denmark and was originally intended to be a closed youth detention centre, but when the prison was finished, the Danish Borstal system had been abolished. Instead, Ringe became a prison for young prisoners who had been given a prison sentence.

Today, almost half a century after Ringe State Prison opened, four practices especially stand out as important and novel (Andersen, 1992, p. 49; Philip, 2020):

1. Mixed-sex prison wings: in Ringe, male and female prisoners not only served their time in the same prison, but also on the same prison wings.
2. Self-catering: as far as possible, prisoners should be self-managed, which included responsibility for their own meals. The inmates prepared their own food in the kitchens at the departments.
3. The import model played a bigger role than previously: to a much further extent than other Danish prisons, Ringe obtained assistance from the regional public teaching and welfare systems.
4. The general officer:[3] the basic staff were not designated specifically as prison officers or foremen, as in traditional prisons, but rather as general officers who not only worked in the departments as guards and administrative assistants, but also ran leisure and occupational activities. All general officers had to have a vocational background, and they were each responsible for administrating specific inmates.

As we shall see in the following, all these practices first and foremost reflected a novel and intensive application of the principle of normalization and hence a rights-based approach to prison management.

The background of Ringe State Prison

After the Second World War, the Danish prison system was expanded with a number of open institutions with low levels of physical security. Gradually the idea also emerged to create closed prisons with more liberal regimes. Furthermore, in the mid-1950s, there was a dramatic increase in the number of young people sent into detention (Borstal) instead of a regular prison. The idea of these Borstal institutions was that young people could be given a partially indefinite sentence, with rehabilitation as the main priority. The Danish Criminal Code Commission (*Straffelovskommissionen*), which consisted of Denmark's leading experts within the criminal justice system, submitted a report on youth crime in 1959 arguing for even further use of these youth detention centres instead of regular prisons. Hence, a 1962 report on the organization of the Danish prison system included a proposal to establish a new, central reception prison for the youth detention centres. In 1964, a site for the purpose was purchased south of the railway town Ringe on central Funen. Ringe was a good choice in terms of the requirements, and placing the prison in a railway town provided sufficient mobility for the staff, so that it would not be necessary to build service accommodation, which had otherwise been normal for other Danish prison projects.

However, more than ten years would pass before the prison was completed, and during this period the requirements for the prison changed completely. Soon after the purchase of the site, the Criminal Code Committee (*Straffelovsrådet*), which had replaced the Criminal Code Commission, recommended that instead of being a reception prison for youth prisoners, the prison in Ringe should be a closed prison. This would make it possible to avoid placing youth prisoners in the 'adult' prison in Nyborg. But even more radical changes were underway. From the mid-1960s, the prison ideology of treatment and rehabilitation came under severe pressure. The idea of disciplining and re-socializing prisoners was criticised internationally for having none or miniscule effect on recidivism and seemed increasingly meaningless for experts within and outside the prison system (Martinson, 1974). Accordingly, from the mid-1960s, the various treatment programmes proscribed by the Danish Criminal Code and by penal law were criticised and as a result the indefinite sanctions were now increasingly considered inhumane (Fransen, 2010, pp. 88–89).

In 1969, Lars Nordskov Nielsen was appointed director of the Danish prison and probation service and he worked specifically towards abolishing the youth detention centre scheme (Fransen, 2021a, p. 85). He also wanted to improve the physical prison conditions, and a new prison was the obvious solution (Fransen, 2017b, pp. 92–97). Despite an economic boom, it was difficult to raise funding. The Danish welfare state was characterized by explosive expansion of public building and construction, but prisons were not prioritized. For many years, the Danish Ministry of Finance and Housing laconically stated that the youth prison in Ringe would have to be postponed every time the annual Finance Act was negotiated.[4] Not until 1972 did the finance committee give the project the go-ahead, and the tendering procedure could start.[5] Actual construction started in spring 1973, paradoxically a couple of months after the youth detention centres had been abolished.

Planning the prison – on the way to extensive reforms

The plans for the physical framework of the prison were in place, but these did not include plans for the type of prisoners the prison was to cater for, nor for the regime and how the prisoners were to be treated. In 1971, H. H. Brydensholt became director of the Danish prison and probation service and he was clearly interested in launching the experiments in Ringe (Brydensholt, 2007, pp. 10–12). Brydensholt had come across Erik Andersen in 1972 as a unique deputy governor of the open prison in Renbæk in southern Denmark. While most prison governors had a law degree, Andersen had majored in literature. Brydensholt encouraged Erik Andersen to apply for the position as the governor in Ringe and to help plan the guidelines for the prison.

Indeed, the planning was initially put in the hands of a working group headed by Andersen and it soon became clear that he had many novel ideas for how to run the prison. Andersen hand-picked several of his previous colleagues from Renbæk prison to the working group and demanded that they were later employed at Ringe. The terms of reference for the working group also reflected Andersen's ambitions for the prison. In addition to addressing questions regarding the physical buildings, furniture and equipment, the group was mandated to design the staffing of the prison, make proposals for teaching prisoners, and suggest how the prison was to be operated. In other words, the group had to determine almost everything about the new prison, and could summon experts where appropriate.[6]

Self-catering on the drawing board

In spring 1974, the plan was to populate the new prison with sentenced disadvantaged young people between 17 and around 25 years.[7] At that time, there were no plans for allowing women prisoners into Ringe. Also, another of the later high-profile Ringe experiments – self-catering – had not been developed and planned yet. In September 1973 Erik Andersen had sought to clarify the issue of whether there should be a central kitchen and as the ring wall went up – made up of elements supplied by the factory in the open state prison at Kragskovhede – this issue became urgent.

One of the original arguments for purchasing the site in Ringe was that the central kitchen could be shared with the prison at Søbysøgaard, only 10 km from Ringe. Erik Andersen argued that the individual departments should have kitchenettes, so the prisoners could prepare their own breakfast and perhaps even lunch. At that time, he believed that it would be neither practicable nor desirable for the prisoners to prepare their own hot meals as well. Whether the central kitchen was in Ringe or at Søbysøgaard was less important for Andersen, as he saw little educational value in such work.[8]

When it was decided that Ringe would not have a central kitchen, the kitchenettes at the departments were upgraded. The working group was still unsure whether they should go all the way and let the prisoners prepare their hot meals as well. They were worried about low hygienic standards and that some prisoners would not get enough to eat. However, as discussions progressed the attitude towards this activity became more positive, and preparing hot meals was increasingly viewed as a welcome challenge for the prisoners to assume responsibility and manage their own lives. Nevertheless, the working group remained sceptical at this stage.[9]

The general officer

The working group wanted to revolutionize the way prison staff worked *vis-à-vis* the prisoners. The prison should consist of so-called autonomous units, in which both prisoners and staff were to have significant influence. This influence would be extended to the planned workshop, which would be the main place of work. To put this participatory philosophy into practice Andersen wanted to establish so-called 'general officers' ('enhedsfunktionærer'). According to this scheme the basic staff were not to be designated specifically as prison officers or foremen, as in traditional prisons, but rather as general officers who worked in the departments as guards and administrative assistants and ran leisure and occupational activities as well. The general officer would also perform a significant amount of welfare work, although the plan was to also have offices in the prison for a number of social workers made available when required by the municipal authorities.

All general officers had to have a vocational background and they were each responsible for administrating specific prisoners, hence maintaining more intimate contact. The idea was to completely change the relationship between prisoners and staff. In the workshop, the prisoners were surrounded by specialists, who would also play a key role in other aspects of the prisoners' lives.

The ideas concerning general officers can be traced back to a previous committee that had worked with the personnel structure within the prison service.[10] However, here reform efforts were thwarted by a hierarchical organizational structure with sharply defined roles and status.[11] Erik Andersen had been on the committee from its establishment in 1970, and he took over as chair of the committee in 1973. The work in this committee gave him an in-depth knowledge about staff groups in Danish prisons and convinced him that fundamental reforms in a prison required completely new staff structures. Specifically, this meant that, apart from a few hand-picked people, he wanted to start up Ringe prison with a new staff corps with no previous prison experience and no ties with the Danish Prison Officers' Union, which organised prison officers and foremen. A whole new group of staff had to be established: general officers. With the emphasis he wanted to put on vocational training and the planned prison furniture workshop, he had his mind set on skilled people. Prison experience would come with time.

Resisting reforms

The plan drafted by the working group was subsequently processed several times by the Danish Ministry of Justice's central cooperation committee for the prison system and met strong resistance from the Danish Prison Officers' Union. The Officers' Union feared that the general officer could cause problems in relation to the rest of the prison system, and that the workshops would not function efficiently.[12] However, the union of governors and deputy governors as well as the union for civilian staff (*Kriminalforsorgsforeningen*) supported the working group's memorandum, provided that the new general officers would be required to undergo prison training.

Following this, the Ringe working group was supplemented with representatives from all these three unions, who then had to work out an agreement on the personnel issue. On 18 December 1974, members of the group – including representatives from the Officers' Union – recommended to the directorate in a memorandum that the experiment with general officers be carried out at Ringe. However, this was subsequently overruled by the executive committee of the Officers' Union, and this meant that the unions of governors and the civilian staff also backed out. This sparked strong reaction from Director Brydensholt, and he asked straight out whether all organizations considered it pointless to make further attempts to come to an agreement. This was confirmed and the experiment was now hanging by a thread, but Brydensholt had no intention of giving up the general officer, so the decision was now left to the directorate.[13]

After recovering from this, and to break the deadlock, in spring 1975 Brydensholt decided to permanently supplement the working group with representatives from relevant organizations. The result was the so-called Ringe Committee, with 11 members, who subsequently set up a number of sub-committees to make recommendations on specific issues. These recommendations would then, through the main committee, form the basis for the final wording of the guidelines for the prison. In this way, Brydensholt once again succeeded in reviving the negotiations, and he maintained the directorate's support for the general officers proposed by Erik Andersen. However, it was still difficult to come to an agreement, and this was clearly reflected in the final minutes from the Ringe Committee in summer 1975. The lines drawn between the sides for general officers were still the same, but now there was also disagreement about the prison population.

Female prisoners in Ringe?

In 1966, a building committee for the greater Copenhagen area was set up under the Directorate of the Prison Service, which began to discuss possibilities for housing female prisoners. When Ringe prison went from drawing board to reality, the committee saw a possibility to place women prisoners unfit for open regimes there. Erik Andersen supported the idea based on his strong belief in the principle of normalization and in late 1974 the working group recommended the full integration of female inmates in the prison. This was a radical break from the original plan. The recommendation was thoroughly discussed at a meeting in the directorate in February 1975 attended by no fewer than 16 high-ranking people from the Danish Prison and Probation Service, including the governor of the prison in Horserød, Erik Christensen.[14]

Christensen became governor in 1973, and he belonged to the new generation of prison governors who pressed for more liberal conditions. In Horserød, efforts to establish a community for both sexes was well underway but the open prison needed to solve the problem of female prisoners who were only deemed fit to serve in closed regimes (Fransen, 2017a, pp. 172–174). Horserød had established joint workplaces for men and women (a furniture workshop, a storage facility, a laundry, and a kitchen) and there had been general satisfaction with the scheme. There were also experiments with joint leisure activities and, with proper management, these caused no problems. The working group under the building committee had concluded that there was a need for a closed women's prison, and the group recommended that the experiments with a mixed population be taken further at the closed prison in Ringe.

The arguments for a mixed population included a) the experience from workplaces in Horserød, as well as in psychiatric hospitals, where mixing the two sexes had improved conditions; b) reference to prisons in the US with mixed populations; c) that sexual tensions arising from lack of contact with the other sex would be avoided; and d) that life in prison would become more normal.

The arguments against mixed populations included a) the risk of prostitution; b) that prisoners would find a new partner in prison and threaten existing marriages; c) that association with the men would pose a criminogenic risk to women prisoners; d) that centralizing all closed spaces for female prisoners in Ringe would disrupt the principle of prisoners serving their sentence close to their homes and families; and finally e) that it would be difficult to attract enough qualified women general officers with the necessary vocational training.

At the meeting of the central cooperation committee in February 1975, all the organizations agreed to the proposal to conduct an experiment with a mixed population in Ringe prison.[15] The decisive paper regarding the female prisoners came in June 1975.[16] The committee had visited institutions with mixed populations in psychiatric hospitals and a reformatory for disadvantaged (criminal) children and young people. The assessment was positive. The committee intensively discussed the issue of possible sexual relations between the prisoners. Ringe would be a closed prison, where prisoners would be locked in at night, and there were no concerns that such 'problems' would occur during working hours either. However, when it came to the issue of banning sex between prisoners or establishing rules, the group made it clear that this was absolutely out of the question. It should be entirely up to the prisoners themselves whether they wanted to have sex in the prison. As a possible consequence of sex in the prison, the group expected a spread of sexually transmitted diseases, but again the attitude was very liberal, and the group did not want to tighten rules by imposing compulsory periodic medical examinations on prisoners.

The concern that marriages could break up in prisons, where prisoners often worried about the possible escapades of their partner had now been replaced by the other extreme: what if two prisoners wanted to marry? The attitude of the group was that they did not want to oppose this, but they would try to convince the prisoners to postpone the event until after their release. However, it was pointed out that this was only a recommendation and not a requirement. Pregnancy on arrival at prison as well as during imprisonment was also to be expected – and this had to be accepted. Again, the principle of normalization and the rights of prisoners prevailed. The group also anticipated prostitution and pimping, but the group did not want to propose in advance detailed measures against such activities – the problems would have to be solved along the way. In the final recommendation from the Ringe Committee a month later, the majority supported these views.

This decision later received significant criticism from within the prison service. The care manager at Søbysøgaard, Svend Heden Andersen, wrote a long response to the committee fearing, among other things, strong tensions between the prisoners, which in turn could lead to jealousy, violence, and extortion. Heden Andersen also thought that the experiment would 'give rise to much public debate'.[17] However, this protest did not change any plans. The experiment was scheduled to continue with a clientele of disadvantaged young women and men who were to live in small self-governing units with a planned gender distribution of 15 men to three women per unit.

The state prison in Ringe opens

In his speech at the official opening of the prison on 4 December 1975, one month before the first prisoners arrived, the Social Democratic Minister of Justice at the time, Orla Møller, explained how he hoped that the new prison would succeed, and that the values it was based on would spread in ever-widening circles (in Danish 'ringe' means 'circles', which made the pun obvious).[18]

News of the prison certainly did spread quickly in ever-widening circles across the globe. The experiments in Ringe attracted world-wide interest and articles were published in journals and newspapers all over Scandinavia, in Western European countries such as Germany, England, France, and Italy, as well as in, for example, US, Australia, New Zealand, and Venezuela.[19] What especially caught the interest of media was, unsurprisingly, the fact that men and women served time together in the prison. Some of the headlines were sensational: 'The sex prison', 'Sex makes prisoners happy', 'Sex, alcohol and drugs', but Erik Andersen generally managed to explain about the experiments at Ringe in more detail in the newspaper columns. In general, the new prison was surprisingly successful in branding itself in the media. But what actually went on in Ringe after the prison opened?

The mixed population

After the first year, Erik Andersen rightly believed that it was too early to evaluate the experiment of letting men and women serve time in the same prison. As a strong advocate for the principle of normalization and the rights of prisoners he stressed that there was no reason to assume that there were significantly different norms for the young prisoners than there were for young people outside prison. Nevertheless, virtually all the concerns that had been raised in advance towards a mixed gender prison had proved real: There was sex and there were sexual relationships in the prison and one couple in particular, who wanted to get married in the prison, had received a lot of media attention (Andersen, 1977 p. 128 and Scrapbook: Newspaper articles e.g., from the Danish *Politiken*, *BT*, *Ekstrabladet*, *Aktuelt* all the 6 November 1976, the Norwegian *Arbeiderbladet* 15. November

1976 and the Swedish *Expressen* 12 November and *Dagbladet* 20 November 1976). Furthermore, the limited number of women meant that they as a minority received a lot of attention from the male prisoners – and couples could cause jealousy. In some cases, women were threatened by other prisoners (typically in connection with debt incurred before imprisonment). Prostitution did not come to light at first, but with the large number of female drug addicts who could earn money by prostituting themselves, the prison authorities assumed that prostitution did take place (Philip, 2020, p. 10).

In reality, relatively few women served in Ringe. The number was not expected to exceed 15, divided between two of the prison's six departments, out of a total maximum population of 90 prisoners. However, this did not prevent the prison from being strongly attacked by members of the Danish Parliament for the mixed gender population. The Minister of Justice had to answer questions about the alleged wild relationships – even sex orgies – in the prison.[20] However, Erik Andersen had no difficulty providing the Minister with objective documentation from everyday life in the prison that clearly refuted these particular notions.

Self-management and self-catering

The part of the prisoners' self-management, which was undoubtedly a success, was the experiment with self-catering – i.e., giving prisoners responsibility for buying groceries as well as planning, preparing, and cooking their own meals. This model was highly valued by prisoners and staff in Ringe, and subsequently it was implemented in other Danish prisons (Fransen, 2017b, pp. 193–196). Today, self-catering is considered a matter of course and has been integrated in all open and closed prisons in Denmark. Furthermore, it is standard practice in many prisons in Sweden and Norway and for outsiders it is considered one of the hallmarks of Nordic penal culture (Smith and Ugelvik, 2017, p. 6; Minke and Smoyer, 2017, p. 373) along with kitchens with knives, prison grocery stores etc. Although the model has posed some challenges it is likely to be one of the greatest successes of the Danish Prison and Probation Service (Minke and Smoyer, 2017, pp. 359–361).

In Ringe, kitchens were established on the individual wings, where prisoners could prepare their meals individually or in groups. This required a store and the prison entered into an agreement with the local grocery store and the prisoners were given allowances to shop groceries. To the great amusement of the public, rumours began to circulate during 1976 that the grocery store did not make any money because of its losses. In other words, the prisoners were allegedly stealing. The actual reason, though, was primarily that the first shop manager was not able to make the profit he had expected because the customer base was simply not large enough. The prison later succeeded in finding another manager who opted for a smaller scale store (Scrapbook: Newspaper articles Fyns Stiftstidende 27 and 29 March and 10 June 1976, and Andersen, 1977 p. 124).

There were limitations on the products that could be sold, and beer and spirits were disallowed because many prisoners had a drinking problem. Nevertheless, huge amounts of yeast were sold in the prison grocery store and used to produce alcoholic drinks. This news also reached the public, and the issue was brought up in the Danish Parliament, where the Minister had to answer questions about whether the prisoners were drinking and were intoxicated in the prison. The Minister had to admit that there had been problems with home brew in the prison, which had resulted in yeast being removed from the shelves in the prison shop (Brydensholt, 2007, p. 32). This, of course, gave rise to much dissatisfaction among the prisoners, who were then not able to bake their own bread either.

Self-management also included less spectacular day-to-day chores, such as doing the laundry and cleaning, while more extensive plans were never realised. The plans for the prison to be run using autonomous units never materialized. However, there is no doubt that prisoners' rights were high on the agenda in the 1970s and this was a high priority for both the Directors of the prison service during that decade, Nordskov Nielsen and his successor Brydensholt (Fransen 2021a, p. 84 ff.). There were also strikes among the prisoners in Ringe. This was a fairly common phenomenon in Danish prisons during the 1970s – more rights for the prisoners led to greater self-awareness and greater resistance to the system.

The import model

The plan was that social workers from Ringe Municipality would have a core function in fulfilling action plans for the prisoners, if the situation required specialist insight. However, this system never really worked. It seemed that the relatively small municipality could not cope with the task, and the issue of payment from the state prison system to the municipal system also caused problems. In the long term, however, the import model became the preferred method for specialized treatment in both Ringe and in other prisons – for example in the case of treatment for drug addiction where private suppliers were hired. However, this was not a product of the Ringe model. Also, the import model with regard to social workers from the municipality was never implemented in the Danish prison and probation service, which, unlike in Norway, continues to rely on social workers hired by the prison service.

The general officers

At the opening, the prison had a total of 68 employees, 46 of whom were general officers and almost all of them had no prison experience, but instead had a background as tradesmen. The idea was that the work for the prisoners at the furniture workshop should resemble a working day for an ordinary industrial worker. The prisoners would then also meet the same officer at the department during their time off. There were considerable start-up problems, and the scheme met a lot of resistance from the Danish Prison Officers' Union, but was nevertheless maintained. For many years, the furniture workshop produced office furniture for the state according to the motto 'from state operations to state utilisation' ('fra statsdrift til statsbrug'). However, over the years, the prison had to recognize that this undertaking was too difficult, and it therefore switched to easier tasks. From the 1990s, production had to be on market terms, and the prison production could not cope in this competitive environment. Furthermore, over the following years many industrial workplaces were shut down.

In the 1970s the scheme generally received a positive evaluation from the staff in Ringe, but not from their colleagues in the other prisons. Nevertheless, over the next decades, there were attempts to export the general officer model to other state prisons, although with varying degrees of success. However, the general officer model was never fully implemented in the Danish prisons, and has now been given up completely. The cognitive skills programmes and the treatment of drug addiction that came in force during the 1990s required other competences than what a tradesman background could supply.

Rehabilitation or rights? Contemporary discussions about the project

Already in the planning phase, it was decided that the experiments in Ringe should be evaluated to establish whether they were to continue as permanent schemes. The Danish Prison and Probation Service was very interested in having the issue scientifically evaluated and had transferred the task to a sociological consultancy firm ('Rådgivende Sociologer A/S'), who, in 1980, were working on a comprehensive report on the experiments in Ringe State Prison 1975–1979. Historically, external private management consultants made their entry into the public sector in the 1970s, including the Danish Prison and Probation Service. However, some of the sociologists working on the evaluation had been involved also during the Ringe planning phase.

The sociologists concluded that the many attempts at reforming prison operations in Ringe had succeeded, almost without any exception (Holstein, 1980, p. 8). This was a controversial conclusion, and far from everyone agreed. As mentioned, the general officer scheme in particular had caused problems. The report from the external consultants also met criticism from criminologists at the University of Copenhagen.[21] The Ringe experiments also became the subject of later political discussion which interestingly revealed, that now, on the verge to a new decade, Ringe would likely be subject to a somewhat different evaluative standard than originally conceived. As already mentioned, the principle of normalization and the rights of prisoners had several times prevailed over the ideology of treatment and rehabilitation during the planning and construction of Ringe. But this could clearly look somewhat different from a political vantage point, where normalization and prisoner rights were easily seen as possible rehabilitative instruments rather than aims in their own right. On 11 December 1979, Mimi Jakobsen, member of the Danish Parliament (and later government minister) said from the parliament rostrum:

> Like many other spokesmen today, I've visited some of our prisons, and I must admit that my visits left me somewhat depressed. Not because the physical framework in Horsens State Prison was poor [the prison in East Jutland

> was in use from 1853–2006], although it was, but because we visited Ringe State Prison first, where in many ways they had tried to create better conditions with small family-like groups, and they really tried working with the young people there. We saw Horsens as a sharp contrast to Ringe, but despite this – if I haven't completely misunderstood the governor – Ringe had to realise that their rate of recidivism was no lower than for any other prisons. In other words, are we in a situation where we have to accept – and this is a question – that providing treatment doesn't help; that these much more humane and congenial measures for which I have great sympathy don't help? Is the relapse rate the same, regardless of how liberal the system is, of how many programmes are offered to prisoners, or of how the system is otherwise organised? I thought that was a very depressing experience.[22]

It was this feeling of despair that the Danish Prison and Probation Service was challenged by. However, Erik Andersen was ready with an answer:

> Imprisonment in itself is first and foremost a negative sanction with mostly negative effects on the prisoners. Therefore, no ambitious goals have been set for the activities of this new prison in terms of preventing relapse into crime (…) The goal of the activities in this prison is instead to limit the negative consequences of imprisonment by adding some positive elements such as training, teaching, building responsibility and social understanding
> (Holstein, 1980, p. 5).

Nevertheless, Mimi Jakobsen's verdict clearly signalled, that the rights-based approach and the principle of normalization could be judged politically within a logic of rehabilitation and treatment. As we shall see below, the rehabilitative understanding has since taken a back seat once again, but not because of a renewed interest in prisoners' rights but as a result of the rise of penal populism which has favoured a much more retributive approach during the last two decades.

Nordic exceptionalism, welfare states, and Ringe State Prison

Previous studies on and theories about Nordic exceptionalism have not been based on thorough empirical historical accounts of how the Nordic prison practices associated with such exceptionalism have actually evolved. When doing such an empirical study of the conception and development of some of the important prison practices in this regard one is struck by how many diverse factors that needed to line-up and how many challenges that had to be overcome, before the radical reform project at Ringe could be carried out. Among these factors a number of key elements stand out, which have received little attention in previous research in this area:

1) The importance of risk-willing and strong individual leadership – in this particular case both at Ringe prison and in the directorate of the Danish prison service;

2) How this leadership was willing to break with Danish penal history and tradition;
3) The ad-hoc development of the project (self-catering and mixing genders came at a late stage of the planning);
4) The degree to which the reform project at Ringe was based on a rights-based approach that prioritized the principle of normalization, rather than a treatment-model approach, that prioritized rehabilitation.

Rehabilitation and normalization were, of course, not seen as mutually exclusive approaches, but when clashes occurred normalization and the rights or prisoners tended to carry the day when Ringe State Prison was conceived and planned, as well as during the early years of its operation. Seen from today's vantage point, this was a relatively short-lived window of opportunity in the sense that rehabilitation had been a primary objective in the preceding more than 100 years (and especially from the 1930s to the 1960s) and came to the fore again during the 1980s and 1990s before both rehabilitation and prisoner rights had to retreat again in the face of the rise of penal populism in the present millennium (Smith, 2003, 2014; Fransen, 2021b, pp. 30–35).

Taken together, Ringe State Prison in important ways does not look like a direct and natural product of a social democratic welfare state *per se*, despite the way in which Nordic penal exceptionalism is often portrayed as a child of the Nordic social democratic welfare state. The degree to which the Danish welfare state itself was a social-democratic project, it was clearly a product of the extensive scientific society building schemes so well-known of the Nordic social democratic tradition. A tradition that favoured intricate and far-reaching social engineering rather than a focus on individual civil rights. A rehabilitative treatment model in prisons would fit naturally with this form of social engineering and state building. The principle of normalization, on the other hand, was more a product of the international rights revolution in the 1970s (Smith, 2016) and indeed, this principle is clearly stipulated in international law (Engbo, 2017). In other words, there is nothing specifically Nordic or Scandinavian about the principle of normalization as such – it is part of international human rights law and a core principle especially within European prison law (Zyl Smit and Snacken, 2011).

In fact, our case study clearly reveals that the central decision makers, including Erik Andersen, and the actual policies and practices they helped create in Ringe Prison, granted prisoners (and staff) more autonomy and more powers of participation specifically without requiring or prioritizing rehabilitative goals. Often this philosophy created problems and posed clear criminogenic risks – as when it was decided to have cash in the prison and a prison population of both women and men – but nevertheless, the principle of normalization prevailed.

It is still possible, however, that the principle of normalization gained particular traction in Scandinavia (and in this case in Denmark) because of a peculiar local context, which could include the Nordic welfare state as an important backdrop. In other words, it is still possible to argue, that the Danish welfare state – social democratic or not – helped create or maintain a context that made the experiments at Ringe State Prison possible: a small and relatively peaceful society with an efficient bureaucracy and citizens who generally trusted their government and the authorities. Indeed, the social democratic party had itself come a long way in the 1970s and was ready to embrace the experiments at Ringe and their rights-based foundation when they were launched. In his previously mentioned opening speech in December 1975, the Social Democratic Minister of Justice at the time, Orla Møller, explained how "we have moved from wanting to indoctrinate inmates through treatment to a point where we now relate to them human to human".[23] In other words, the welfare state and the social democrats along with it, had apparently also been influenced by the international rights revolution and for a couple of decades it was possible to prioritize rights over treatment and rehabilitation, on the one hand, and retribution on the other hand. And it is quite possible, that the Nordic welfare state context, despite being originally conceived as a top-down project of social engineering conducted by a strong state, in the end provided especially fertile ground for creating a rights-based humanistic prison practise in the 1970s. Nevertheless, it remains the case that the rights-based turn in the 1960s and 70s was primarily an international phenomenon, as demonstrated by several international studies on the history and development of human rights (Hopgood, 2013; Moyn, 2012).

Indeed, current events clearly illustrate how Danish penal policy, as well as the Danish social democratic party for that matter, can be very open to influence from very different international penological tendencies – in the contemporary case in the form penal populism and tough on crime policies. Ironically, no other institution in the Danish prison estate symbolizes this turn of events more dramatically than the once so 'exceptional' prison in Ringe.

The downfall of exceptionalism – Ringe State Prison and the detention of unwanted migrants

As already touched upon, recent decades have witnessed a move towards tougher sentencing and penal populism in Denmark (Fransen, 2010, p. 127). This tendency gained ground in the late 1990s under a social democratic government and took off in earnest under several liberal-conservative governments from 2001 and onwards (Balvig, 2005; Smith, 2012; Smith, 2017). As a result, sentences have been stiffened, the prison population has gone up, and prison conditions have become stricter and tougher. An illustrative example of this tendency is the explosion in the use of punitive solitary confinement in Danish prisons in recent years (Engbo, 2021). At the same time, the focus on both rehabilitation and prisoner rights has abated.

Importantly, these policies are a direct product of political initiatives that can only be characterized as penal populism. On top of this development anti-immigration policies have caused an expansion of penal practices towards migrants, which in itself has begun to change the Danish penal estate and its more or less exceptional prison practices (Barker and Smith, 2021).

The history of Ringe State Prison is a perfect illustration of these tendencies. Today, one will have a hard time finding very much except the physical buildings that resemble the original practices and the original philosophy behind the prison. Ringe has been transformed into an institution for unwanted immigrants. Since October 2018, Ringe Prison has been a closed deportation prison that offers no programmes or initiatives aimed at rehabilitation. The number of employees in the prison has been reduced and the prison guards are no longer attached to a specific department/wing. Accordingly, the relational work, which was previously a high priority in Ringe, is no longer prioritized.

The penal revolution that took place in Funen in Denmark in the 1970s has, in other words, been replaced by another dramatic change, in some ways no less revolutionary. The result is a prison which has abandoned all pretence of trying to improve the lives of its inhabitants. Ringe State Prison is now simply supposed to warehouse its inmates until they can be shipped off to a remote destination outside Denmark's borders out of sight of the Danish welfare state. It is difficult to imagine a starker contrast to the notion of Nordic penal exceptionalism.

In a sense, both the opening of Ringe Prison in the 1970s and the recent regime changes in a much more punitive direction bear witness to the same thing, namely the way in which Danish prison practice is not developed in a national vacuum but rather takes form in an international and increasingly globalized context. Our historical case suggests that the international rights revolution constitutes an important backdrop and paradigm for understanding the focus on the principle of normalization in Scandinavia and in Ringe in the 1970s, and similarly, the internationally informed phenomena of penal populism and 'crimmigration' clearly help us explain the downfall of the original Ringe regime and the way that penal exceptionalism has been left in disarray in this historically important institution of Nordic punishment.

Notes

1 Danish Prison and Probation Service (DfK) 1.ktr, 133–1973, 20 May 1974. Prison and Probation Service 1st Office file 133-1973 and 2nd Office file 966-2 are collective cases about Ringe State Prison. National Archives of Copenhagen.
2 https://www.reasonstobecheerful.world/article/2018/3/15/prison-reform (assessed 13 January 2019).
3 The governor Erik Andersen himself called these "Standard Officers" in English, but there was nothing 'standard' about them given the broad responsibilities that they were granted. Also, the Danish term was 'Enhedsfunktionær' which translates better into 'general officer'.
4 Dkf 1st Office, file 206/1963.
5 Dkf 1st Office, file 112/1969 document regarding the construction.
6 DfK 1.ktr, 133-1973, 16 November 1973.
7 DfK 1.ktr, 133-1973, 20 May 1973.
8 DfK 1.ktr, 133-1973, 12 September 1973.
9 DfK 1.ktr, 133-1973, 20 May 1974.
10 The department of administration was part of the Danish Ministry of Finance. It was set up to manage public finances. This was a difficult task during the explosive develop-

ment of the Danish welfare society, which was conceived in the 1950s and rolled out in the 1960s and 1970s.

11 The Danish Ministry of Finance's department of administration case records 1. Institution cases.

12 DfK 1.ktr, 133-1973, 16 February 1975.

13 DfK 1.ktr, 133-1973, 19 February 1975.

14 State prison in Ringe: General record (microfilm) (1976–1983) 2008–128: 01 00 – 13 21, record group 13–17 Female prisoners.

15 DfK 1.ktr, 133-1973, 19 February 1975.

16 DfK 1.ktr, 133-1973, 9–11 June 1975.

17 DfK 2. k. 966-2, 5 August 1975.

18 DfK 2. k. 966-2, 4 December 1975.

19 With the state prison in Ringe's planning and later opening in 1976, prison inspector Erik Andersen created a scrapbook, which Bodil Philip continued upon her accession in 1989. The scrapbooks contain articles mainly from the local newspapers, but also the nationwide newspapers, science magazines, and foreign newspapers. Now at the National Archives of Odense.

20 Official Report of Danish Parliamentary Proceedings 1975/76 qs. 11577–11579.

21 DfK 2. k. 966-2 *Information*, 22 October 1980 and Rentzmanns' response.

22 Official Report of Danish Parliamentary Proceedings 1979/80 (2nd assembly), *Forhandlingerne spalte* (negotiation column), 2061–2062.

23 DfK 2. k. 966–2, 4 December 1975.

References

Andersen, E. (1977) Statsfængslet i Ringe. In: Direktoratet for Kriminalforsorgen. *Kriminalforsorgen 1976*. København, Direktoratet for Kriminalforsorgen, pp. 122–129.

Andersen, E. (1992) Den lange vej. Kriminalforsorgen efter straffelovsreformen 1933 *Bikrerød, Kriminalforsorgens Uddannelsescenter*.

Balvig, F. (2005) When Law and Order Returned to Denmark. *Journal of Scandinavian Studies in Criminology and Crime Prevention* 5(2), pp. 167–187.

Barker, V. (2012) Nordic Exceptionalism Revisited: Explaining the Paradox of a Janus-Faced Penal Regime. *Theoretical Criminology* 17(1), pp. 5–25.

Barker, V. and Smith, P. S. (2021) This is Denmark: Prison Islands and the Detention of Immigrants. *British Journal of Criminology* 61(6), pp. 1540–1556.

Brydensholt, H. H. (2007) Tilblivelsen af Statsfængslet i Ringe. *Fængselshistorisk Selskab* 2007, pp. 7–35.

Cavadino, M. and Dignan, J. (2006) *Penal Systems: A Comparative Approach*. London, Sage Publications.

Engbo, H. J. (2017) Normalisation in Nordic Prisons: From a Prison Governor's Perspective. In: P. S. Smith and T. Ugelvik, eds. *Scandinavian Penal History, Culture and Prison Practice: Embraced by the Welfare State?* London, Palgrave MacMillan, pp. 327–352.

Engbo, H. J. (2021) Disciplinærretlig skyld og straf i danske fængsler. *Nordisk Tidsskrift for Kriminalvidenskab* 108(1), pp. 136–156.

Fransen, P. (2010) Altid en noget urolig etat. In: M. Henze, ed. *Direktoratet for Kriminalforsorgen 1910–2010*. København, Direktoratet for Kriminalforsorgen, pp. 37–152.

Fransen, P. (2013) *Borgen med de mange ansigter: Statsfængslet i Nyborg 1913–2013*. Nyborg, Statsfængslet i Nyborg.

Fransen, P. (2017a) *Livet i de Røde Barakker: Horserød 1917-2017*. Odense, Syddansk Universitetsforlag.

Fransen, P. (2017b) The Rise of the Open Prisons and the Breakthrough of the Principle of Normalisation from the 1930s Until Today. In: P. S. Smith and T. Ugelvik, eds. *Scandinavian Penal History, Culture and Prison Practice: Embraced by the Welfare State?* London, Palgrave MacMillan, pp. 81–102.

Fransen, P. (2021a) Hvem styrer fængslerne og fangehåndteringen i Danmark? Stillingen som direktør for fængselsvæsenet/kriminalforsorgen gennem 111 år. *Nordisk Tidsskrift for Kriminalvidenskab* 108(1), pp. 77–98.

Fransen, P. (2021b) Danske fængsler og fængselsideologi i det 20. og 21. Århundrede. *Noter – Forbrydelse og Straf* 228, pp. 30–35.

Holstein, B. E. (Ed.). (1980) Ledelse og menneskeværd. Beskrivelse og vurdering af forsøgsvirksomheden ved Statsfængslet i Ringe 1975–1979. Direktoratet for Kriminalforsorgen.

Hopgood, S. (2013) *The Endtimes of Human Rights*. Ithaca, NY, Cornell Press.

https://www.thedanishparliament.dk/en/folketing-hansard.

Lappi-Seppälä, T. (2008) Trust, Welfare, and Political Culture: Explaining Differences in National Penal Policies. In: M. Tonry, ed. *Crime and Justice: A Review of Research*, Vol. 37. Chicago, The University of Chicago Press, pp. 313–387.

Lappi-Seppälä, T. and Tonry, M. (2011) Crime, Criminal Justice, and Criminology in the Nordic Countries. *Crime and Justice* 40(1), pp. 1–32.

Martinson, R. (1974) What Works? Questions and Answers about Prison Reform. *The Public Interest*, 1974-04-01, 35, pp. 22–54.

Mathiesen, T. (2012) Scandinavian Exceptionalism in Penal Matters: Reality or Wishful Thinking? In: T. Ugelvik and J. Dullum, eds. *Penal Exceptionalism? Nordic Prison Policy and Practice*. Abingdon, Routledge, pp. 13–37.

Minke, L. K. and Smoyer, A. B. (2017) Prison Food in Denmark: Normal Responsibility or Ethnocentric Imaginations? In: P. S. Smith and T. Ugelvik, eds. *Scandinavian Penal History, Culture and Prison Practice: Embraced by the Welfare State?* London, Palgrave MacMillan, pp. 353–376.

Moyn, S. (2012) *The Last Utopia: Human Rights in History*. Cambridge, MA, Harvard University Press.

Philip, B. (2020) *Statsfængslet i Ringe 1975–2015 Set i Lyset Af Fængslets Scrapbog (Manus I Statsfængslet I Ringe: Fængselsinspektør Bodil Philips Materiale (1972–2015) Pakke 4: Scrapbog 1975–1996)*.

Pratt, J. (2008a) Scandinavian Exceptionalism in an Era of Penal Excess: Part I: The Nature and Roots of Scandinavian Exceptionalism. *British Journal of Criminology* 48(2), pp. 119–137.

Pratt, J. (2008b) Scandinavian Exceptionalism in an Era of Penal Excess: Part II: Does Scandinavian Exceptionalism Have a Future? *British Journal of Criminology* 48(3), pp. 275–292.

Pratt, J. and Eriksson, A. (2013) *Contrasts in Punishment: An Explanation of Anglophone Excess and Nordic Exceptionalism*. London, Routledge.

Smith, P. S. (2003) *Moralske hospitaler: Det moderne fængselsvæsens gennembrud 1770–1870*. København, Forum.

Smith, P. S. (2012) A Critical Look at Scandinavian Exceptionalism: Welfare State Theories, Penal Populism, and Prison Conditions in Denmark and Scandinavia. In: T. Ugelvik and J. Dullum, eds. *Penal Exceptionalism? Nordic Prison Policy and Practice*. Abingdon, Routledge, pp. 38–57.

Smith, P. S. (2014) *When the Innocent are Punished: The Children of Imprisoned Parents*. London: Palgrave Macmillan.

Smith, P. S. (2016) Prisons and Human Rights: Past, Present and Future Challenges. In: L. Weber, E. Fishwick, and M. Marmo, eds. *The Routledge International Handbook of Criminology and Human Rights*. London, Routledge, pp. 525–535.

Smith, P. S. (2017) Punishment Without Conviction? Scandinavian Pre-trial Practices and the Power of the "Benevolent" State. In: P. Scharff Smith and T. Ugelvik, eds. *Scandinavian Penal History, Culture and Prison Practice*. Palgrave Studies in Prisons and Penology. London, Palgrave Macmillan, pp. 129–156.

Smith, P. S. and Ugelvik, T., eds. (2017) *Scandinavian Penal History, Culture and Prison Practice: Embraced by the Welfare State?* London, Palgrave MacMillan.

Wacquant, L. J. D. (2008) *Urban Outcasts: A Comparative Sociology of Advanced Marginality*. Cambridge, Polity Press.

Zyl Smit, D. and Snacken, S. (2011) *Principles of European Prison Law and Policy: Penology and Human Rights*. Oxford, Oxford University Press.

Unprinted sources

National Archives of Copenhagen:

By- og Boligministeriet, Statsbyggekontoret: Journalsager (Statsbyggesager) (1950-1972) Pakke 288: 1963 5 19 - 6 3.

Direktoratet for Kriminalforsorgen (DfK), 1. Kontor: Journalsager (1946-1979) Pakke 590: 1973 126 – 165.

Direktoratet for Kriminalforsorgen (DfK), 1. Kontor: Journalsager (1946-1979) Pakke 528: 1969 92 10 – 118.

Direktoratet for Kriminalforsorgen, (DfK) 2. afdeling: Journalsager (1972 -1989) Pakke 204 og 205: 966 2 – 2.

Finansministeriet, Administrationsdepartementet: Journalsager I. (Institutionssager m.m.) (1965-1974) 19.

National Archives of Odense

Statsfængslet i Ringe: Generel journal (mikrofilm) (1976-1983) 2008-128: 01 00 - 13 21.

Statsfængslet i Ringe: Fængselsinspektør Bodil Philips materiale (1972-2015) Pakke 4: Scrapbog 1975 – 1996.

3 Nordic perspectives on international criminal law and international humanitarian law

Mark Klamberg

There is a common Nordic perspective on international humanitarian law (IHL) and international criminal law (ICL) which may be explained by a common historical and cultural heritage as well as by conscious and close Nordic cooperation in the field of legislation, including criminal law. Noteworthy is the 1872 congress of Nordic jurists, convened in Copenhagen with the express purpose of advancing the legal unification of Scandinavia. Since that time, cooperation among the Nordic countries has evolved, especially after the 1940s. Following the establishment of the Nordic Council in 1952, cooperation in legal matters has been on a permanent basis. Cooperation concerning criminal matters has been facilitated by a like-minded approach in relation to areas such as extradition, mutual legal aid, execution of sentence, criminality, and criminal policy.[1]

Nordic countries are seen as belonging to the continental European law tradition, although separate from the Romanistic and German legal families. They tend to avoid undue conceptualism and the construction of large-scale integrated theoretical systems, which places them somewhere between the continental European law tradition and the common law tradition.[2] This is also manifested in criminal law and criminal procedure; although the law is based on statutes, the criminal proceedings are adversarial, and the legal vocabulary is close to the common law tradition. Moreover, the Scandinavian countries have a similar approach with each other when it comes to legal sources with the particular role that preparatory works have. Preparatory works are not only a source of law, they also often contain a comparative outlook where particular attention is made to similar legislative processes and statutes in other Nordic countries, all in an effort of harmonization among the Nordic countries.

Thus, when a Nordic country introduces a law relating to IHL or ICL the legislator will consider how it has been done in the neighbouring countries. This has been facilitated by the fact that Scandinavian languages, except for Finnish, are very closely related. Swedish is a recognized minority language in Finland, taught also to those who have Finnish as their first language and Finnish legislation is available in Swedish. This means that Scandinavian lawyers can speak and write in their own language and still understand each other quite well.[3]

The Nordic countries also share their approach to public international law in several regards: a dualist approach to the relationship between national law and

DOI: 10.4324/9781003195504-5

public international law and the political will to ratify relevant international treaties at an early phase. This means that the relevant IHL and ICL, to a large extent, have been implemented in national legislation from the 1950s and onwards. With the exception of Sweden, Nordic countries share the history of being involved in the Second World War. The end of the war triggered legal proceedings in all three countries, although these proceedings had different scope, legal frameworks, aims, and results.

In modern times, Nordic countries share the experience of peace within their countries and with their neighbours. They have all received immigrants, including refugees from conflict areas, arriving in distinct periods depending on the conflict at hand and the availability of migrant routes. The international crimes that have been investigated and prosecuted in Nordic countries have thus – to a very large extent – related to conflict areas of these immigrants. Since the immigrants arrived from distinct areas and in distinct periods, weaknesses were revealed and the need for legal reform became clear at these times in Scandinavia. This has been reinforced by the Nordic countries joining relevant international legal regimes at similar periods of time. The Nordic countries also perceive and promote themselves as progressive, law-abiding, and good citizens in a global context.

Thus, one would expect the Nordic countries to have almost identical legislation implementing IHL and ICL. In a global comparison, this might appear somewhat true, however when looking closer at the differences within Scandinavia a puzzle appears – how can we explain the differences that exist within Scandinavia in their implementation of IHL and ICL?

While there have been some early examples of scholarly works,[4] it is primarily two decades when scholars have examined how ICL and IHL is implemented in the Nordic countries[5] and pursued at the domestic level.[6] The current chapter certainly builds on existing scholarship, while it also provides for a comparison which has not really been done yet.

The current chapter will examine how ICL and IHL has been implemented in a domestic context in relation to three themes: 1) implementing legislation; 2) prosecutorial discretion, jurisdiction, and government involvement, and 3) situations investigated and cases adjudicated by courts in the Nordic countries. This will be based on separate country and thematic studies previously conducted by several scholars.[7] For each of the three themes there will be an initial account for each of the Nordic countries, followed by a comparative analysis. Particular attention will be paid to transplants from one Nordic country to another.

State of the relevant legal frameworks in the Nordic countries

This section will focus on when domestic legislation was introduced and how it implements ICL and IHL. As such it examines the domestic implementation of international legal frameworks, differences, and similarities in Nordics. It includes an account of the evolution of domestic legislation which is not only of historical interest, it may also have determinative practical significance in current and future cases since some of the acts to be prosecuted may relate to events committed several years ago. In such cases the old legislation may still be applicable pursuant to principle of legality which provides that a person may only be convicted for acts that were criminalized at the time when the act was committed. Next there will be a description of the evolution and state of the relevant legal frameworks in each of the Nordic countries. This will allow for a subsequent comparative analysis. Four observations and arguments will be made: first, all major revisions of domestic legalisation in the Nordic countries appear to have been done as responses to the adoption and ratification of/accession to international treaties. Second, the Nordic countries have all from at least from the early 1950s criminalized violations against IHL, i.e., war crimes. Third, domestic legislation in Finland, Sweden, and Denmark initially made references to customary international law as basis for criminal responsibility which made the criminalization in the mentioned countries somewhat open-ended. Finally, the Nordic tradition of trying to harmonize legislation appears to be present. In their preparatory works, Sweden, Finland, and Norway explicitly reference other Nordic laws and ongoing reforms in this area.

Sweden

The Swedish penal regulation 'crime against international law' was introduced with the reform of Swedish penal law in 1948.[8] Chapter 27 section 11 of the Penal law provided for sanctioning war crimes on the basis of treaties as well as customary international law.[9] This made the criminalization somewhat open-ended and continuously adaptive to changes in customary international law. The Swedish Government was inspired by Danish legislation in this area.[10] As a result of the adoption of the four Geneva Conventions in 1949 and Sweden's accession to these conventions the law was amended in 1954. When the Criminal Code (Brottsbalken) was adopted in 1962 the same wording of crime against international law was used in its chapter 22 section 11 as had been used previously in chapter 27 section 11 of the Penal Law. A separate Law on Genocide was introduced 1964.[11] The provision on crime against international law was amended in 1986 and the scope of crime against international law was limited to serious violations, and the provision at that time contained a non-exhaustive list of criminalized acts. The provision was also moved to chapter 22 section 6 of the Criminal Code. The term 'serious violations' in chapter 22 section 6 of the Criminal Code goes beyond the scope of the 'grave breaches' regime of the 1949 Geneva Conventions and Additional Protocol I.[12] With the adoption of the Rome Statute of the International Criminal Court in 1998 and Sweden's impending accession thereto, the government initiated a review on the Swedish legislation on criminal responsibility for international crimes and Swedish criminal jurisdiction, resulting in the report SOU 2002:98.[13] Some of the Commission's proposals were implemented in separate legal amendments, for example 2010 on statute of limitations preserving jurisdiction for alleged international crimes committed after 1985.[14] The substantial change was made in 2014 by the introduction of the Act on Criminal Responsibility for Genocide, Crimes against Humanity and War Crimes (2014:406) and chapter 22 section 6 of the

Criminal Code was repealed. The new law better harmonized the criminalization of genocide with the wording in the UN Genocide Convention and the Rome Statute.[15] The change was greater in relation to war crimes, since, instead of having an open-ended penal regulation with the legal characterization 'crimes against international law', the new law gives an exhaustive list of what is meant by war crimes; and the reference to customary international law has been removed. In the 2014 Act, the legislator placed those acts which may amount to war crimes in an International Armed Conflict as well as in Non-International Armed Conflict in the same provisions, i.e., sections 3, 4, and 6, while the offences which amount to war crimes only in IAC are in sections 5 and 7. This differs from how the provision on war crimes is structured in article 8 of the Rome Statute. This was an acknowledgement of the development, on a domestic level and international level, towards making the two types of armed conflict equal in terms of the applicability of rules in IHL.[16] The preparatory works states Finland and Norway as examples of the same approach.[17] The Act also contains a new penal regulation on crimes against humanity.[18]

Finland

Finland had three major amendments to the Criminal Code relevant for the prosecution of international crimes.[19] The first major broadly applicable legislation was adopted in 1974 which included a penal provision on war crime, petty warfare crime, violations of human rights, aggravated violation of human rights, and genocide.[20] Similar to the Swedish law, the Finnish law was open-ended and provided for sanctioning war crimes on the basis of treaties as well as customary international law.[21] The legislation was revised in 1995 as part of a larger reform of the Criminal Code. After the revision the Criminal Code contained provisions on warfare crime, aggravated warfare crime, petty warfare crime, violations of human rights in a state of emergency, aggravated violations of human rights in a state of emergency, genocide, and preparation of genocide.[22] The provision retained its open-ended character, sanctioning of war crimes was based in treaties as well as customary international law.[23] When Finland ratified the Rome Statute in 2000 there was a perception that the existing substantial definitions of crime sufficiently corresponded to international law.[24] However, the Criminal Code was eventually amended in 2008. The Rome Statute and the ICC elements of crime had a major role in this revision; however, the new legislation also includes a reference to customary international law.[25] The reference to customary international law is in the chapeau of chapter 11 section 5, however, it does not appear to make the provision open-ended as the provision contains a list of 14 specified acts that amount to war crimes. It is rather a means for interpreting the crimes listed in section 5.[26]

Denmark

When Denmark acceded to the Rome Statute in 2001, it introduced implementing legislation[27] in order to meet the obligations relating to cooperation with the International Criminal Court (ICC) and criminal responsibility for offences directed against the Court's administration of justice (article 70 of the Rome Statute). However, the implementing legislation at that time did not entail any additional consequences for Danish legislation. There were already other laws in place at that time. In order to implement the 1948 Genocide Convention, genocide has been criminalized in Denmark since 1955 in a special law.[28] Other international crimes are criminalized in separate statutes, instead they are partially criminalized through the Danish Criminal Code[29] and the Danish Military Penal Code.[30] The Military Penal Code provides for criminal responsibility for certain acts committed during armed conflict, for example abuse of protected characteristics or designations, use of war methods or procedures contrary to an international agreement, or international customary law and plundering.[31] These provisions are also applicable for civilians who commit these acts as indicated by the use of the words 'anybody'. There are no specific provisions on crimes against humanity, instead such acts must be prosecuted under domestic provisions such as murder or rape.[32] The Danish approach – having a somewhat open-ended provision in Military Penal Code where criminal responsibility can be based on customary international law – appears similar to the situations in Finland prior to 2008 and Sweden prior to 2014.

Norway

The Norwegian military penal law had, in sections 100–108, provisions that could be used to sanction war crimes.[33] This was clarified in 1954 in an amendment adopted in the context of Norway ratifying the four Geneva Conventions in 1951.[34] However, the law did not cover genocide or crimes against humanity. This became a particular problem in relation to the 1994 Genocide, as later illustrated by the *Bugingo* case.[35] In 2001, when Norway adopted legislation to regulate its relationship with the ICC, the Ministry of Justice noted that the Norwegian criminal code did not correspond to the Rome Statute.[36] The Ministry also stated that Finland and Sweden had penal provisions at the time that corresponded better with the Rome Statute than Norwegian law.[37] This probably referred to the existence of Swedish Law on Genocide from 1964 and the Finnish law from 1974; no such law had been adopted in Norway. A more thorough regulation of international crimes into Norwegian legislation became part of the greater project of introduction a new Norwegian civil penal code. This was a project that started in 1980, the code was adopted in 2005 and came into effect first in 2015. However, the Norwegian Government decided to bring forward the entry into force of chapter 16 of the new penal code on international crimes already in March 2008.[38] The preparatory works have references to legislation and similar reform project in Sweden, Denmark, and Germany, including the Swedish report SOU 2002:98 mentioned above.[39] When it comes to war crimes, Norway decided to depart from the structure in article 8 of the Rome Statute and instead followed the German example and the draft law in SOU 2002:98.[40] This meant that some acts are in the provision regardless if committed in a IAC or NIAC, war crimes are grouped based on the prohibited acts or types of legal goods which are to be protected.[41]

There are at least four observations that can be made in a comparative assessment. First, all major revisions of domestic legalisation in the Nordic countries appear to have been done as responses to the adoption and ratification of/accession to international treaties. This is obvious in relation to the 1948 Genocide Convention, 1949 Geneva Convention, and the 1998 Rome Statute. It is less clear when it comes to 1977 Additional Protocols to the 1949 Geneva Convention which did not prompt immediate specific domestic legislation at the time of their adoption and ratification.[42] One plausible explanation as to why it did not happen after 1977 was that references in domestic legislation to customary international law could accommodate evolution in international humanitarian law. Second, the Nordic countries have all from at least from the early 1950s criminalized violations against IHL, i.e., war crimes. Except for Norway, they have also criminalized genocide as a distinct crime for several decades. It was only recently that Sweden, Finland, and Norway criminalized crimes against humanity. Finland had admittedly already criminalized 'kränkning av mänskliga rättigheter' (violation against human rights) in 1974, however this was only if committed in the context of armed conflict and the specific acts constituted what we today would describe as war crimes. Today, all Nordic countries have criminalized the core international crimes of genocide, war crimes, and crimes against humanity, except for Denmark in relation to the later crime. Third, domestic legislation in Finland, Sweden, and Denmark initially contained references to customary international law as basis for criminal responsibility which made the criminalization somewhat open-ended, this has been replaced in Finland and Sweden by lists enumerating the criminalized acts that may amount to war crimes. The Finnish law still has a reference to customary international law, but this is arguably to be used as a means to interpret the listed crimes and not as a self-standing basis for criminal responsibility. Norway never had a law with this open-ended character, when chapter 16 in the penal code was introduced on international crimes it also contained a closed list on war crimes. Denmark has not, to this date, changed its domestic legislation and thus the open-ended character of its law remains. Moreover, it may be noted that in the three countries that have changed its legislation in recent times, the structure of the provisions on war crimes have not followed the structure of article 8 of the Rome Statute when it comes to distinguishing between NIACs and IACs. Finally, the Nordic tradition of trying to harmonize legislation appears to be present. In their preparatory works, Sweden, Finland, and Norway explicitly reference other Nordic laws and ongoing reforms in this area.[43] In the Norwegian and Finnish preparatory works there also frequent references to German law.[44] Thus, with Denmark a bit lagging, there appears to be a Nordic approach and inter-Nordic discussion on how to implement ICL and IHL in domestic legislation.

Jurisdiction, prosecutorial discretion and government involvement in investigation and prosecution

As indicated at the beginning of this chapter, there is a common tradition and history in the Nordic countries when it comes to criminal matters and procedure.

However, differences may still be found. In a global comparison, some of these differences may be associated with diverging approaches found either in common law countries or continental European countries.

Moreover, in the context of domestic investigation and prosecution of international crimes, prosecutorial discretion, jurisdiction, and government involvement are interrelated for the following reason. All of the Nordic countries allow for prosecution of international criminals based on universal jurisdiction. If this is combined with the obligation to prosecute, as in Sweden and Finland, there is an obvious opportunity (or risk) that prosecutions will be brought against military and political leaders of other countries. This may create a problem for the government of the country where the prosecution is made and is not necessarily resolved by rules on immunity for foreign officials. Thus, there may be a need for the government to screen cases before the prosecution is allowed to bring them forward, which in turn creates challenges to principles of prosecutorial independence.

Prosecutorial discretion

The Nordic countries, to various degrees, limit the discretion and instead impose an obligation on the prosecutor to prosecute alleged crimes. In Sweden, unless otherwise prescribed, prosecutors must prosecute offences falling within the domain of public prosecution.[45] In Finland, there is a similar obligation.[46] Both systems have traditionally been described as containing an *absolute* obligation to prosecute – which is a familiar feature of continental European countries. However, this rule has been supplemented with caveats,[47] thus it is more correct to describe it in terms of a *relative* obligation.[48] In contrast to Finland and Sweden, there is no obligation to prosecute in Norway and Denmark. Instead, the later apply the principle of opportunity (*opportunitetsprincipen*) which grants a wider discretion for the prosecutor,[49] more like the approach in common law countries.

Extraterritorial jurisdiction

The same countries also allow for prosecution based on the active nationality principles and the principle of universal jurisdiction,[50] i.e., forms of extraterritorial jurisdiction. Combining extraterritorial jurisdiction and an obligation to prosecute creates a wide potential to prosecute international crimes.

Government involvement

In view of the wide potential to prosecute international crimes, states may perceive an obligation in relation to international law on immunities as well as political interests to limit jurisdiction or at least have some checks on the prosecutor. However, this triggers questions relating to arbitrariness: it may raise doubt about the independence and impartiality of the legal proceedings.[51] A system requiring an authorization to prosecute, which is controlled by the government, opens political considerations. What are the relevant public international law considerations? The obligation of states either to prosecute international crimes or to surrender them to a state capable of investigating and prosecuting such crimes (*aut dedere aut judicare*) would favour a system where prosecutors have an absolute duty to prosecute without the need for prior authorization. The *aut dedere aut judicare* principle is applicable for grave breaches of international humanitarian law,[52] torture,[53] and genocide.[54] In contrast, obligations relating to immunity for a foreign head of state, head of government, minister of foreign affairs, and other state representatives suggest that prior government authorization to prosecute should be required.

The Swedish Criminal Code, chapter 2 section 7, provides that prosecution based on extraterritorial jurisdiction may only be initiated with authorization by the Prosecutor-General or the government (the national cabinet of ministers).[55] The default approach is that the Prosecutor-General should authorize prosecutions for crimes committed outside of Sweden.[56] However, if the decision may affect Sweden's foreign and security policy, prosecution is dependent upon authorization by the national cabinet of ministers.[57] This requirement for an authorization to prosecute (*åtalsförordnande*) indicates that the intent was never that prosecutions should be pressed home to the extent that the jurisdictional rules suggest. The relevant provision provides that the following should be considered when deciding whether to authorise a prosecution.

1. whether a prosecution in this country is compatible with Sweden's obligations under public international law;
2. the extent to which the offences or the suspect are linked to Sweden;
3. whether measures for legal proceedings have been or will be initiated in another state or before an international court; and
4. what actual possibilities there are to investigate the offence and bring legal proceedings against the suspect here.[58]

The Criminal Code of Finland similarly provides that prosecution based on extraterritorial jurisdiction may only be initiated by the Prosecutor-General.[59] However, such authorization is exempted in certain, limited situations, for example if the offence was committed by a Finnish citizen or a foreigner residing in Finland and a criminal act was directed at Finland, a Finnish citizen, a foreigner permanently resident in Finland, or a Finnish corporation, foundation, or other legal entity.[60]

Under section 13 of the 1902 Norwegian Penal Code (repealed), the King (i.e., the government) had to authorise prosecution in relation to certain crimes (for example murder, assault, and rape) committed by foreigners outside of Norway.[61] Prosecution relating to crimes committed outside of Norway shall, pursuant to section 5 of the 2005 Norwegian Penal Code (in force), only be instituted when in the public interest. Normally, this determination is made by the prosecutor handling the case. The authority to authorize prosecution which previously belonged to the King (i.e., the government) has been transferred to the Director of Public Prosecutions (Riksadvokaten).[62]

To summarize, prosecutorial discretion, jurisdiction, and government involvement are interrelated matters. The fact that the prosecutors in Finland and Sweden have an obligation to prosecute and, thus, less direction than their Norwegian and Danish counterparts may warrant some kind of centralized control over prosecutions in Finland and Sweden in order to avoid diplomatic meltdowns with other countries.

Having set out the relevant legal frameworks in the Nordics, in relation to which crimes and under which conditions they may be prosecuted, the next section will examine how these rules play out in the situations investigated and cases adjudicated.

Situations investigated and cases adjudicated by courts in the Nordic countries

Although none of the Scandinavian countries have had armed conflicts on their soil since the Second World War, there have still been trials relating to events in the last decades. Among the war criminals, witnesses, and victims of atrocity crimes that are here, many have come to the Nordic countries as asylum seekers. Others, who have been born and raised in the Nordics, travel to conflict areas and later return. The common geographic position of the Nordic countries, as well as their shared international travel routes and somewhat similar refugee policies, probably explain why the cases in the Nordic countries originate from conflicts in the same regions: former Yugoslavia, Rwanda, and Syria/Iraq. The cases that follow are ones where the prosecution and/or the judgment has concerned core international crimes (genocide, war crimes, crimes against humanity), not prosecutions which exclusively have been brought forward as terrorist cases.

In total, four cases have originated from Yugoslavia, three adjudicated in Sweden,[63] one in Norway.[64] Notably, the two Swedish cases *Arklöv* and *Makitan* concerned crimes in the same prison camp in Bosnia as the *Repak* case before the Oslo District Court and later before Norway's Supreme Court.[65] Thus, they allow for a comparison of how almost identical cases were adjudicated in two different countries. All three defendants in three separate trials were members of the Croatian Defence Forces (HOS) and they were prosecuted for similar criminality, namely illegal detention. The Swedish and Norwegian authorities cooperated in the investigation of these cases, which is evidenced in several references in the *Makitan* case (Stockholm District Court) to legal and factual matters in the *Repak* case (Oslo District Court).[66] There are some interesting differences between the facts and the court's findings in the three cases. The *Makitan* case and *Repak* case concerned alleged crimes in the same prison camp as in the *Arklöv* case but committed at a different point of time (summer 1992 in Makitan and Repak, July 1993 in Arklöv). Makitan and Repak were – like Arklöv – members of HOS, a paramilitary Croatian organization, with the difference that the victims in the *Arklöv* case were Bosnian Muslims while the victims in the *Makitan* case and Repak case were Serbs. The deprivation of the Serbs' liberty was part of the effort to pressurise the Federal Republic of

Yugoslavia to exchange prisoners.[67] The criminal acts in the *Arklöv* case were characterized as part of an NIAC,[68] while the acts in the *Repak* case and the *Makitan* case were characterized as part of an IAC.[69] In other words, it was the same prison camp run by the same group, but the courts in the two cases characterized the conflict differently, and this had consequences in the Swedish cases for the applicable law as it differs between the two types of conflict. The difference in classification of the conflict may be explained by the fact that the parties to the conflict at the time of the alleged acts were different and thus the conflict was different. An alternative explanation is that the district court in the *Arklöv* case viewed HOS as more independent from the Croatian state than did the courts in the *Repak* case and the *Makitan* case.[70] The changes in the Norwegian legislation presented particular problems in the *Repak* case, while the District Court initially ruled that it could apply the law which was in force from 2008, the Supreme Court ruled that it could not be applied retroactively.[71]

Eight cases have originated from Rwanda, one adjudicated in Finland,[72] three in Sweden,[73] one in Norway[74] and three cases initiated but not adjudicated in Denmark.[75] While the Swedish and Finnish district courts could convict for genocide, the Norwegian court – due to absence of criminalization of genocide prior to 2008 – could only convict the defendant for 'ordinary' premediated murder under the Norwegian penal code. However, the defendant did receive the maximum prison sentence available under Norwegian law (21 years).[76] Danish authorities have dealt with three cases concerning the genocide in Rwanda. The Special International Crimes Office (*Statsadvokaten for Særlige Internationale Straffesager* – SAIS) initiated investigations in the first case in 2006 but it was terminated in 2007 due to lack of evidence. A second case was initiated in 2010 with an arrest of a Rwandan citizen who was transferred to Rwanda in 2014 following a decision by the Supreme Court of Denmark. In a third case, a Danish citizen of Rwandan origin was extradited to Rwanda for prosecution, following a decision in 2018 by the High Court of Eastern Denmark.[77]

In total, eleven cases have originated from Syria/Iraq following the so-called 'Arab spring' and the rise of multiple rebel and jihadi groups, four cases have been adjudicated in Finland[78] and seven in Sweden.[79] Several of the photographs – invoked as evidence in the trials – show dead bodies being used as trophies with the defendants visible next to them. The cases involve multiple interesting matters. A question in the *Saaed* case was whether the dead are protected persons under IHL and ICL, a question that appeared to be of general relevance. The Swedish Supreme Court ruled that the dead are protected persons.[80] The Stockholm District Court, confirmed by the Appeal Court in the *Haisam-Sakhanh* case, ruled that armed non-state actors can establish courts and issue judgments involving death sentences under IHL and ICL if the court is independent and impartial and guarantees certain fair trial requirements.[81] Almost all of the cases involved photographs or videos either taken by the defendants themselves or by the group they belong to. These photographs or videos have, in different ways, reached the Finnish or Swedish authorities which subsequently resulted in investigations and trial. The fact that such evidence has not, in all of these cases, been obtained directly by the police may raise concern regarding the authenticity and reliability of that evidence. However, this has proven to be less of a problem in most of these cases since several of the defendants admitted the alleged acts without necessarily criminal guilt,[82] and in at least one case the defendants also denied the alleged acts.[83]

There is one case that originated in Iran, relating to events in 1988 relating to the Iraq-Iran war and mass executions of opponents to the Iranian Government. The district court of Stockholm convicted Noury for war crimes and murder,[84] a conviction that was appealed by the defendant, and the outcome is still pending.

Conclusions

There is a tendency in legal scholarship to assume that a certain legal regime – for example, international criminal law – is on an evolutionary trajectory towards ever-increasing harmonization, commonality between countries, and greater domestic implementation of international norms. Studying the implementation of IHL and ICL in the Nordic countries may in some ways prove this assumption true, for example, when international crimes have been subject to ever-expanding and more detailed criminalization in domestic statutes. This may have occurred at different points of time in the Nordic countries, yet the common trend is clear. However, in some regards, differences in national traditions persist as illustrated on how prosecutorial discretion has been and probably will remain greater in Denmark and Norway compared to Finland and Sweden. Setbacks, regression, and discontinuity are also possible.[85] Despite the national characteristics, there is arguably a common Nordic approach to IHL and ICL with several similar regulatory features, policies, and experiences. The Nordic countries all allow for prosecution based on the active nationality principles and the principle of universal jurisdiction. They have all – from at least the early 1950s – criminalized violations against IHL, i.e., war crimes. The domestic legislation in Finland, Sweden, and Denmark initially made references to customary international law as a basis for criminal responsibility which made their criminalization processes somewhat open-ended. All major revisions of domestic legalisation in the Nordic countries appear to have been done in response to the adoption and ratification of/accession to international treaties. The Nordic tradition of trying to harmonize legislation appears to be present. In their preparatory works, Sweden, Finland, and Norway explicitly reference other Nordic laws and ongoing reforms in this area. All of the countries were early to ratify the Rome Statute, all between 2000 and 2001. As noted above, Nordic countries have a common geographic position, shared international travel routes, and somewhat similar refugee policies which probably explain why the cases in Nordic countries originate from conflicts in the same regions: former Yugoslavia, Rwanda, and Syria/Iraq.

In a global comparison, the Nordic countries may provide an example of how the domestic investigation and prosecution of international crimes may become well integrated with existing structures of criminal justice. Countries outside Scandinavia have already, or will, meet similar challenges; the need to exchange experience and scrutinize one's own assumptions will remain. This is not only an endeavour for practitioners and state organs – it also a worthy scholarly enterprise to undertake comparative studies of the domestic investigation and prosecution of international crimes, asking how different countries sanction international crimes. Hopefully the current chapter will invite further comparative research.

Notes

1 Zweigert, Konrad and Kötz, Hein, *Introduction to Comparative Law* (Second Edition, Oxford: Clarendon Press, 1987), p. 291; Suominen, Annika, *The Principle of Mutual Recognition in Cooperation in Criminal Matters* (Intersentia, 2011), p. 41; see Hurwitz, Stephan, 'Nordisk kriminalretligt samarbejde', *Nordisk tidsskrift for kriminalvidenskab* (1949), 36(1), 74–75 on meetings in Stockholm and Copenhagen on legislative coordination in the field of criminal matters.
2 Zweigert & Kötz (1987), pp. 287, 291, and 295.
3 Ibid, p. 291.
4 Gihl, Torsten, 'Angående begreppet "folkrättsbrott"', *Nordic Journal of International Law* (1952), 22(1), 240–256.
5 Hannikainen, Lauri, 'Implementation of International Humanitarian Law in Finnish Law' in Hannikainen, Lauri (ed), *Implementing Humanitarian Law Applicable in Armed Conflicts: The Case of Finland* (Dordrecht: Martinus Nijhoff Publishers, 1992), 114–145; Cameron, Iain, 'Swedish Investigations for Gross Human Rights Violations, Actual and Possible' in Asp, Petter, Herlitz, Carl Erik, and Holmqvist, Lena (eds), *Flores juris et legum: festskrift till Nils Jareborg* (Uppsala: Iustus, 2002), 123–149; Friman, Håkan, 'Political and Legal Considerations in Sweden Relating to the Rome Statute for the International Criminal Court' in Lee, Roy S. (ed), *States' Responses to Issues Arising from the ICC Statute, Constitutional, Sovereignty, Judicial Cooperation and Criminal Law, 121–145* (Ardsley: Transnational Publishers, 2005); Plum, Lars and Laursen, Andreas (eds), *Enhver Stats pligt...*(København: Jurist- og Økonomiforbundets Forlag, 2007); Bring, Ove and Körlof, Anna, *Folkrätt i krig, kris och fredsoperationer* (Fourth Edition, Stockholm: Norstedts Juridik, 2010); Kimpimäki, Minna, 'Taking International Criminal Law Seriously: A Decade of Finnish Criminal Legislation' in Elholm, Thomas (ed), *Liber Amicarum et Amicorum Karin Cornils: Glimt af Nordisk Strafrätt og Straffeprocessrett* (Copenhagen: Djøf, 2010), 1–17; Cameron, Iain et al., *International Criminal Law from a Swedish Perspective* (Cambridge-Antwerp-Portland: Intersentia, 2011); Kimpimäki, Minna, 'Sotarikollisia ja merirosvoja – Suomen rikosoikeudellisen toimivallan rajat', *Lakimies* (2011), 5; Asp, Petter, *Internationell straffrätt* (Uppsala: Iustus Förlag, 2011); Asp, Petter, 'Folkrätten och den svenska straffrätten' in Stern, Rebecca and Österdahl, Inger (eds), *Folkrätten i Svensk rätt* (Malmö: Liber, 2012), 58–73; Høgestøl, Sofie, 'En generell kriminalisering av fremmedkrigere: den norske modellen og påtaleskjønn i straffeloven § 145' in Andersson, Anna, Høgestøl, Sofie, and Lie, Anne (eds), *Fremmedkrigere: forebygging, straffeforfølgning og rehabilitering i Skandinavia* (Oslo: Gyldendal Juridisk, 2018).
6 Plum, Lars, 'SAIS – Statsadvokaten for Særlige Internationale Straffesager' in Motzfeldt, Hanne Marie (ed), *Mod og mening, Hyldestskrift til Frederik Harhoff* (København: Jurist- og Økonomforbundets Forlag, 2016), 435–454; Jarle Christensen, Mikkel, 'Anklagemyndigheden og internationalt samarbejde: En retssociologisk analyse af kampen mellem det nationale og internationale', *Retfærd: Nordisk Juridisk Tidsskrift* (2017), 40(1), 3–14; Jarle Christensen, Mikkel, 'International Prosecution and National Bureaucracy: The Contest to Define International Practices within the Danish Prosecution Service', *Law and Social Inquiry* (2018), 43(1), 152–181; Österdahl, Inger, 'Folkrättsbrott i svenska domstolar: En våldsam utveckling' in Samuelsson Kääntä,

Jenny et al. (eds), *Vänbok till Lena Holmqvist* (Uppsala: Iustus Förlag, 2019), 357–381; Klamberg, Mark (ed), *Lagföring i Sverige av internationella brott*, (Stockholm: Jure, 2020); Lundstedt, Lydia (ed), *Investigation and Prosecution in Scandinavia of international crimes*, Scandinavian Studies in Law(2020), 66.

7 Klamberg, *Lagföring i Sverige av internationella brott*, 2020; Lundstedt (2020) with the current author acting as the scientific coordinator.

8 Chapter 27, Section 11 of the Penal Law (Strafflagen).

9 The provision refers to 'allmänt erkända folkrättsliga grundsatser' (generally recognized principles or tenets of international law). From the preparatory works, doctrine, and case law, it is clear that this is an old expression for customary international law, see Prop. 1948:144 om strafflagstiftning för krigsmakten, pp. 59 and 165; Gihl, Torsten, 'Angående begreppet "folkrättsbrott"', *Nordic Journal of International Law* (1952), 22(1), 240–256, p. 246.

10 See p. 166 in Prop. 1948:144 on the inspiration from Danish law.

11 Act on Criminal Responsibility for Genocide (1964:169).

12 *Prosecutor ./. M.M.*, Stockholms tingsrätt, Mål B 5373-10, dom den 20 januari 2012, pp. 47 and 53; Österdahl (2019), p. 363. See also Klamberg, Mark and Andersson, Anna, 'Swedish Case Law on the Contextual Elements Relating to War Crimes', *Scandinavian Studies in Law* (2020), 66, 217–244, p. 229.

13 International Crimes and Swedish Jurisdiction (*Internationella brott och svensk jurisdiction*), SOU 2002:98.

14 Prop. 2009/10:50, bet. 2009/10:JuU10, rskr. 2009/10:180, SFS 2010:60.

15 Nilsson, Jonas, 'The Crime of Genocide Before Swedish Courts', *Scandinavian Studies in Law* (2020), 66, 307–325.

16 Prop. 2013/14:146, p. 127. See also Klamberg and Andersson (2020), pp. 218–219.

17 *Regeringens proposition 2013/14:146 om Straffansvar för folkmord, brott mot mänskligheten och krigsförbrytelser* (2013/2014), p. 127.

18 For a more detailed account, see Klamberg, Mark, 'The Evolution of Swedish Legislation on International Crimes', *Scandinavian Studies in Law* (2020), 66, 205–215.

19 Based on account in Heikkilä, Mikaela, 'The Criminalisation and Prosecution of International Core Crimes in Finland', *Scandinavian Studies in Law* (2020), 66, 458–477.

20 Law No. 987/1974 and Governmental Bill 241/1973, p. 4. See also Heikkilä (2020), p. 460.

21 The provisions in Chapter 13, Sections 1 and 2 of the Criminal Code refers to 'allmänt erkända folkrättsliga grundsatser' (generally recognized principles or tenets of international law) which is the exact same wording as the Swedish law from 1948.

22 Law No. 578/1995 and Governmental Bill 94/1993, p. 25.

23 Chapter 11, Section 1(3) of the Criminal Code.

24 E.g., Council of Europe, the Implications for Council of Europe Member States of the Ratification of the Rome Statute of the International Criminal Court: Progress Report by Finland, 11 September 2001, Consult/ICC (2001) 13 rev., p. 4. See also Hannikainen, Lauri, 'Finland', *Yearbook of International Humanitarian Law 2000* 3, 498, p. 499; Nuutila, Ari-Matti, 'RL 11: Sotarikokset ja rikokset ihmisyyttä vastaan' in Heinonen, Olavi et al. (eds), Rikosoikeus, pp. 559–579 (Second Edition, Helsinki: WSOY Lakitieto, 2002), p. 560 and Heikkilä (2020), p. 460.

25 Government Bill 55/2007, pp. 12–13.

26 Compare with Heikkilä (2020), p. 463: 'With this reference to international law, it is ensured that all acts that are internationally criminalised as war crimes also are criminal in Finland'.

27 Lag om Den Internationale Straffedomstol (Lov nr 342 af 16/05/2001).

28 Lov nr. 132 af 29 april 1955 om straf for folkedrab.

29 Straffeloven, 15 April 1930 (Denmark).

30 Militær straffelov, lov nr. 530 af 24 juni 2005 (Denmark).

31 Ibid., Sections 36 and 37.

32 Plum, Lars, 'Investigation and Prosecution in Denmark of International Crimes', *Scandinavian Studies in Law* (2020), 66, 435–455, p. 438; see comparative outlook, which includes Denmark, in Proposition 2013/14:146 (Sweden), p. 67.
33 Miltary Penal Law, 22 May 1902 nr. 13; Ot. prp. nr. 95 (2000–2001), Om lov om gjennomføring i norsk rett av Den internasjonale straffedomstols vedtekter 17 juli 1998 (Romavedtektene), p. 14.
34 Ot. prp. nr. 8 (2007–2008) Om lov om endringer i straffeloven 20. mai 2005 nr. 28 mv. (skjerpende og formildende omstendigheter, folkemord, rikets selvstendighet, terrorhandlinger, ro, orden og sikkerhet, og offentlig myndighet), p. 87.
35 Oslo tingrett dom 14 februar 2013 (TOSLO-2012-106377); Borgarting lagmannsretts dom 16 januar 2015 (LB-2013-41556).
36 Ot. prp. nr. 95 (2000–2001).
37 Ibid., p. 16.
38 Høgestøl, Sofie A. E., 'A Norwegian Perspective on the Prosecution of International Crimes', *Scandinavian Studies in Law* (2020), 66, 407–434, pp. 413–415.
39 Ot. prp. nr. 8 (2007–2008), p. 52
40 Ibid., p. 88.
41 Høgestøl (2020), p. 418.
42 However, the Swedish amendment in 1986 was at least partially a response to the Swedish ratification of the additional protocols, see SOU 1983:2 Nytt militärt ansvarssystem, p. 113.
43 See for example Norway: Ot. prp. nr. 8 (2007–2008), pp. 52, 75–76, 87, and 88; Sweden: Proposition 2013/14:146, pp. 64–67 and 127; RP 55/2007 rd Regeringens proposition till Riksdagen med förslag till ändring av strafflagens bestämmelser om krigsförbrytelser och brott mot humaniteten samt vissa lagar som har samband med dem, pp. 10–12.
44 See for example Norway: Ot. prp. nr. 8 (2007–2008), pp. 75–76; Finland: RP 55/2007 rd, pp. 10–12.
45 Code of Judicial Procedure (Sweden), Chapter 20, Section 6.
46 Criminal Procedure Act (Finland), Chapter 1, Section 6.
47 Code of Judicial Procedure (Sweden), Chapter 20, Section 7; Criminal Procedure Act (Finland), Chapter 1, Section 6.
48 Wennberg, Suzanne, *Introduktion till straffrätten* (Twelfth Edition, Stockholm: Norstedts Juridik, 2020), pp. 20–21; Frände, Dan, *Grunddragen i den Finska Kriminalrätten* (Helsingfors: Juridiska fakulteten vid Helsingfors universitet, 2017), pp. 212–218.
49 *Straffrättslig jurisdiktion i Norden* (København: Nordic Council of Ministers, 1992), p. 63; Justitiedepartementet, Åtalsförordnande enligt 2 kap. brottsbalken, Ds 2014:13, p. 55.
50 Swedish Penal Code, Chapter 2, Sections 3(2) and 3(6)–(7); Norwegian Penal Code, Section 5; Criminal Code of Finland, Sections 6 and 7; Danish Criminal Code, Sections 7 and 8a. See also Martinsson, Dennis and Klamberg, Mark, 'Jurisdiction and Immunities in Sweden When Investigating and Prosecuting International Crimes', *Scandinavian Studies in Law* (2020), 66, 51–78, pp. 54–61; Plum (2020), pp. 440–441.
51 Ingeson, Miriam and Kather, Alexandra Lily, 'The Road Less Traveled: How Corporate Directors Could be Held Individually Liable in Sweden for Corporate Atrocity Crimes Abroad' *EJIL*, 13 November 2018; Martinsson and Klamberg (2020), p. 69.
52 Geneva Convention for the Amelioration of the Condition of the Wounded and Sick in Armed Forces in the Field of 12 August 1949, Article 49; Geneva Convention for the Amelioration of the Condition of Wounded, Sick and Shipwrecked Members of Armed Forces at Sea of 12 August 1949, Article 50; Geneva Convention Relative to the Treatment of Prisoners of War of 12 August 1949, Article 129; Geneva Convention Relative to the Protection of Civilian Persons in Time of War of 12 August 1949, Article 146.

53 Convention against Torture and Other Cruel, Inhuman or Degrading Treatment or Punishment adopted 10 December 1984, 1465 UNTS 85, Article 7.
54 Convention on the Prevention and Punishment of the Crime of Genocide, Article VI.
55 Regulation (1993:1467).
56 Swedish Penal Code, Chapter 2, Sections 2(8).
57 Swedish Penal Code, Chapter 2, Sections 2(8)(4).
58 Swedish Penal Code, Chapter 2, Sections 2(8)(2).
59 Criminal Code of Finland, Section 12(1).
60 Ibid., Section 12(2). See account in Ds 2014:13, pp. 51–53.
61 Ds 2014:13, p. 55.
62 Criminal Procedure Act (Norway), Section 65 (6). See also Ot. prp. nr. 90 (2003–2004), p. 404; Ds 2014:13, p. 55.
63 *Prosecutor v. Jackie Arklöv*, Stockholm district court, Case No. B 4084-04, Judgment of 18 December 2006; *Prosecutor ./. M.M.*, Svea Hovrätt, Mål B 1248-12, Judgment of 19 December 2012; *Prosecutor ./. Ahmet Makitan*, Stockholms tingsrätt, Mål B 382-10, Judgment of 8 April 2011.
64 *Prosecutor v Repak*, Oslo District Court, LB-2009-24039, Judgment 12 April 2010; *Prosecutor v Repak*, Supreme Court of Norway, HR-2010-02057-P, Judgment 3 December 2010.
65 *Prosecutor v Repak*, Oslo District Court, Judgment 12 April 2010.
66 *Makitan*, Judgment 8 April 2011, pp. 79, 81, 83, 85, 93, 107–108, 110, 159, 183, 188, 200, 201, 203, 206, 209, 214–215.
67 *Prosecutor v Repak*, Oslo District Court, 08-018985MED-OTIR/08, Judgment 2 December 2008, para. 18; *Makitan*, Judgment 8 April 2011, p. 26.
68 *Arklöv*, Stockholm district court, Judgment of 18 December 2006, pp. 52–56.
69 *Prosecutor v Repak*, Oslo District Court, Judgment 2 December 2008, para. 46; *Makitan*, Judgment 8 April 2011, pp. 6, 42–43.
70 Klamberg and Andersson (2020), pp. 224–225.
71 *Prosecutor v Repak*, Supreme Court of Norway, Judgment 3 December 2010, paras. 29, 75, 96, 106–113, 119–122. See comment by Høgestøl (2020), pp. 424–425.
72 *Prosecutor v. Bazaramba*, Helsinki Court of Appeal, Case R 10/2555, Judgment 30 March 2012.
73 *Prosecutor ./. Mbanenande*, Svea Hovrätt, Mål B 6659-13, Judgment 19 June 2014; *Prosecutor ./. Berinkindi*, Svea Hovrätt, Mål B 4951-16, Judgment 15 February 2017; *Prosecutor ./. Tabaro*, Svea Hovrätt, Mål B 6814-18, Judgment, 29 April 2019.
74 *Prosecutor v Bugingo*, Oslo District Court, TOSLO-2012-106377, Judgment 14 February 2013. See comment by Heikkilä (2020), pp. 470–472.
75 UfR.2014.423H; *Prosecutor v T*, Østre Landsrets 17, Decision 21 September 2018, S-623-18.
76 *Prosecutor v Bugingo*, Oslo District Court, Judgment 14 February 2013, part 5.7.
77 *Prosecutor v T*, Østre Landsrets 17, Decision 21 September 2018, S-623-18. For comments on the Danish cases, see Plum (2020), pp. 448–449.
78 *Prosecutor v. Jebbar-Salman*, District Court of Pirkanmaa, Case R 16/1304, Judgment 18 March 2016; *Prosecutor v. Habeeb Hilal*, Case No. R 16/214, Judgment, District Court of Kanta-Häme, 22 March 2016; *Prosecutor v. Jabbar Hasan*, Case No. R 18/6593, Judgment, District Court of Helsinki, 10 January 2019; *Prosecutor v. S.H. & S. H.*, Case No. R 17/1229, Judgment, Appeal Court of Turku, 28 February 2020.
79 *Prosecutor ./. Al-Mandlawi och Sultan*, Hovrätten för Västra Sverige, Mål B 5306-15, Judgment 30 March 2016; *Prosecutor ./. Droubi*, Svea Hovrätt, Mål B 4770-16, Judgment 5 August 2016; *Prosecutor ./. Abdulkareem*, Hovrätten över Skåne och Blekinge, Mål B 3187-16, Judgment 11 April 2017; *Prosecutor v. Omar Sakhanh Haisam Sakhanh*, Svea Hovrätt (Svea Appeal Court), B 2259-17, Judgment 31 May 2017; *Prosecutor ./. Abdullah*, Södertörns tingsrätt, Mål B 11191-17, Judgment

25 September 2017; *Prosecutor ./. Saeed*, Högsta Domstolen, Mål B 5595-19, Judgment 5 May 2021; *Prosecutor v. Ishaq*, Stockholms tingsrätt (Stockholm District Court), B 20218-20, Judgment 4 March 2012.

80 *Prosecutor ./. Saeed*, Högsta Domstolen, Judgment 5 May 2021, para. 27.

81 *Prosecutor v. Omar Haisam Sakhanh*, Stockholms tingsrätt (Stockholm District Court), B 3787-16, Judgment 16 February 2017, paras. 27, 30, and 34, see comment by Klamberg, Mark, 'The Legality of Rebel Courts during Non-International Armed Conflicts', *Journal of International Criminal Justice* (2018), 16(1), 235–263.

82 *Prosecutor v. Jebbar-Salman*, District Court of Pirkanmaa, Judgment 18 March 2016, p. 2; *Prosecutor v. Habeeb Hilal*, District Court of Kanta-Häme, 22 March 2016, p. 2. For comment and analysis of the Finnish cases, see Heikkilä (2020), pp. 472–475. *Prosecutor ./. Droubi*, Svea Hovrätt, Judgment 5 August 2016; *Prosecutor ./. Abdulkareem*, Hovrätten över Skåne och Blekinge, Judgment 11 April 2017; *Haisam Sakhanh*, Svea Hovrätt (Svea Appeal Court), 31 May 2017; *Prosecutor ./. Abdullah*, Judgment 25 September 2017; *Prosecutor ./. Saeed*, Högsta Domstolen, Judgment 5 May 2021. For comment and analysis of the Swedish cases, see Klamberg, Mark, 'Evidentiary Matters in the Context of Investigating and Prosecuting International Crimes in Sweden: Admissibility, Digital Evidence and Judicial Notice', *Scandinavian Studies in Law* (2020), 66, 367–383.

83 *Prosecutor ./. Al-Mandlawi och Sultan*, Hovrätten för Västra Sverige, Judgment 30 March 2016.

84 *Prosecutor v. Noury*, Stockholms tingsrätt (Stockholm District Court), B 15255-19, Judgment 14 July 2022.

85 Grewe, Wilhelm G., *The Epochs of International Law (Translated and revised by Michael Byers)* (Berlin: De Gruyter, 2000), p. 9; Klamberg, Mark, 'Evolution of rules and concepts in international humanitarian law: navigating through legal gaps and fault lines' in Deland, Mats, Klamberg, Mark, and Wrange, Pål (eds), *Historical and sociological perspectives on international humanitarian law and justice* (Routledge, 2018), 79–84, pp. 80 and 82.

References

Asp, Petter, *Internationell straffrätt* (Uppsala: Iustus Förlag, 2011).

Asp, Petter, 'Folkrätten och den svenska straffrätten', in: Stern, Rebecca and Österdahl, Inger (eds), *Folkrätten i Svensk rätt* (Malmö: Liber, 2012), 58–73.

Bring, Ove and Körlof-Askholt, Anna, *Folkrätt i krig, kris och fredsoperationer*, Fourth Edition (Stockholm: Norstedts Juridik, 2010).

Cameron, Iain, 'Swedish Investigations for Gross Human Rights Violations, Actual and Possible', in: Asp, Petter, Herlitz, Carl Erik and Holmqvist, Lena (eds), *Flores juris et legum: festskrift till Nils Jareborg* (Uppsala: Iustus, 2002), 123–149.

Cameron, Iain, Thunberg Schunke, Malin, Påle-Bartes, Karin, Wong, Christoffer, and Asp, Petter, *International Criminal Law from a Swedish Perspective* (Cambridge-Antwerp-Portland: Intersentia, 2011).

Friman, Håkan, 'Political and Legal Considerations in Sweden Relating to the Rome Statute for the International Criminal Court', in: Lee, Roy S. (ed.), *States' Responses to Issues Arising from the ICC Statute, Constitutional, Sovereignty, Judicial Cooperation and Criminal Law* (Ardsley: Transnational Publishers, 2005), 121–145.

Frände, Dan, *Grunddragen i den Finska Kriminalrätten* (Helsingfors: Juridiska fakulteten vid Helsingfors universitet, 2017)

Gihl, Torsten, 'Angående begreppet "folkrättsbrott"', *Nordic Journal of International Law*, 22(1), 1952, 240–256.

Grewe, Wilhelm G., *The Epochs of International Law (Translated and revised by Michael Byers)* (Berlin: De Gruyter, 2000)

Hannikainen, Lauri, 'Implementation of International Humanitarian Law in Finnish Law', in: Hannikainen, Lauri (ed.), *Implementing Humanitarian Law Applicable in Armed Conflicts: The Case of Finland* (Dordrecht: Martinus Nijhoff Publishers, 1992), 114–145.

Hannikainen, Lauri, 'Finland', *Yearbook of International Humanitarian Law*, 3, 2000, 498–499.

Heikkilä, Mikaela, 'The Criminalisation and Prosecution of International Core Crimes in Finland', *Scandinavian Studies in Law*, 66, 2020, 458–477.

Hurwitz, Stephan, 'Nordisk kriminalretligt samarbejde', *Nordisk tidsskrift for kriminalvidenskab*, 36(1), 1949, 74–75.

Høgestøl, Sofie, 'En generell kriminalisering av fremmedkrigere: den norske modellen og påtaleskjønn i straffeloven § 145', in: Andersson, Anna, Høgestøl, Sofie, and Lie, Anne (eds), *Fremmedkrigere: forebygging, straffeforfølgning og rehabilitering i Skandinavia* (Oslo: Gyldendal Juridisk, 2018).

Høgestøl, Sofie A. E., 'A Norwegian Perspective on the Prosecution of International Crimes', *Scandinavian Studies in Law*, 66, 2020, 407–434.

Ingeson, Miriam and Kather, Alexandra Lily, *'The Road Less Traveled: How Corporate Directors Could be Held Individually Liable in Sweden for Corporate Atrocity Crimes Abroad' EJIL*, 13 November 2018.

Jarle Christensen, Mikkel, 'Anklagemyndigheden og internationalt samarbejde: En retssociologisk analyse af kampen mellem det nationale og internationale', *Retfærd: Nordisk Juridisk Tidsskrift*, 40(1), 2017, 3–14.

Jarle Christensen, Mikkel, 'International Prosecution and National Bureaucracy: The Contest to Define International Practices within the Danish Prosecution Service', *Law and Social Inquiry*, 43(1), 2018, 152–181.

Kimpimäki, Minna, 'Taking International Criminal Law Seriously: A Decade of Finnish Criminal Legislation', in: Elholm, Thomas (ed.), *Liber Amicarum et Amicorum Karin Cornils: Glimt af Nordisk straffrätt og Straffeprocessrett* (Copenhagen: Djøf, 2010), 1–17.

Kimpimäki, Minna, 'Sotarikollisia ja merirosvoja – Suomen rikosoikeudellisen toimivallan rajat', *Lakimies*, 5, 2011, 888–911.

Klamberg, Mark, 'Evolution of Rules and Concepts in International Humanitarian Law: Navigating through Legal Gaps and Fault Lines', in: Deland, Mats, Klamberg, Mark, and Wrange, Pål (eds), *Historical and Sociological Perspectives on International Humanitarian Law and Justice* (London: Routledge, 2018), 79–84.

Klamberg, Mark, 'The Legality of Rebel Courts during Non-international Armed Conflicts', *Journal of International Criminal Justice*, 16(1), 2018, 235–263.

Klamberg, Mark, 'Evidentiary Matters in the Context of Investigating and Prosecuting International Crimes in Sweden: Admissibility, Digital Evidence and Judicial Notice', *Scandinavian Studies in Law*, 66, 2020a, 367–383.

Klamberg, Mark, 'The Evolution of Swedish Legislation on International Crimes', *Scandinavian Studies in Law*, 66, 2020b, 205–215.

Klamberg, Mark, 'Trials in Sweden, Participants in the Proceedings and other Actors', *Scandinavian Studies in Law*, 66, 2020c, 28–39.

Klamberg, Mark (ed), *Lagföring i Sverige av internationella brott* (Jure 2020).

Klamberg, Mark and Andersson, Anna, 'Swedish Case Law on the Contextual Elements Relating to War Crimes', *Scandinavian Studies in Law*, 66, 2020, 217–244.

Lundstedt, Lydia (ed) *Investigation and Prosecution in Scandinavia of International Crimes*, 66, 2020.

Martinsson, Dennis and Klamberg, Mark, 'Jurisdiction and Immunities in Sweden When Investigating and Prosecuting International Crimes', *Scandinavian Studies in Law*, 66, 2020, 51–78.

Nilsson, Jonas, 'The Crime of Genocide Before Swedish Courts', *Scandinavian Studies in Law*, 66, 2020, 307–325.

Österdahl, Inger, 'Folkrättsbrott i svenska domstolar: En våldsam utveckling', in: Samuelsson Kääntä, Jenny and others (eds), *Vänbok till Lena Holmqvist* (Uppsala: Iustus Förlag, 2019), 357–381.

Plum, Lars, 'SAIS - Statsadvokaten for Særlige Internationale Straffesager', in: Motzfeldt, Hanne Marie (ed.), *Mod og mening, Hyldestskrift til Frederik Harhoff* (København: Jurist- og Økonomforbundets Forlag, 2016), 435–454.

Plum, Lars, 'Investigation and Prosecution in Denmark of International Crimes', *Scandinavian Studies in Law*, 66, 2020, 435–455.

Plum, Lars and Laursen, Andreas (eds), *Enhver Stats pligt ...* (København: Jurist- og Økonomiforbundets Forlag, 2007).

Suominen, Annika, *The Principle of Mutual Recognition in Cooperation in Criminal Matters* (Cambridge: Intersentia, 2011).

Wennberg, Suzanne, *Introduktion till straffrätten*, Twelfth Edition (Stockholm: Norstedts Juridik, 2020).

Zweigert, Konrad and Kötz, Hein, *Introduction to Comparative Law*, Second Edition (Oxford: Clarendon Press, 1987).

Part 2

Promoting Nordic criminal justice

4 To be both in the world and yet not of it

Swedish drug policy and the international context

Henrik Tham and Johan Edman

Sweden has a high international profile in drug policy. The country has taken a quite restrictive line in relation to many other Western countries. Sweden has also been seen internationally as claiming a successful drug policy in relation to other countries, and it has almost launched a crusade both at home and abroad. The claimed success seems to have culminated in the 1990s, thereafter losing its political attractiveness.

In this chapter, we try to understand the connection between Sweden's very restrictive drug policy and this international commitment. The materials used are primarily media debates, official government investigations, and government instructions to Swedish delegates participating in European and international meetings on drug policy. We begin by briefly describing and explaining the development of Swedish drug policy. We then get to grips with the connection to the international arena in which Sweden becomes active after the mid-1980s. The first part of the analysis describes the international launch of a successful Swedish drug policy culminating in the UN-meeting in 1998. The second part illustrates how Sweden retreats from the argument of an effective policy in relation to drug abuse and instead defends its policy by references to the protections of general values like democracy, welfare, and human rights. The third and final part demonstrates how Sweden's international entrepreneurship serves as a national resource and is a moral mission with long historical roots.

The domestic logic

Early, an *epidemic* model for the spread of drugs was launched where one drug user would be claimed to 'infect' others with the habit who would then carry the use of drugs on to more people. The drug user then had to be stopped as a link in the chain with dealers, smugglers, producers, and corrupt regimes in different parts of the world (Bejerot 1975). This theory of the spread of drugs clearly inspired the change in policy from around 1980 focusing the drug user in the street and stressing the demand side in drug policy. Eventually, the epidemic theory and the stress on the demand side lead to criminalization of use, as such, and the police getting the powers to by force take tests of body fluids (Tham 2021).

DOI: 10.4324/9781003195504-7

The tradition from the *temperance movement* probably played a role (Lenke 1991). The movement having been quite strong in Sweden began losing ground in the 1960s but associated and eventually merged with hard-line NGOs in the drug field. The total abstinence ideal of the temperance movement was carried on into the drug movement. The stepping-stone or gateway theory also justified that no distinction should be made between 'soft' and 'hard' drugs. While the earlier restrictive Swedish alcohol policy has become liberal, the drug policy has moved in the opposite direction (Edman 2021).

The welfare state is *an interventionist state*. The promise of the welfare state is to give help and care to those who are in need. This is also a mark of Swedish drug policy. The person with a problematic drug use is not left by him or herself in the street but is given economic help and offers of treatment. The welfare state spirit promotes early intervention to prevent possible risks of marginalization even when the risks might be small. Both the epidemic model and the model from the temperance movement are quite compatible with this welfare state risk-perspective. Non-intervention is not a natural option in the welfare state and intervention can be intrusive (see also Barker 2013; Smith 2017). The promise of care is also an expansive offer. Almost everyone has to work and contribute with high taxes to make the welfare state possible. The risks that someone might 'drop out' at an early age and require economic support and treatment for the rest of their life has to be prevented even if that requires penal law and coercion.

A final contributing explanation of the Swedish drug policy could be to regard it as a *national project*. In the drug policy discourse, there are clear themes of specific 'Swedish virtues' and 'Sweden versus abroad'. Drugs are pictured as coming from abroad and being alien to Swedish culture and working-class morals. Also, the ideas to liberalize the drug policy come from outside Sweden and should be combatted. In a situation where 'the Swedish model' has become less self-evident and the welfare-state ideas are being increasingly criticized, a restrictive drug policy has been named 'the Swedish model' and seems to become a project for reinforcing a threatened national identity (Tham 1995).[1]

The international arena

From around 1980, the drug policy was as described markedly sharpened by measures directed against the drug user. Such measures risked being criticized for being repressive but could perhaps be justified if shown to be effective. Drug abuse was by the government also described as one of the biggest social problems in Sweden in the early 1980's. This description continued in the budget bills but from the mid-1980s with the addition that 'the drug policy is successful and that drug abuse is being pushed back' (GB 1985/86:100, app. 4, p. 18). This constituted a rhetorical challenge for the Swedish Government: was this still the worst of problems or was the Swedish drug policy successful, as in solving the problem? This is where the international perspective becomes a useful resource for the government and domestic drug policy.

Threats from abroad

In 1989 the government appointed an action group against drugs consisting of the highest representatives of a number of authorities involved in the drug issue. The report published by the group carried the name *We Will Never Surrender* with a cover image of the outermost beach before the see separating Sweden from the continent (Regeringens aktionsgrupp, 1991). The situation was described as serious but not as bad as in other countries. Tendencies towards liberalization around the world was regarded as particularly threatening. Even though the situation was serious, the preparedness of Sweden was good: 'we have in Sweden this far been successful in our fight against drugs' (op. cit. p. 8).

The story of a successful Swedish drug policy, particularly in relation to other countries, was being formed. In 1993 the Swedish Institute of Public Health published a brochure on drug policy, *A Restrictive Drug Policy. The Swedish Experience* (Folkhälsoinstitutet 1993). The brochure was published except for in Swedish in three other languages with the obvious intent to describe a successful policy to other states. The success of the Swedish drug policy was in the brochure claimed mainly on the basis of the development of life time prevalence and last month use of drugs among schoolchildren 15 years old which are shown to have dropped markedly since around 1980. The drop was regarded to be an effect of massive information, extensive treatment, and a population united around the motto 'Sweden a drug-free society'. The theory on which the policy was based was an epidemiological assumption that by limiting the number who ever try drugs the bases for new recruitment to careers in drug consumption would be prevented. The future risks for the Swedish policy were seen in an increase in international drug trafficking and in liberalization movements.

The restrictive and successful policy was pictured against an earlier period of a less restrictive drug policy (Folkhälsoinstitutet 1993). An experiment in Stockholm in the mid-1960s was described as having had negative results (a conclusion that was refuted in a study by Lenke and Olsson, 1998) and being a reason for not liberalizing the Swedish policy. A permissive attitude of the Prosecutor-General that allowed for waivers of prosecution was seen as negative. A marked increase in problematic use in the 1980s was explained by pointing to that the population mainly consisted of users entering drugs during the 1960s and 1970s while new recruits among the young during the 1980s was low. The marked rise in drug related deaths in the 1980s was not mentioned (Folkhälsoinstitutet 1993).

Sweden as the good example

Sweden in the 1990s increasingly embarked on a road of picturing itself as a successful country in drug policy and trying to influence other countries to adopt the same policies. Sweden in this respect probably reached its peak in the late 1990s. A United Nation Special Session on drugs was held in New York in June 1998—one of different types of recurrent UNGASS where world leaders meet for policy decisions on central world problems. Sweden participated with a large delegation headed by the Minister of Health and Social Affairs from the Social Democrats. The delegation consisted of three members of the Swedish parliament, including a former Minister of Justice from the Moderates (the conservative party), two ambassadors, and two more diplomats and 15 advisors. Among the advisors there were two representatives for NGOs and organizations taking a hard line in drug policy (Regeringsprotokoll 1998). No representative from the liberal NGO RFHL was invited.[2]

The Swedish Queen Silvia also participated at the UNGASS. The General Secretary of the UN, Kofi Annan, tried to engage the Queen in a *Comité des Sages* consisting of persons of very high status that should be engaged in fund-raising and opinion formation. The General Secretary referred to the engagement by the Queen in the international drug issue. The Swedish Government was in favour of the Queen engaging herself in this committee. The Queen was interested but would not participate in fundraising. Eventually, not enough people accepted offers of membership of the committee and the project was postponed (Utrikesdepartementet).

Another person who was approached by the General Secretary was Queen Sofia of Spain. The Spanish Queen turned down the offer on constitutional grounds saying that she could not make a public statement in an issue like this (op. cit.). In a constitutional monarchy like Sweden the royalties cannot engage themselves in politically controversial questions. Had the Swedish Queen engaged herself in, for instance, the alcohol policy where different political opinions exist that could have led to a constitutional crisis. The fact that the Queen could consider the proposal from the General Secretary shows that the drug issue in Sweden was regarded as an issue of complete consensus. This consensual culture was further stressed by the Swedish Minister of Health and Social Affairs in a statement given at the UNGASS:

> It may be difficult and it may be costly, but we, the political leaders of the UN member-states, must make it very clear that we will not allow ourselves to be influenced by those who promote illicit drugs. I firmly believe that giving in for such ideas will undermine our common effort. Let us not lose sight of our goal—a drugfree society. That is a responsibility we have towards the younger generations as we lead our countries into the next millennium.
>
> (Wallström 1998a, p. 3)

A brochure on the Swedish drug policy was presented at UNGASS, *A Preventive Strategy. Swedish Drug policy in the 1990s* (Regeringskansliet, 1998). In a preface the Minster of Health and Social Affairs wrote that the aim of the brochure was 'to communicate Sweden's policy on drugs to interested persons in other countries' (op. cit., p. 3) and that the drug policy is strongly supported by the Swedish public. The brochure claimed the relative success of the Swedish drug policy, that there was no distinction or opposition between measures against supply and demand, and that no drugs were regarded as 'soft' since cannabis increased the risk for use of hard drugs. The risk of punishment was said to be an important aspect of the policy and police action at street level had an important effect on public opinion showing that drug abuse and trafficking was not accepted by society. The brochure ended by pointing to the global character of the drug problem 'which in turn heightens the importance of stronger international co-operation' (op. cit., p. 18).

From the good example to the extreme example

The quest from Sweden for consensus, a joint fight against liberal tendencies and position Sweden as the morally good example was however immediately scattered during the UN-meeting. The same day that UNGASS started, a two-page call appeared in *The New York Times*, paid for by the Lindesmith Centre (*The New York Times*, 1998). The call was formed as a letter to the General Secretary of the UN with the main message: 'We believe the global war on drugs is now causing more harm than drug abuse itself'. Some 650 persons from all over the world had signed the call of which half were listed in the newspaper. The signatories mainly consisted of two categories. One group was constituted by retired high-ranking politicians and civil servants like presidents, prime ministers and other cabinet members, members of parliament, chiefs of police and one Secretary General of the UN, Javier Perez de Cuellar. The other group was made up by active academics, doctors, lawyers, and others who wouldn't risk their jobs. Kofi Annan was annoyed but did after his resignation as Secretary General join The Global Commission on Drug Policy, an organization with the same aim as the call in *The New York Times*.

Twelve of the signatories came from Sweden. It was seen as important by the organizers to include all these names in *The New York Times*. Sweden was perceived as a particularly strong Western representative for zero-tolerance and the publication would show a crack in the Swedish consensus. A consequence of the publication was also a fierce debate in Swedish media. The signatories were claimed to be cowards and misled, and it was questioned if they were at their senses in a tabloid that also quoted the Minister and an MP in the delegation (*Expressen* 1998-06-10 & 16). Particular attention was given to the fact that the Director General of the National Board of Health and Welfare had signed the call the day after leaving office. The Minister of Health and Social affairs wrote in a debate article commenting on the Swedish signatories and their demand for rethinking the drug policy: 'No, it would according to me be a disaster. It is a totally wrong road to hit. We cannot allow the drug liberal forces in Europe and in other parts of the world to spread out' (Wallström, 1998b).

The strong reaction against the signatories was in a way surprising. The majority of the Swedes who signed the call were university professors and in addition there was a judge, a poet, and a retired editor in chief. The name of the General Director did of course carry weight but he withdrew his support to the call claiming that he had signed by mistake. Moreover, the strict zero-tolerance policy advocated by the UN was not shared by all countries at the UNGASS in New York. An analysis based on the large number of documents published by the UN before the UNGASS shows that the 'common ground' was not that clear, the

North–South divide remained, prohibition was questioned, and that there were voices for reviews of the UN conventions against cannabis and coca (Jelsma 2003). The dissenting Swedes cannot have been such a surprise.

An interpretation of the strong political and media reactions to the Swedish signatories could be that it revealed an internal critique of the drug policy. Even if the critique in reality hardly reached outside the country it was an action that was perceived to challenge the claimed consensus in Sweden. The call could question the Minister's statement of the strong public support for Swedish drug policy and the emphasis in the distributed brochure that the drug policy would demonstrate a united society. The political reaction to an international appeal, including some Swedes, against the war on drugs could be seen as an attack on Sweden and also as an attempt to undermine the authority of Sweden in the field of international drug policy.

Sweden losing ground

A month before the UNGASS the Minister of Health and Social Affairs had appointed a commission to evaluate the Swedish drug policy. The directives included suggestions of how to strengthen the Swedish policy internationally and to give possibilities for a large impact of the Swedish restrictive line in international policies. The result of the work of the commission was published two years later with the title *At a Crossroads* (SOU 2000:126). The introduction to the English summary started:

> Swedish drug policy has come to a crossroads. One direction calls for a significant augmentation of resources in the form of commitment, direction, competence and funding. The other implies a lowering of sights and a considerable acceptance of drug abuse.
>
> (p. 33)

The report emphasized, again, the importance of a common stand: 'In Sweden the importance has been stressed of a united distancing from drugs' (p. 109). Sweden, according to the report, had through its consistent attitude become a symbol for a restrictive drug policy and much weight was given to Swedish points of view internationally. A prioritized area for Swedish drug policy efforts was to strengthen the international control of illegal drugs. Thus, it was most important for the Swedish international credibility to maintain a correspondence between rhetoric and praxis at the national level. The report referred to Sweden's role internationally as an argument for an increase in resources for fighting drug use in Sweden.[3]

The name of the state report, *At a Crossroads*, could alternatively have been 'At the end of the road'. There was a clear change in tone in relation to the optimism expressed in New York just two years earlier. Even if the Swedish official position was repeated there was an undertone of Sweden losing ground internationally, 'the ordeals Swedish drug policy at times has been exposed to in international contexts' (SOU 2000:126, p. 74). The Swedish claimed success (op. cit., p. 75) had also become more difficult to demonstrate. The proportion of 15 years old trying drugs had doubled in the 1990s. The number of persons with a problematic drug use had increased substantially. The committee was forced by the critique to address the question of the high number of drug-related deaths and had to admit the higher figures than in relation to other European countries (Curman et al. 1998; SOU 2000:126, PM nr 3).

Rescue operations

The status of Sweden as a successful state in the field of drug policy was however lifted once more and this time from abroad. UNODC, the United Nation Office of Drugs and Crime, in 2007 published the report *Sweden's Successful Drug Policy. A Review of the Evidence* (UNODC 2007). In a foreword, the Executive Director notes that in a possibly failed European drug police 'Sweden is a notable exception' and '[i]t is my firm belief that the general positive situation of Sweden is a result of policy that has been applied to address the problem' (p. 5). The report describes the development of the Swedish drug policy, stresses the active contribution of Sweden in the forming of the UN conventions in 1961 and 1971 and highlights the setting of the vision of a drug-free society. The main indicator of the success is the marked decrease and low level of drug use among schoolchildren. The increase in problematic use and drug-related deaths are noted but explained by a cut in health services in the 1990s and referring to a small drop in the deaths in the 2000s.

The report was critically reviewed by Börje Olsson, professor of alcohol and drug research at Stockholm University (Olsson 2009). Olsson criticizes the report for, among other things, attributing a decrease in drug use to the restrictive Swedish policy even before it was introduced, not distinguishing between medical, experimental, and occasional use, repeating the inaccurate conclusions of the experiment with legal prescription, giving wrong interpretations of the development of drug use, and presenting facts that are outright wrong.

> The concluding description of the Swedish drug policy development covering the last 15 years is quite superficial, idyllic, without analyses of critical approach, and the wording not only reminds the reader of the formal and empty style of an overriding committee report, is basically a summary and translation of the national action plan on drugs.
>
> (Olsson 2009, p. 6)

The critique might not have reached outside the academic community and influenced the perception of Sweden's dug policy internationally. It does however once more demonstrate the efforts of Sweden to claim a successful policy through a biased and incomplete presentation.

The report from the UNODC came from an international organization and not from Sweden, However, it is not likely that it was produced without help from

Sweden. One of the two prefaces in the report is written by the Swedish Minister for Elderly Care and Public Health who says: 'I am of course proud that the overall judgement is positive'. Likewise, the Minister of Public Health up to 2006 at a press conference where the Executive Director of the UNODC presented the report said: 'I become embarrassed and proud by the praise' (Olsson 2009, p. 1). An international evaluation done in collaboration with Sweden could be used to boast Swedish drug policy both abroad and at home.

In 2010 a state commission of inquiry was charged with charting Sweden's international commitments in the drug field. The work of the committee was according to the directives to be pursued within the frame of Swedish drug policy, namely zero-tolerance. The UN conventions on drugs should be a starting point, meaning that drugs could be used for medical and scientific reasons but not for recreational use. The directives were clearly formulated in a feeling that the Swedish voice in international drug policy was being weakened and needed to be strengthened. (SOU 2011:66, Bilaga 1).

The report was delivered a year later (SOU 2011:66). Sweden was described as over the years having been active in international drug policy. Sweden contributed to the second UN convention on psychotropic drugs and Sweden was one of the large contributors to the UNODC. The international movement towards liberalization was described as a real threat to the international drug policy as the zero-tolerance goal was seriously questioned.

Official Sweden must have felt that the market for its model has shrunk. There was in debates on international drug policies disagreement over the use of the words 'user' and 'abuser' and if 'soft' drugs should be separated from 'hard' drugs. The debate was seen as one-sided in favour of the advocates of liberalization. The international critique of existing Swedish drug policy was said not to recognize the importance of a policy aiming towards a drug-free society that, even if unattainable, means sending an important signal and supporting the UN conventions. Sweden and other states therefore had to react against this worrying development: 'It cannot continue like this' (SOU 2011:66, p. 49).

Different arguments were being put forward in the report about why Sweden had to act more strongly in international organizations concerned with drug policy. Sweden praised itself for having been a strong advocate of focusing also the demand side and particularly of stressing the need of treatment. This meant stressing public health thereby showing a human and caring side of drug policy. The Swedish practice of police controls of body liquids for proving consumption of drugs could be justified as both a defence of the UN conventions and a means for improving public health.

The report was an inquiry into Sweden's engagement in international drug policy. It was however clear that the task of Sweden had changed. Sweden had, according to the report, been very driving and even successful: '[I]s it worth aiming at freedom from drugs or should we reduce ambitions and settle for limiting medical and social harm?' (SOU 2011:66, p. 61). Sweden had gone from being a driving to a guarding country, but this did not have to be:

> The choice does however not have to stand between only to see to that no formulations inappropriate to Sweden slips into the resolution texts and to be the foremost on the barricade. By cooperating with other likeminded countries, we can drive our questions at the same time.
>
> (op. cit. p. 107)

Despite this vision, it was clear that for Sweden as a result of international movements there was a change from having been a front-line agent internationally in the war against drugs and actively forming more intervening polices to a position of defending conquered territory. This change became increasingly clear in the years that followed when Sweden's engagement in the international drug policy increasingly took place with EU.

UN conventions as an argument in the European Union

Sweden entered the European Union in 1995. The attempts of Sweden to influence international drug policy have since then been relatively more oriented toward the EU than the UN. For the EU member states it is important to try to speak with one voice in international contexts. The work mainly takes place in the called Horizontal Narcotics Group (HNG). The participants in the HNG-meetings but also in other international drug-fora receive instructions before every meeting, mainly from the Ministry of Social Affairs.[4]

The instructions to the Swedish representatives have, through the years, stressed different but interlinked positions and strategies. It is, however, clear from the turn of the century that Sweden faces a new situation, and the country now has increasing difficulties arguing for its claimed successful drug policy. Sweden still tries to defend its zero-tolerance stand but increasingly links the drug policy to wider issues and especially to UN drug conventions and to other goals of the UN.

Sweden should, according to the instructions, combat any attempts to decriminalize or legalize and look out for formulations in common documents that would indicate liberalization (PM 1998-04-30; Instruktion 2016-01-05, 2016-03-09, 2016-09-16, 2017-11-28, 2019-09-04, 2019-10-04, 2020-01-20). Different lines of defence can be detected in the instructions to the HNG. These include delaying decisions by referring to international opinions, defence of the UN conventions, enlarging the issue to further underline the importance of a fast stand, drug control as a means for fighting organized crime, and stressing the use of drugs as a threat to UN human rights.

Sweden counteracts EU tendencies to liberalize cannabis policy by claiming that the work on that issue should be done in an orderly manner, and that an international group of experts should be set up on the issue of a possible reclassification of the conventions. Sweden repeatedly stresses the importance of demand reduction, including both treatment and police interventions. The country also presents itself as a strong supporter of the UN conventions and claims that legalisation is incompatible with the conventions (Instruktion 2017-02-21, 2020-01-20). That Sweden in international fora stands up for the UN conventions on drugs and at the same time legitimizes the zero-tolerance policy at home.

Sweden links drug issues with poverty, equality, and democracy (Instruktion 2016-04-07/08, 2017-03-10, 2017-05-02, 2019-01-14). Thereby, the drug use and the drug market are claimed to be obstacles toward sustainable development in a broad sense and international cooperation and strict enforcement of the UN conventions become even more important. As further arguments to the penalization and world-wide resistance to drugs, Sweden points to the connection between the drug market and organized crime and terrorism (Instruktion, 2017-05-02). These phenomena are clearly cross-border and demand consensus among nations to fight drugs and ultimately create a drug-free world as formulated in the UN meetings.

Recurrent Swedish lines of argument internationally are public health and human rights (Direktiv 2017-03-23, Förslag 2016-05-02, 2017-01-04; Instruktion 2016-01-05, 2016-03-01, 2016-05-11, 2017-03-10; Svenska synpunkter på UNGASS). By stressing good health as a human right, Sweden again can show support for UN conventions concerning good material living conditions as a right for all human beings. Since the use of drugs can be detrimental to the health of citizens, drugs must be forbidden and prevented even with penal law and criminal justice.

A particularly good demonstration of this this line of argument is when Sweden was criticized by the UN before UNGASS 2016 for not upholding the human rights of the drug user (*The Local* 2015). In a brochure in English to the UNGASS-meeting, Sweden took a human rights stand in order to defend its strict drug policy:

> The UN Convention on the Rights of the Child recognizes a child's right to grow up in a drug-free environment as a human right. The UN International Covenant on Social, Economic and Cultural Rights talks about the right to health. All societies attempt to protect their citizens from risks that they cannot foresee; these may be anything from additives in food to seat belts in cars. This is part of the duty of society and of governments to protect citizens from risks.
>
> (Government Office of Sweden, 2016, p. 9)

The Swedish Government justifies its drug policy by prioritizing positive human rights over negative human rights. The right of the child and other citizens to a decent life without risks for physical or psychological health problems is set up against the protection of the citizen against the state. This is in line with the overall justification of Swedish drug policy. Caring for the weal and woe of the population is at the centre of welfare state ideology. In the government's national action plan for alcohol and drugs it says:

> The drugs policy is based on people's right to a dignified life in a society that stands up for the individuals needs for security and safety. Illegal drugs

> must never be allowed to threaten health, quality of life and security of the individual or public welfare and democratic development.
>
> (GB 2005/06:30; Hallam 2010, p. 2)

This quote could then perhaps both illustrate a continued fast stand and a possible retreat as long as the liberalization does not jeopardize the health and public welfare.

To be both in the world and yet not of it

> And when domestic problems prove intractable, to show that something has been achieved on the international level may become a political necessity, especially if the problem is seen to have originated from outside the country.
>
> (Bruun, Pan & Rexed 1975, p. 133)

For a short period at the end of the 20th century, Sweden was the self-proclaimed shining star of international drug policy. It was the hard but good example of how drug policy should be conducted, a model to put on display to an international audience. But Sweden hardly influenced drug policy outside the country's borders. The clear effect was instead seen in Sweden, where the international status made it possible to pursue the distinctive Swedish drug policy further and further away from the international development.

Sweden's international involvement in drug problems appears to us a kind of mission, a quest for status in the international arena through moral supremacy (e.g., Dahl 2006; Wohlforth et al. 2018). The moral and religious undertones of drug resistance are well suited to this model, something that is also seen in the early transnational temperance movement's engagement in the drug consumption of Indigenous peoples (Edman 2015). But it is also a model for international action that has been used by various countries on several issues since at least the transnational revolution of the 19th century when technological, economic, social, and cultural development made it possible for both people and information to travel faster and farther, thereby creating new possibilities across national borders for state officials, scientists, and various interest groups (Edman 2015).

This was particularly noticeable in the United States. The US made efforts early, and for a long time was the initiator of many international actions, not least against the 'morally reprehensible', whether it was slavery or prostitution, tobacco, or drunkenness (Tyrrell 2010). When the United States took the initiative for the 1909 Shanghai Opium Commission, drugs really weren't seen as a Swedish problem (Barop 2015), and they still weren't when Sweden signed the 1912 International Opium Convention in The Hague. Nevertheless, Sweden's signing of the Hague Convention was the direct reason for Sweden's first drug law, the 1923 Drug Proclamation (Edman 2017). This connection between, on the one hand, international initiatives and commitments and, on the other hand, domestic legislation and policy, is central to our understanding of Sweden's international involvement in the drug issue. As historian Ian Tyrrell (2010, p. 236) states, speaking of US moral imperialism, these foreign policy initiatives have 'many feedback effects'.

An international involvement in the drug issue is understandable as national prohibition legislation has made drugs a global and highly profitable commodity. International agreements have therefore aimed to prevent the production and smuggling of drugs. But an international commitment also becomes a binding commitment and not only in the formal sense as when the ratification of an international convention takes place in national legislation. At least as important is the anchoring of a domestic issue in a larger context, which helps to legitimize domestic polices and makes otherwise provincial policy appear universal and beyond domestic quarrel. The transnational context and the very use of an international discourse provides a resource for political struggle and debate (af Petersens 2006) and, as political scientist Mark Lawrence Schrad (2010, p. 46) has shown regarding the temperance movement, references to a global community serves 'to legitimize temperance activity as a worldwide moral battle between universal principles of good and evil, right and wrong'. Schrad (2007, p. 388 f) claims that 'domestic actors in effect "anchor" their positions on domestic policy considerations to the fate of policy developments abroad, which are out of their own jurisdiction and control'. But the intention (or at least the effect depending on what intentions we attribute to our actors) is also not to influence other countries' legislation as much as to 'dignify and generalize claims that might otherwise remain narrow and parochial' (Tarrow 2005, p. 76). In that manner, Sweden's foreign drug policy initiatives have contributed to the domestic political consensus on the drug issue established by previous research and previously noted (Tham 1995; Edman 2012).

Sweden's involvement in the drug issue bears resemblance to the United States' previous temperance missionary. Using an international point of view and being able to exemplify what other countries have already implemented domestically is a strength, as the problem and the solution then appear to be universal and beyond national conflict. The path towards US prohibition was, for example, taken by pointing to the previously introduced Russian alcohol ban (Schrad 2007). Problems only arise when you are already leading the development, when your own country is the extreme example of what you want to achieve. In that situation, the motives for international action are reasonably changed to be about influencing other countries to implement a stricter policy. When Tyrrell (2010, p. 237) tries to understand the United States' international commitment to temperance more than 100 years ago, he therefore starts with the duality that often characterizes missionary work, the ambition to be part of something bigger and the impulsion to something that must be understood as the opposite, the extreme position from which you try to enforce your agenda:

> moral reformers had bequeathed to the American nation a tradition of entanglement with the wider world; this tradition included the urge to be part of the world and yet at the same time superior to other countries. This experience imparted a streak of moral interventionism that cast the United States as

> an exception to the norms of empire and that urged higher moral standards on Americans. Paradoxically, this spirit of moral particularism encouraged a mission to change the world. The United States was seen to be both in the world and yet not of it.

'To be both in the world and yet not of it' could also fit as a description of Sweden's international involvement in the drug issue a century later. The international anchoring of Swedish drug policy has blended well with Sweden's self-image as a moral superpower. In addition, the Swedish model—the notion of an epidemic spread of drug abuse—has fit in well with the global public health framework of substance misuse problems that has grown strong during the post-war period (Edman 2018). Finally, this international involvement has also been a clear resource in the consensus-oriented Swedish drug policy, where dissenting views on a reasonable drug policy have been externalized to something propagated by countries described as uniformed. The question that arises is how long that model lasts, at what time you are no longer 'in the world', but only 'not of it'.

Notes

1 For a more detailed description of the development of Sweden's drug policy, see Tham, 2021.
2 Communication with Annika Mansnérus, member of the delegation as an expert in the Ministry of Social Affairs and also a board member of RFHL, the National Association for Help and Assistance to Drug Addicts.
3 A further example of a Swedish effort to influence European drug policy should be mentioned. The Major of Stockholm in 1992 took the initiative to the organization European Cities Against Drugs (ECAD), in order to fight the Frankfurt Resolution and efforts to liberalize drug policies. ECAD has received economic support from the city of Stockholm, the government, SIDA (The Swedish International Development Cooperation Agency) and The Swedish Institute and has been active in trying to influence the drug polices of the former communist regimes in Central and Eastern Europe, thereby exporting the Swedish model.
4 Documents relevant to Swedish participation in international bodies on drug policies were asked for at the Ministry of Social affairs. In all 58 documents were delivered. Most concern instructions to HNG-meetings but also to CND-meetings. Some documents have the Ministry of Foreign Affairs as sender. One document was classified as secret and not disclosed. The documents have been compiled by the Ministry, scanned, and sent to us. We are grateful for the service provided.

References

Barker, Vanessa (2013), "Nordic Exceptionalism Revisited: Explaining the Paradox of a Janus-Faced Penal Regime", *Theoretical Criminology*, 17(1): 5–25.

Barop, Helena (2015), "Building the 'Opium Evil' Consensus—The International Opium Commission of Shanghai", *Journal of Modern European History*, 3(1): 115–137.

Bejerot, Nils (1975), *Narkotika och narkomani*. 3 aktualiserade upplagan. Stockholm: Aldus/Bonnier.

Bruun, Kettil, Lynn Pan & Ingemar Rexed (1975), *The Gentlemen's Club. International Control of Drugs and Alcohol*, Chicago, IL: University of Chicago Press.
Curman, Peter et al. (1998), "Ingen kräver kokain på Konsum". Dagens Nyheter, DN .debatt 998-06-29.
Dahl, Ann-Sofie (2006), "Sweden", *International Journal*, 61(4): 895–908.
Direktiv 2017-03-23 till Horisontella narkotikaarbetsgruppen (HNG) 2017. Regeringskansliet, Socialdepartementet.
ECAD, European Cities Against Drugs. http://www.ecad.net/
Edman, Johan (2012), *Vård och ideologi. Narkomanvården som politiskt slagfält*, Umeå: Borea.
Edman, Johan (2015), "Temperance and Modernity: Alcohol Consumption as a Collective Problem 1885–1913", *Journal of Social History*, 49(1): 20–52.
Edman, Johan (2017), "Swedish Drug Policy", in: Renaud Colson & Henri Bergeron (eds.), *European Drug Policies: The Ways of Reform*, New York: Routledge, 195–205.
Edman, Johan (2018), "Alcohol Consumption as a Public Health Problem 1885–1992", in: Johannes Kananen, Sophy Bergenheim & Merle Wessel (eds.), *Conceptualising Public Health: Historical and Contemporary Struggles over Key Concepts*, London: Routledge, 135–155.
Edman, Johan (2021), "A Century of Dissonance and Harmony in Swedish Intoxication Policy", in: Henrik Tham (ed.), *Retreat or Entrenchment? Drug policies in the Nordic countries at a crossroads*, Stockholm: Stockholm University Press, 239–265.
Expressen, 1998-06-10 & 16.
Folkhälsoinstitutet. (1993), *Narkotikapolitik. De svenska erfarenheterna*. Rapport 1993: 3. Stockholm: Folkhälsoinstitutet.
Förslag 2016-05-02 till instruktion till möte i Horisontella narkotikaarbetsgruppen (HNG), 7 december 2016, Bryssel. Regeringskansliet, Socialdepartementet.
Förslag 2017-01-04 till instruktion till Horisontella narkotikaarbetsgruppen (HNG) 2017. Regeringskansliet, Socialdepartementet.
Government Bill [GB] 1985/86:100, *Förslag till statsbudget för budgetåret 1986/87*.
Government Bill [GB] 2005/06:30, *Nationella alkohol- och narkotikahandlingsplaner*.
Government Office of Sweden. (2016), *Swedish Drug Policy—A Balanced Policy Based on Health and Human Rights*, Ministry of Health and Social Affairs. https://www.government.se/496f5b/contentassets/89b85401ed204484832fb1808cad6012/rk_21164_broschyr_narkotika_a4_en_3_tillg.pdf
Hallam, Christopher (2010), "What Can We Learn from Sweden's Drug Policy Experience?", *The Beckley Foundation Drug Policy Program*, Briefing paper 20, January. http://fileserver.idpc.net/library/Sweden%20Briefing%20Paper%20final.pdf
Instruktion 2016-01-05 till Horisontella narkotikaarbetsgruppen (HNG), 7–8 januari 2016, Bryssel. Regeringskansliet, Socialdepartementet.
Instruktion 2016-03-01 till Horisontella narkotikagruppen (HNG), 17 februari 2016, Bryssel. Regeringskansliet, Socialdepartementet.
Instruktion 2016-03-09 inför Commission on Narcotic Drugs 59:e session 14–22 mars 2016. Regeringskansliet, Socialdepartementet.
Instruktion 2016-04-07/08. Horisontella narkotikagruppen (HNG), 17 februari 2016, Bryssel. Regeringskansliet, Socialdepartementet.
Instruktion 2016-05-11 till Horisontella narkotikagruppen (HNG), 9 juni 2016, Bryssel. Regeringskansliet, Socialdepartementet.

Instruktion 2016-09-16 till Horisontella narkotikaarbetsgruppen (HNG), 21–22 september 2016, Bryssel. Regeringskansliet, Socialdepartementet.

Instruktion 2017-02-21 till Horisontella narkotikaarbetsgruppen (HNG) 2017 (Attachémöte). Regeringskansliet, Socialdepartementet.

Instruktion 2017-03-10. FN:s narkotikakommission (CND) 13–17 mars 2017. Regeringskansliet, Socialdepartementet.

Instruktion 2017-05-02 till Horisontella narkotikaarbetsgruppen (HNG) 2017. Regeringskansliet, Socialdepartementet.

Instruktion 2017-11-28 till Horisontella narkotikaarbetsgruppen (HNG) 2018. Regeringskansliet, Socialdepartementet.

Instruktion 2019-01-14 till Horisontella narkotikaarbetsgruppen (HNG). Regeringskansliet, Socialdepartementet.

Instruktion 2019-09-04 till Horisontella narkotikaarbetsgruppen (HNG). Regeringskansliet, Socialdepartementet.

Instruktion 2019-10-04 till Horisontella narkotikaarbetsgruppen (HNG), den 9–10 oktober 2019. Regeringskansliet, Socialdepartementet.

Instruktion 2020-01-20 till möte i den horisontella narkotikaarbetsgruppen (HNG) den 21–22 januari 2020. Regeringskansliet, Socialdepartementet.

Jelsma, Martin (2003), "Drugs in the UN System: The Unwritten History of the 1998 United Nations General Assembly Special Session on Drugs", *International Journal of Drug Policy*, 14(2): 181–195.

Lenke, Leif (1991), "Dryckesmönster, nykterhetsrörelser och narkotikapolitik", *Sociologisk Forskning*, 28(4): 34–47.

Lenke, Leif & Börje Olsson (1998), "Drugs on Prescription—The Swedish Experiment of 1965–1967 in Retrospect", *European Addiction Research*, 4, 183–189.

The Local (2015–11–08), "UN: Sweden's drug rules violate human rights", https://www.thelocal.se/20151108/un-swedish-drug-policy-violates-human-rights

New York Times, June 6, 1998. Open letter to Mr. Kofi Annan, Secretary General, United Nations.

Olsson, Börje (2009), "Dressed for Success? A critical review of "Sweden's Successful Drug Policy: A Review of the Evidence (UNODC, 2007)", Paper presented at the third annual conference of the International Society for the Study of Drug Policy (ISSDP), Vienna, Austria.

af Petersens, Lovisa (2006), *Formering för offentlighet. Kvinnokonferenser och Svenska kvinnornas nationalförbund kring sekelskiftet 1900*, Stockholm: Acta Universitatis Stockholmiensis.

PM 1998-04-30, Instruktion inför den Horisontella narkotikaarbetsgruppens möte den 4 maj 1998. Regeringskansliet, Socialdepartementet.

Regeringens aktionsgrupp mot narkotika. (1991), *Vi ger oss aldrig!* Stockholm: Socialdepartementet.

Regeringskansliet. (1998), *A Preventive Strategy. Swedish Drug Policy in the 1990s*.

Regeringsprotokoll. (1998-06-04), Socialdepartementet. Förordnande av Sveriges delegation vid Förenta Nationernas Generalförsamlings extra möte 8–19 juni 1998.

Schrad, Mark Lawrence (2007), *The Prohibition Option. Transnational Temperance and National Policymaking in Russia, Sweden and the United States*, Madison: University of Wisconsin.

Schrad, Mark Lawrence (2010), *The Political Power of Bad Ideas*, Oxford: Oxford University Press.

Smith, Peter Scharff (2017), "Punishment Without Conviction? Scandinavian Pre-Trial Practices and the Power of the 'Benevolent' State", in: Peter Scharff Smith and Thomas Ugelvik, (eds.), *Scandinavian Penal History, Culture and Prison Practice*, 129–155. London: Palgrave Macmillan.

SOU 2000:126, *Vägvalet—den narkotikapolitiska utmaningen*, Stockholm: Statens Offentliga Utredningar.

SOU 2000:126, *Vägvalet—den narkotikapolitiska utmaningen*. PM nr 3. Narkotikarelaterad död, juni 1999, Stockholm: Statens Offentliga Utredningar.

SOU 2011:66, *Sveriges internationella engagemang på narkotikaområdet*, Stockholm: Statens Offentliga Utredningar.

Svenska synpunkter på UNGASS deklarationen efter input från civila samhället (2016).

Tarrow, Sidney (2005), *The New Transnational Activism*, Cambridge: Cambridge University Press.

Tham, Henrik (1995), "Drug Control as a National Project: The Case of Sweden", *The Journal of Drug Issues*, 25(1): 113–128.

Tham, Henrik (2021), "On the Possible Deconstruction of the Swedish Drug Policy", in: Henrik Tham (ed.), *Retreat or Entrenchment? Drug Policies in the Nordic Countries at a Crossroads*, Stockholm: Stockholm University Press, 129–158.

Tyrrell, Ian (2010), *Reforming the World: The Creation of America's Moral Empire*, Princeton, NJ: Princeton University Press.

UNODC (2007), *Sweden's Successful Drug Policy: A Review of the Evidence*. United Nations, Office on Drugs and Crime. https://www.unodc.org/pdf/research/Swedish_drug_control.pdf

Utrikesdepartementet. (1998-01-09), Telefax från Sveriges ständiga representation vid Förenta Nationerna: "FN:s generalsekreterare bjuder in drottningen att ingå i en kommitté om drogbekämpning" samt följande fax i frågan samlade av Socialdepartementet.

Wallström, Margot (1998a), "Statement", *Twentieth Special Session of the United Nations General Assembly 9 June 1998*.

Wallström, Margit (1998b), "Svenskar måste förklara knarkupprop", DN Debatt, *Dagens Nyheter* 1998-06-21.

Wohlforth, William C., Benjamin de Carvalho, Halvard Leira & Iver B. Neumann (2018), "Moral Authority and Status in International Relations: Good States and the Social Dimension of Status Seeking", *Review of International Studies*, 44(3): 526–546.

5 Swedish, Nordic, European

The journey of a 'model' to abolish prostitution

Isabel Crowhurst and May-Len Skilbrei

Introduction

The governance of prostitution across Europe is characterized by different regulatory approaches and models of intervention that are shaped by, amongst other factors, national traditions and histories, contingent problem definitions, specificities of local prostitution markets, as well as by the global influence of policy models and discourses. In the past two decades, prostitution has become a highly contentious and divisive policy area in Europe. Animated political and public debates have been unfolding around which of the prostitution policy approaches currently in place is the most effective and whether there is scope for legal harmonization across the region. While sex worker advocacy groups and alliances, and many prominent international organizations, academics, and some politicians have been advocating for the decriminalization of sex work, the criminalization of sex buyers with a view to abolishing prostitution and promoting gender equality has gained particularly strong political support in and beyond Europe. This approach was first conceptualized in Sweden where it was passed into law (the Swedish Sex Purchase Act) in 1999 and has since been hailed as a model for other countries to conform to. But conform to what? As we show in this chapter, the original scope of the Swedish approach has been detached from its actual application in Sweden and throughout its rise to global popularity. Nevertheless, in its multiple redefinitions as Swedish, Nordic, pan-European, end demand, or equality 'model' it has acquired potent symbolic capital globally, serving as a tool of convergence and consensus for the many who ascribe to it a superior moral status and who view it as the solution to the 'problem of prostitution'.

In presenting the increasing global popularity and application of the 'Swedish model',[1] in this chapter we show how key ideas underpinning it evolved and were adapted over time, and how currently the adoption of its multiple interpretations is pursued by countries with limited or no proximity and little socio-economic, political, and social welfare resemblance to the Nordic region. In this journeying from one context to another, the 'model' has taken a life of its own in at least three meaningful ways which we introduce here and further discuss in the rest of the chapter.

DOI: 10.4324/9781003195504-8

Firstly, the 'Swedish model' as it is conceptualized and understood globally today is very much detached from its empirical roots and shows limited resemblance to its original intention. However, while the link to Sweden and the Nordic countries has been severed and the 'weight' of Swedish-ness and/or Nordic-ness has lost importance, the symbolic capital of the 'Swedish model' has stayed, even if the intent of the original approach is diluted or strayed from. Such symbolic capital is used to validate and build consensus around new model adaptations and new model brands, such as 'gender equality model' or 'end demand model', that can appeal and make better sense globally.

Secondly, today, those who promote the 'Swedish model' more vigorously are political actors far removed from the Swedish and Nordic contexts. In the name of the gender equality that the model claims to promote and defend, these advocates invoke its moral superiority and go as far as shaming the values and character of their *own* nations for not having implemented it yet.

Thirdly, the Swedish approach was conceptualized at a particular historical moment, and a lot has changed since then, both politically and in the shape and organization of sex industries across the world. Debates about the best way to regulate prostitution and prostitution policy conformity remain unabated, but new problem definitions and actors have come into the picture, sex markets have become increasingly international, and prostitution as a policy sphere has become more and more entangled with the issues of migration and human trafficking. The Swedish feminism of the late 1990s that contributed to conceptualizing 'the model' was exclusively focussed on cis men's violence against cis women, which was assumed to be experienced in the same way by all cis women and to damage all cis women's worth in society, all the while neglecting intersectionality and the much more diverse landscape of people who buy and sell sex. The strong commitment that was later made by Sweden to be an LGBTQI+ inclusive society (for a critique of this, see Lilja and Johansson, 2018) does not sit comfortably with the hetero-cis normativities of 1990s feminist advocacy that led to the Swedish Sex Purchase Act.

It is in this dynamic context that harm reduction, not contemplated until recently as a practice to be pursued by social workers operating in this field in Sweden and very much against the ethos of the law (Florin 2012), is no longer seen so unfavourably, approaches to prostitution are diversifying, and the Sex Purchase Act is no longer as unassailable as it appeared just a decade ago, even in Sweden.

Prostitution policy conformity and the appeal of a uniform 'model': an overview

The precedent for prostitution policy conformity in modern Europe takes us back to the 19th century, when the widespread optimism about the effectiveness of regulationism resulted in the containment and regulation of prostitution across many European cities. Regulationism was a system whereby national penal law was set aside and only applied if women who sold sex did not abide by local police by-laws and health regimes that controlled where they lived and how they worked, and subjected them to regular checks for sexually transmitted infections. The aim of this approach was public harm reduction: under this widespread public health regime, 'common women' were tolerated as long as they operated in ways that were not seen as harmful for society at large (Harsin 1985; Levine 2003). Public health, more specifically ill-health prevention, had become a legitimate argument for policies, including repressive ones (Porter 1998). While some European countries retained a regulationist approach well into the 20th century—including Sweden which maintained it in Stockholm until 1918 (Svanström 2017)—many others gave in to the demands of the movement to abolish regulationism. With few exceptions, by the mid 20th century regulationism had been formally repealed, effectively putting an end to the one time in modern history when most European nation states had a shared understanding of prostitution primarily as a public health issue and implemented very similar prostitution policy approaches.

The idea that Europe *should* have a common understanding of, and approach to, prostitution re-emerged in the 21st century when the aspiration for a unified European policy approach to prostitution returned to the political agenda of supranational entities, as well as national and non-governmental actors. This time, however, debates about harmonization have been taking place in the context of deep disagreements over what approach is best, and for whom. In the 19th century, policy harmonization had been facilitated by the shared identification of 'common enemies': syphilis and the de-domestication of sexuality, both viewed as a threat to the normative family. Today prostitution policies have different objectives. Some aim to eradicate or limit commercial sex through criminal law, others aim to integrate it into society and tightly control it (Östergren 2017a). Moreover, even when policy goals are shared, there are substantial differences over how these can be achieved. To align policies across Europe mandates a harmonization of problem definitions, a difficult task to achieve. Nevertheless, the allure of having a unified model of prostitution regulation, expected to have the same standardized outcome no matter where it is implemented, continues to drive prostitution policy agendas in and beyond Europe. Despite the fact that an expanding body of research warns against pursuing a one-size-fit-all 'harmonized' approach in prostitution regulation that would end up ignoring the unique conditions and needs of the different contexts to which it is applied (Scoular 2015; Östergren 2017a; Crowhurst and Skilbrei 2018; Wagenaar 2018), attempts to promote a uniform understanding of, and response to, prostitution across highly diverse jurisdictions have been prompted and promoted around what has become known as the 'Swedish model'. Self-proclaimed as a superior policy approach, the 'Swedish model' has served as a space of ideological convergence by framing prostitution as a matter of gender inequality and as the best viable way to abolish prostitution once and for all.

Given the ideological and symbolic capital of policy models (Bowling 2011), it is not uncommon for their proposers to expect them to exhibit a nation's character and core values, both to its citizens and globally. Much energy is invested in presenting principles and understandings that inform policy models as more sophisticated and/or more enlightened than others, and in ensuring that they are effective, or at least viewed as such. This is especially the case with morality politics, in which prostitution is viewed as an archetypal case that rouses uncompromizing value conflicts in both societal and political spheres (Foret and Calligaro 2018; Wagenaar 2018). With the passing of the Sex Purchase Act in 1999, Sweden asserted its moral authority as the pioneer of a conceptualization of prostitution that it viewed as transcending religious moralizing and sexual double standards, has gender equality as its key objective instead, and has the capacity to 'contribute to changing debates [on prostitution] also in Europe' (the Swedish Minister of Social Affairs, Lars Engqvist as cited in Langford and Skilbrei 2022: page 178).

The popularity of this model, the efforts invested by Sweden to advertise and export it, the implementation of (some of) its principles in a number of other countries globally, the enhanced appeal it garnered in its extended configuration as 'Nordic model', and the momentum this has given to the abolitionist movement that supports it, are all factors that have contributed to enhancing divisiveness and confrontations over whether this is really the model of prostitution governance that all countries should aspire to have. As mentioned earlier, sex workers' rights movements and various esteemed international organizations, amongst others, have condemned this approach for producing, rather than reducing, harm to sex workers (see, for example, World Health Organization 2012; Amnesty International 2016; Human Rights Watch 2019). However, if anything, the popularity of the 'Swedish model' has expanded over the past two decades and many countries (Canada, Finland, France, Iceland, the Republic of Ireland, Israel, Northern Ireland, and Norway) have adopted the key principles that constitute it (with crucial variations)[2]: that buyers of sexual services should be criminalized and punished, not sellers.

The 'Swedish model': origin, ethos, and contestations

In 1999, with the Sex Purchase Act, Sweden introduced a unilateral ban on the purchase of sex. It did so after several years of discussion of how prostitution is best regulated, and in the process, prostitution became firmly situated as an issue to do with gender equality. This marked a notable shift away from dominant perspectives that had previously guided how states and societies approached prostitution, i.e., as a matter of public health or as related to sexual morality. Within this framework of understanding, the link between gender equality and prostitution works both ways: it is gender inequality that causes prostitution to exist, and the existence of prostitution itself perpetuates gender inequality. Other matters were also drawn into national debates preceding the passing of the law,[3] but in the end, the Sex Purchase Act was integrated into a larger law package on women's rights, the Women's Peace Bill (for an analysis of the debates, see Svanström 2004; Östergren 2017b; Erikson 2018), and this firmly severed the ties between prostitution policy and previous problem definitions.

The Sex Purchase Act builds on an abolitionist stance on prostitution, in other words, the aim was to design a policy that would ultimately abolish prostitution, although not at any cost. The view that prostitution results from gender inequality and is harmful for women who sell sex meant that completely criminalizing the sale of sex was politically impossible. The Act was intended to work toward gender equality by combating prostitution: in the short run by curbing the market, and in the long run by changing social norms. Importantly, it was also introduced to set an example for other countries to follow (Holmström and Skilbrei 2017), something we return to below. Policy making on prostitution in various contexts has considered gender equality (see e.g., Dodillet 2005), but the latter is especially and explicitly central in the Swedish approach with the clear formulation of the Sex Purchase Act as a gender equality legislation designed to protect sellers specifically, and gender and sexuality norms more generally. As mentioned previously, prostitution has historically been defined as different kinds of problems, and Swedish policy makers wanted to make a clear break with earlier understandings of prostitution as immoral and especially so as pertaining to the immorality of the seller. The law emerged from several decades of feminist debates wherein the aim to destigmatize sellers became increasingly important.[4]

The scope of the 'Swedish model' is presented differently in different contexts (Langford and Skilbrei 2022), but the common denominator is the criminalization of the purchase of sex. While there are many policy approaches globally where only one party in prostitution is criminalized, this is usually the seller, whereas in other instances, both parties are criminalized. The unilateral ban on sex buyers, therefore, represented a novelty in the contemporary prostitution policy landscape.[5] Sometimes, however, the 'Swedish model' and its extended version the 'Nordic model' are wrongly presented in debates outside the region as being about criminalizing buyers and decriminalizing sellers. Indeed, selling sex is not illegal per se in Sweden, but this has been the case already since 1918—the Sex Purchase Act did not decriminalize the selling of sex, selling sex was already legal in Swedish law (Östergren 2017b). Similarly, in Finland, Norway, and Iceland, partial criminalisation of the sale of sex was removed in the last two decades through policy initiatives that were unrelated to the introduction of bans against buying sex. The mis-representation of the Swedish approach as being one of simultaneously criminalizing the purchase and decriminalizing the sale of sex can be observed in the European Parliament resolution recommending that EU Member States follow the Nordic lead, which stated: 'Sweden changed its prostitution laws in 1999 to prohibit the purchase of sex and decriminalize the prostituted person' (European Parliament 2014: 17, for more on this, see below). Scholars have misrepresented this too (see e.g., Waltman 2011) by portraying the decriminalization of the sale of sex as part of the legal shift taking place in Sweden, and later in other Nordic countries, which, as explained, amounts to a factual error. Such widespread misrepresentation of the Act contributes to reinforcing the symbolic power of 'the model' as an approach that is conceived specifically in the interest of sellers as victims. Furthermore, the premise that 'the Swedish model' only aims at enforcing punitive approaches against clients and never at sellers, is also not accurate. While the sale of sex is in itself legal across the region, there are prohibitions in place that target the sale of sex, for example third country nationals are forbidden from selling sex in Sweden and are at risk of deportation and banned from re-entry if they do sell sex, even though selling sex is legal *per se* (Skilbrei and Holmström 2013). This predicament shows the incorrectness of claims made about the 'Swedish model' that it works in ways that people who sell sex are supported with welfare measures rather than being punished (see e.g., European Women's Lobby 2017). Indeed, the Sex Purchase Act in Sweden was intended to be followed by investments in social work to aid sex sellers, but this did not materialize (Florin 2012), and to this day, support services are mainly offered to women in street prostitution in the three largest cities in Sweden, and migrants and sex workers who do not wish to/are not able to exit prostitution face obstacles in accessing assistance (Vuolajärvi 2019).

Assumptions that the 'the Swedish model' entails the active policing of sex purchasing is also not entirely correct. Looking at law in action, it is evident that the Sex Purchase Act is not uniformly implemented across Sweden, but mainly enforced in the three largest cities. Moreover, over 20 years (1999–2019) only 3,594 individuals have been convicted of buying sex and almost all of them received a fine, not a prison sentence (Olsson 2021). This is the background for the claim made by some that in Sweden buying sex is *de facto* legal (if not *de jure*), as most men who buy sex do not have much to fear as far as being criminalized (see e.g., Lööf and Hedin 2021). This has, in part, contributed to the Swedish Parliament voting in the summer of 2022 to exacerbate punishments for sex buyers, removing fines from the list of punishments, leaving only imprisonment (The Swedish Government 2022).

Finally, the 'Swedish model' is discussed in international scholarship on prostitution, in policy debates, and in various jurisdictions as either a negative or positive example depending on how its end results are considered, something that for over two decades has been highly contested. When assessing its effects, some have argued that the Sex Purchase Act has dramatically reduced the extent of prostitution in Sweden (Waltman 2011), while others argue that it has made conditions worse and more dangerous for people who sell sex (Levy 2014). As far as the normative goals of the Sex Purchase Act are concerned, some have argued that the Act has shifted societal norms on prostitution and people involved in it in Sweden (Jacobsson and Kotsadam 2011), although there isn't more recent research on this. Relevant to our argument here, as shown further in the paragraphs that follow, is that the Act and its promotion have contributed to positioning Sweden as the homeland of gender equality, arguably achieving the goal of serving as an inspiration to other countries.

In sum, the Swedish Sex Purchase Act has received much attention because it is considered to be the first law to criminalize only buyers and not sellers of sexual services, and because it is linked to a feminist interpretation that links prostitution to gender inequality and views it as an expression of men's power over women in society. However, there remains much disagreement over the assumed beneficial effects of 'the model' and a number of problematic and wrongful assumptions and claims are made about its scope and effects. Ultimately, the Sex Purchase Act is only one piece of the puzzle if one is to look at how prostitution is approached through hard and soft policies in Sweden. The Act operates in a context where many other developments are also taking place that impact the size, organization and management of the phenomenon, and the prostitution market is also quite resilient to control (Holmström and Skilbrei 2017).

From Swedish to Nordic to European: the transformations of 'the model'

Over time, the 'Swedish model' has become detached from the Swedish context where it originated. After Finland introduced a partial ban against the purchase of sex in 2006 and Norway and Iceland criminalized the purchase of sex in 2009, the 'Swedish model' started being referred to internationally as 'the Nordic model'. As mentioned earlier, however, while some form of client criminalization has been introduced in four of the five Nordic countries, and no general ban exists against selling sex in the region, there is great diversity among these countries in how laws are enacted and how they interact with other legislations, such as the Aliens Act, tax regulations, and police bylaws (Skilbrei and Holmström 2013). Thus, the association to the Nordic region made reference to in 'the Nordic model' is less about how prostitution is actually regulated in the Nordic countries, and rather more about the centrality of welfare and gender equality that exist there and the supposed moral authority/superiority that derives from it.

The international support and popularity for the 'Nordic model' was further enhanced in 2014, when thanks also to the strong backing of Swedish female Members of the European Parliament, a non-binding resolution in favor of the criminalization of the purchase of sex was supported by a majority European Parliament vote. The resolution was based on a controversial report drafted by the MEP Mary Honeyball for the Committee on Women's Rights and Gender Equality (commonly known as the Honeyball report) which condemned the, allegedly, failing prostitution policy approach adopted in the Netherlands and Germany. Instead, the resolution advocated the 'model implemented in Sweden, Finland and Norway (the so-called Nordic model)' which, the motion for the resolution stated (European Parliament 2014: 14), is considered 'the most effective way of combating the trafficking of women and girls for sexual exploitation and improving gender equality [...] where the purchase of sexual services constitutes the criminal act, not the services of the prostituted persons'. The process leading to the 2014 European Parliament resolution to harmonize prostitution policy across Europe was ripe with references to Sweden, to other Nordic countries and to the Nordic region as a whole. Before the European Parliament voted on the resolution, a group of academics published a letter in which they claimed to 'draw on both our practice-based evidence and our academic studies to strongly endorse the Honeyball report and its recommendation to adopt 'the Nordic model' as a pan-European approach to prostitution'.[6] The Nordic model, the letter stated, offers the potential to replicate progress achieved in Nordic countries across Europe, and following their 'pioneering example', it 'has an historic opportunity to act as a global beacon on gender equality'.

What is especially relevant for the scope of this chapter, is the way in which the Nordic model was presented as a symbol of a European commitment to gender equality. The trajectory that the Swedish model has taken over time and through the active advocacy of its supporters shows a progression from representing a nation first (the 'original' Swedish model), a sub-region next (the Nordic model), and finally the aspiration to represent the approach of an entire geographical region and therefore a much larger political unit (a pan-European model). Thus, by championing its implementation across the region and hoping to achieve a European harmonized (neo) abolitionist approach to prostitution, the Nordic model is viewed almost as a 'pivot' which could turn the whole of Europe into a model, indeed a beacon, for the entire globe.

The resolution was firmly opposed by many national and international non-governmental and governmental organizations, social movements and scholars and the evidence used to support its claims was shown to be biased and, in some cases, also inaccurate (see e.g., NSWP 2014). Nevertheless, even if non-binding, it carried 'symbolic and political weight' (Scoular 2015: 10) and gave strong momentum to neo-abolitionists' campaigning in and beyond Europe (Outshoorn 2017).

Indeed, in the context of political debates on prostitution in countries in and outside Europe in the past decade, proposals and preferences for the criminalization of clients have often made reference to either the Swedish or the Nordic models. Already in 2015, in the US, Mosley notes (2019: 353), '11 metropolitan areas pledged to reduce demand for prostitution by using *Nordic strategies*', and we can list more examples of what Kingston and Thomas (2019) refer to as the 'international import', whether successful or attempted, of the Nordic model. Kingston and Thomas (2019) cite the cases of Scotland and Luxembourg—where the model was seriously considered (in 2013 and 2014, respectively) as demonstrated also by visits to Sweden, albeit plans to adopt the model were eventually rejected—and Canada, France, the Republic of Ireland, and Northern Ireland which introduced the criminalization of clients and which consistently made reference to the Nordic model as the approach they wanted to follow. In 2014, when Canada was still debating the introduction of the criminalization of sex buyers, one of its most vocal supporters, the MP Joy Smith reportedly claimed,

> I am pleased that there are many MPs that support the *Nordic model for Canada* [...]. Once you understand the options, the Nordic model is clearly the only approach that effectively addresses the harm and inequality produced by prostitution and targets the buyers of sex[7] (emphasis added).

In 2017, the European Women's Lobby supported the Malta Confederation of Women's Organisations' campaign for a 'Nordic Model for Malta'.[8] In 2018, the Israeli Parliament voted in favour of introducing a ban against the purchase of sex, which became law in 2020 and made Israel, as many reported, the eighth country to adopt the Nordic Model.[9] In September 2020, an alliance of centre/

conservative parties in Switzerland proposed, albeit unsuccessfully, the introduction of a 'Nordic Model for Switzerland'.[10] The list of examples could be longer, but the ones presented here convey the geographical breadth of the reach and popularity of the 'Swedish'/'Nordic' model and desire expressed by some political actors to import it and have their own national version of it.

In recent years, we also find several examples of how policy proposals with an abolitionist aim outside of Europe are addressed as 'equality model' and 'end demand' approach, further detaching the policy from its Nordic geopolitical origin. In these cases, despite the empirical loss of ties to Sweden and the Nordic region, it is reasonable to assume that 'the model's' starting point in the Nordic region has been key in establishing these new 'equality' and 'end demand' model redefinitions as the progressive, gender equal, and modern policy that all countries should apply. However, while 'end demand' and 'equality' models are associated with an abolitionist approach to prostitution whereby only buyers of sex are punished, their critics denounce them as causing sex workers to be aggressively policed and as having detrimental impacts on gender equality. Moreover, third party criminalization, i.e., the criminalization of 'pimping' which is rarely described as a part of 'the Swedish' model, is often included as a key component (see e.g., McBride et al. 2020) in what appear to be substantial adaptations of the 'Swedish model', as opposed to simple re-incarnations or re-definitions. For example, as the Global Network of Sex Work Projects (NSWP) write in their 2018 report 'The Impact of "End Demand" Legislation on Women Sex Workers' (NSWP 2018: 1):

> 'End Demand' legislation ranges from national criminal laws, which can lead to imprisonment, to city laws, which fine or ban individuals from certain areas for a period of time for soliciting or paying for sex; from purchasing sex anywhere in the world to purchasing sexual services in public places, not in licensed brothels or within designated 'prostitution-free' areas. 'End Demand' laws are often accompanied by laws criminalising third parties. Selling sex is criminalized or penalized in all but three countries with 'End Demand' legislation.

Shame on us!

The evolution and international journeying of the 'original' Swedish model unfolded with what can be identified as an ethnocentric intent. By ethnocentrism we mean, to apply Nelken's (2009) definition to this context, 'assuming that what we do, our way of thinking about a [particular policy problem] is universally shared or, at least, that it would be right for everyone else'. Indeed, as discussed earlier, the growth of the 'Swedish model' has been facilitated by the financial and political efforts put by Sweden to promote it 'as part of its own identity-shaping in the international realm' (Ward and Wylie 2017: 4).

What happened next, after the 'Swedish model' became better known as the 'Nordic model' and the appeal of its ideological underpinnings widened and was inscribed in the laws and policies of other countries, is that its most fervent supporters are no longer the Swedes (the other 'Nordics' were never as intent in international proselytizing), but other actors, governmental and non, in countries well beyond the Nordic region. These other Nordic model entrepreneurs have appropriated the symbolic capital of the model and promote its implementation with a strong moralizing rhetoric, as the 'right thing to do', and are able to execute this also through the notable financial support invested globally in neo-abolitionism.[11] A process of shaming, and often of self-shaming, is involved in national campaigns that promote and advocate for the implementation of this approach. Not having implemented it is viewed as an affront to gender equality and women's rights, and this is especially contemptible if the country in question has a regulationist approach in place.

To provide an example of how this process of self-shaming can manifest itself, we describe the campaign video 'A message from Sweden to the people of Switzerland' produced by the Swiss organization Zurich Women's Centre in 2018.[12] The video, produced by the Swiss organization and targeted at a Swiss audience, starts with smiling people of different ages, recognizable as Swedish from their accent, greeting the viewers and stating: 'Switzerland and Sweden are constantly confused with each other. Perhaps you Swiss don't have a problem with this. But we do'. 'We are completely different countries', emphasize the now very serious Swedes. 'Look at how you treat women', a man states, followed by a series of comparisons where the Swiss record is clearly lagging behind the Swedish one and is therefore ridiculed. Women were given the right to vote in 1921 in Sweden and in 1971 in Switzerland. '1971?' some of the actors in the video incredulously ask. In Sweden women who give birth receive 78 weeks' pay, in Switzerland they are paid only for 14 weeks. 'And then there is the sex business': in Sweden 'if a man pays a woman for giving him sex', an actor explains, he is fined or jailed, 'it is forbidden'. 'In your country: it's legal'; 'legal' repeat the actors with a disbelieving expression. 'It's totally crazy', states a woman. Others explain that '75% percent of prostitutes are migrants' and that young girls are brought to 'your country' as cleaners to make pimps rich.

> 'How can something like this be legal?'
> 'Of course anything that makes money is legal in Switzerland' states an actor scornfully;
> 'You guys still live the Middle Ages'
> 'With women as paid sex soldiers'
> 'More than 80% of the prostitutes would like to quit [long pause] if they could'.

Screenshots of the despondent actors are shown in succession, and the video ends with a young girl staring at the camera, pleading: 'please do something about it, Switzerland'. The video ends with these two messages in succession: 'Sweden banned prostitution 20 years ago', and: 'Switzerland, it's time to catch up again'.

The campaign video operates through a strategy of shaming: the core message is delivered by Swedish people who, from a moral high-ground—justified by the progressive and overall positive record and efforts of their country, both contemporary and historical—can afford to chastise the Swiss public for their dismal, regressive, and sexist policies. The focus of the video is not on what the Swedish law is about or what its effects might be on prostitution, but on what supporting gender equality is supposed to entail. Opposing the 'Swedish model' or not supporting it is implicitly equated to being against gender equality. The video, importantly, was not produced by a Swedish organization, but by a Swiss one, so the very act of shaming Switzerland is in fact one of self-shaming, possibly to galvanize national pride and push Swiss citizens to mobilize and follow the illuminated example of Sweden and its model.

There are several examples of analysis of how 'the model' has similarly been used as a rhetorical device in debates elsewhere (Crowhurst and Skilbrei 2018, for individual cases see e.g., Ireland; FitzGerald and McGarry 2015; Kingston and Thomas 2019; and Israel; Langford and Skilbrei 2022). In an article on the mobilization of shame and disgust by abolitionist movements in Germany and Austria, Birgit Sauer (2019), discusses similar affective strategies enacted to promote the Swedish model in these countries. For example, Sauer cites the case of the German abolitionist activist Ingeborg Kraus who appealed to national pride by shaming fellow Germans who decided to pass a regulationist law in 2002 that, she claimed, transformed the country in the brothel of Europe. While Sweden and France felt indignation and outrage at the plight of prostituted women, Kraus argued, Germans shamefully decided to preserve the status quo and, with it, violence against women (Sauer 2019). Also, in this case, the campaigning for the 'Swedish model' is built around how valued gender equality is by a country, its population and leaders, to the extent that aspiring to anything other than these models amounts to a national betrayal of gender equality and of women in particular.

The future of 'the model' at home and abroad

Today there are several countries that present their policy as an adaptation of 'the model', and that used it to create a momentum in debates leading up to domestic law revisions. The last 20 years have demonstrated that 'the model' can be appropriated for diverse political agendas. It is, therefore, a possibility that it will continue to be used as a starting point for debates on prostitution policies in even more countries and in countries very different from Sweden. However, while its international appeal remains strong, various forces and factors are contributing to challenging the 'Swedish'/'Nordic' model. Its hetero-cis normativity is no longer tenable, nor is its lack of applicability to foreign nationals, a situation which creates a double standard that generates even more vulnerability to migrant sex workers. We could even speculate that the strong affective rhetoric deployed in advocating for the 'model' in many countries is a last resort to mobilize followers against the accruing evidence of its ineffectiveness and negative impacts and in light of sex workers' rights movements increasing legitimacy in their advocacy for decriminalization, further supported by prominent organizations. In Europe, as Outshoorn (2017) also points out, resurgent anti-EU sentiments and nationalism might play a role in the future in rejecting any harmonized and super-imposed European approach to prostitution—it is already perhaps harder than before to argue that there might be a pan-European morality that should be expressed in certain policy areas.

Moreover, the context in which the Swedish approach was conceptualized has changed notably, in and beyond Sweden. Over two decades, while the symbolic capital of the model has gained strength internationally, the effectiveness of its implementation and the inclusivity of its equality agenda have been put into question in Sweden itself. In the last few years, critical voices towards the Sex Purchase Act have been growing in numbers in Sweden. A call for broader legislation and harsher punishment against buyers stemming from feminists and the government has been critiqued from several angles, both from within mainstream political parties (e.g., Tolnai 2021), from key media actors (e.g., editorial by chief political editor of *Svenska Dagbladet* Tove Lifvendahl [2019]), and from large civil society actors (e.g., Swedish Federation for Lesbian, Gay, Bisexual, Transgender, Queer and Intersex Rights 2019). Previously, many have stated that it is difficult to voice critique against the Sex Purchase Act in Sweden without being vilified. Sex workers and others are hesitant to take part in debates, and some debaters have chosen to be anonymous or have come forward at great personal cost (Rydström 2021). The Swedish sex workers' rights movement has been critical of the legislation all along but it has been unable to make allies with politicians and other social movements, until recently (Rydström 2021). The first sex workers' rights march in Sweden was organized in 2019 and Swedish sex workers' rights organizations have not had the visibility and traction as those of many other European countries (ibid.). Critique of the 'model' has often been interpreted as neoliberal or conservative, or interpreted as supporting men's right to 'access women's bodies', as the Swedish ambassador Per-Anders Sunesson stated at the governmental conference on the 20th anniversary of the Act, with the noteworthy title 'From controversial law to international model' (Andersson 2019). However, Yttergren and Westerstrand (2016) offer an opposite conclusion, instead arguing that being critical of the Act is the hegemonic position.

The analysis over which position is hegemonic thus differs substantially, and this speaks to the polarization of debates. The 20th anniversary of the Sex Purchase Act in 2019 was itself marked by two separate events. One was organized by sex workers with no participants from governmental bodies, and the other event was organized by the government, with no invited sex workers (Rydström 2021). That two events with opposite approaches to the Act took place during this important anniversary, points to a degree of polarization in Swedish debates on prostitution which was unthinkable just a few years ago, where now claims and demands for sex workers' health, labour, and human rights are gaining a platform and momentum also in Sweden. What impact this might have for the 'Swedish model' and its international adaptations remains to be seen.

Notes

1 We use quotation marks when referring to the 'Swedish model', the 'Nordic model', or 'the model' to reflect the (problematic) social constructed nature of this approach as a coherent and leading model that others should follow.
2 For example, Finland only introduced a partial criminalization of the purchase of sex, i.e. it criminalizes instances of buying sex from victims of human trafficking or from sex sellers who are controlled by pimps.
3 For example organized crime, which was seen as the driving force behind prostitution (Eriksson 2018).
4 For several analyses of how the Swedish sex purchase act came into being, see Gould 2001; Kulick 2005; Skilbrei and Holmström 2013; Scoular 2015; Östergren 2017b; Erikson 2018.
5 It should be noted that the claim that Sweden is the first country to criminalize only the buyer of sex is often repeated, but it has never been investigated empirically. Throughout history and across jurisdictions prostitution has been regulated in a variety of ways. The great diversity in approaches means that we cannot rule out that this particular construction, only criminalizing buyers of sexual services, has happened before.
6 https://www.spaceintl.org/media/submission-in-support-of-mary-honeyballs-report-on-sexual-exploitation.
7 https://ottawacitizen.com/news/local-news/punish-the-clients-not-the-prostitutes-says-tory-mp-joy-smith.
8 https://www.womenlobby.org/Nordic-model-for-Malta.
9 https://www.feministcurrent.com/2020/06/30/whats-current-israel-becomes-8th-country-to-adopt-the-nordic-model-of-prostitution-law/; https://nordicmodelnow.org/2020/06/29/israel-becomes-the-8th-nordic-model-country-as-it-implements-its-prohibition-of-consumption-of-prostitution-services-act.
10 https://www.parlament.ch/it/ratsbetrieb/suche-curia-vista/geschaeft?AffairId=20204216.
11 The political economy of the Nordic Model is an aspect that is beyond the scope of this chapter, nevertheless it needs to be mentioned, as it plays a significant role in subsidizing campaigns and organizations that advocate for it, and therefore their visibility and lobby potential.
12 https://www.youtube.com/watch?v=anflTyvUwBk.

References

Amnesty International. 2016. The human cost of 'crushing the market'. Criminalization of sex work in Norway. Available from: https://www.amnesty.org/download/Documents/EUR3640342016ENGLISH.PDF [accessed 8 July 2021].

Andersson, K. 2019. Sexköpslagen fylle 20 år med fortsatt könsexplosiv potensial. *Feministisk perspektiv*, 23 October 2019. Available from: https://feministisktperspektiv.se/2019/10/23/sexkopslagen-20-ar/ [accessed 26 July 2021].

Bowling, B. 2011. Transnational criminology and the globalization of harm production. In *What is criminology?*, edited by M. Bosworth and C. Hoyle, 361–379. Oxford: Oxford University Press.

Crowhurst, I., and M.-L. Skilbrei. 2018. International comparative explorations of prostitution policies: Lessons from two European projects. *Innovation: The European Journal of Social Science Research* 31(2), 142–161.

Dodillet, S. 2005. Cultural clash on prostitution: Debates on prostitution in Germany and Sweden in the 1990s. In *Genealogies of identity: Interdisciplinary readings on sex and sexuality*, edited by M. Sönser Breen, and F. Peters, 39–56. Amsterdam: Brill.

Erikson, J. 2018. Institutions, gendered perceptions, and frames of meaning: Explaining strategic choices of women MPs in Swedish prostitution policy. *Journal of Women, Politics and Policy* 40(2), 263–285. https://doi.org/10.1080/1554477X.2019.1536599.

European Parliament. 2014. Report on sexual exploitation and prostitution and its impact on gender equality. Committee on Women's Rights and Gender Equality. Available from: https://www.europarl.europa.eu/doceo/document/A-7-2014-0071_EN.pdf [accessed 26 July 2021].

European Women's Lobby. 2017. Nordic model for Malta? Available from: https://www.womenlobby.org/Nordic-model-for-Malta [accessed 30 November 2021].

FitzGerald, S., and K. McGarry. 2015. Problematizing prostitution law and policy in the Republic of Ireland: A case for reframing. *Social and Legal Studies* 1(12), 289–309.

Florin, O. 2012. A particular kind of violence: Swedish social policy puzzles of a multipurpose criminal law. *Sexuality Research and Social Policy* 9(3), 269–278.

Foret, F.O., and O. Calligaro. 2018. *European values: Challenges and opportunities for EU governance. Routledge studies on government and the European Union*. London and New York: Routledge, Taylor & Francis Group.

Gould, A. 2001. The criminalisation of buying sex: The politics of prostitution in Sweden. *Journal of Social Policy* 30(3), 437–456.

Harsin, J. 1985. *Policing prostitution in nineteenth-century Paris*. Edited by Societies American Council of Learned. Princeton, NJ: Princeton University Press.

Holmström, C., and M. L. Skilbrei. 2017. The Swedish sex purchase act: Where does it stand? *Oslo Law Review* 4(2), 82–104.

Human Rights Watch. 2019. Why sex work should be decriminalized. Available from: https://www.hrw.org/news/2019/08/07/why-sex-work-should-be-decriminalized [accessed 22 July 2021].

Jakobsson, N., and A. Kotsadam. 2011. Gender equity and prostitution: An investigation of attitudes in Norway and Sweden. *Feminist Economics* 17(1), 31–58.

Kingston, S., and T. Thomas. 2019. No model in practice: A 'Nordic model' to respond to prostitution? *Crime, Law and Social Change* 71(4), 423–439.

Kulick, D. 2005. Four hundred Swedish perverts. *GLQ: A Journal of Lesbian and Gay Studies* 11(2), 205–235.

Langford, M., and M. L. Skilbrei. 2022. Branding the Nordic model of prostitution policy. In *The making and circulation of Nordic models, ideas and images*, edited by H. Byrkjeflot, L. Mjøset, M. Mordhorst, and K. Petersen, 165–191. London: Routledge.

Levine, P. 2003. *Prostitution, race, and politics: Policing venereal disease in the British Empire / Philippa Levine*. New York: Routledge.

Levy, J. 2014. *Criminalising the purchase of sex: Lessons from Sweden*. London: Routledge.

Lifvendahl, T. 2019. Sexköpslagen befäster kvinnan som omyndig. *Svenska Dagbladet*, 24 May 2019. Available from: https://www.svd.se/sexkopslagen-befaster-kvinnan-som-omyndig [accessed 26 May 2021].

Lilja, M., and E. Johansson. 2018. Feminism as power and resistance: An inquiry into different forms of Swedish feminist resistance and anti-genderist reactions. *Social Inclusion* 6(4), 82–94.

Lööf, A., and J. Hedin. 2021. Skärp straffet för sexköp till fängelse. *Aftonbladet*, 26 May 2021. Available from: https://www.aftonbladet.se/debatt/a/mBAeRp/skarp-straffet-for-sexkop-till-fangelse [accessed 26 July 2021].

McBride, B., K. Shannon, A. Murphy, S. Wu, M. Erickson, S. M. Goldenberg, and A. Krüsi. 2020. Harms of third party criminalisation under end-demand legislation:

Undermining sex workers' safety and rights. *Culture, Health & Sexuality* online first. 1–17. https://doi.org/10.1080/13691058.2020

Mosley, J. L. 2019. The 'John'. Our new folk devil. In *Routledge handbook of sex industry research*, edited by S. Dewey, I. Crowhurst, and C. Izugbara, 352–365. Routledge.

Nelken, D. 2009. Comparative criminal justice. *European Journal of Criminology* 6(4), 291–311.

NSWP. 2014. A critique of the "report on prostitution and sexual exploitation and its impact on gender equality" by Mary Honeyball, MEP. Available from: https://www.nswp.org/sites/nswp.org/files/A%20Critique%20of%20the%20Report%20on%20Prostitution%20and%20Sexual%20Exploitation%20and%20its%20Impact%20on%20Gender%20Equality%20by%20Mary%20Honeyball%20MEP.pdf [accessed 26 July 2021].

NSWP. 2018. *The impact of 'end demand' legislation on women sex workers*. Edinburgh: NSWP. Available from: https://www.nswp.org/sites/nswp.org/files/pb_impact_of_end_demand_on_women_sws_nswp_-_2018.pdf [accessed 26 July 2021].

Olsson, N. 2021. *Crime, punishment, and counselling: A study of the local judicial and social work application of prostitution policy in Sweden*. PhD thesis Department of Social Work. Gothenburg, SE: University of Gothenburg.

Östergren, P. 2017a. From zero-tolerance to full integration: Rethinking prostitution policies. DemandAT Working Paper. Available from: http://www.demandat.eu/sites/default/files/DemandAT_WP10_ProstitutionPoliciesTypology_June2017_0.pdf. [Accessed 24 February 2020].

Östergren, P. 2017b. Sweden. In *Assessing prostitution policies in Europe*, edited by S. Ø. Jahnsen, and H. Wagenaar, 169–184. Abingdon: Routledge.

Outshoorn, J. 2017. European Union and prostitution policy. In *Assessing prostitution policies in Europe*, edited by S. Ø. Jahnsen, and H. Wagenaar, 363–392. Abingdon: Routledge.

Porter, D. 1998. *Health, civilization and the state: A history of public health from ancient to modern times*. London: Routledge.

Rydström, J. 2021. Sociala rörelser i motvind—nordiska sexarbetare och deras allierade 1970–2020. In *Sex mot ersättning—säljare, köpare, makt och moral*, edited by A. de Cabo y Moreda, C. Holmström, and J. Kuosmanen, 37–68. Lund, SE: Studentlitteratur.

Sauer, B. 2019. Mobilizing shame and disgust: Abolitionist affective frames in Austrian and German anti-sex-work movements. *Journal of Political Power* 12(3), 318–338.

Scoular, J. 2015. *The subject of prostitution: Sex work, law and social theory*. Abingdon: Routledge.

Skilbrei, M. L., and C. Holmström. 2013. *Prostitution policy in the Nordic region: Ambiguous sympathies*. Abingdon: Routledge.

Svanström, Y. 2004. Criminalising the John: A Swedish gender model? In *The politics of prostitution: Women's movements, democratic states and the globalisation of sex commerce*, edited by J. Outshoorn, 225–244. Cambridge: Cambridge University Press,

Svanström, Y. 2017. Prostitution in Stockholm: Continuity and change. In *Selling sex in the city: A global history of prostitution, 1600s–2000s*, edited by M. Rodríguez García, L. Heerma van Voss, and E. van Nederveen Meerkerk, 201–229. Amsterdam: Brill.

Swedish Federation for Lesbian, Gay, Bisexual, Transgender, Queer and Intersex Rights. 2019. RFSL on sex for compensation. Available from: https://www.rfsl.se/en/organisation/health-sexuality-and-hiv/rfsl-om-sex-mot-ersattning/ [accessed 26 July 2021].

Swedish Government. 2022. Viktigare lagar och förordningar inför halvårsskiftet 2022. https://www.regeringen.se/informationsmaterial/2022/06/viktigare-lagar-och-forordningar-infor-halvarsskiftet-2022/ [accessed 15 August 2022].

Tolnai, R. 2021. Ovärdigt, Lööf—sexköp borde avkriminaliseras. *Aftonbladet*, 27 May 2021. Available from: https://www.aftonbladet.se/debatt/a/WOwd6k/ovardigt-loof--sexkop-borde-avkriminaliseras [accessed 26 July 2021].

Vuolajärvi, N. 2019. Governing in the name of caring—The Nordic model of prostitution and its punitive consequences for migrants who sell sex. *Sexuality Research and Social Policy* 16, 151–165. https://doi.org/10.1007/s13178-018-0338-9

Wagenaar, H. 2018. Introduction: Prostitution policy in Europe: An overview. In *Assessing prostitution policies in Europe*, edited by S. Ø. Jahnsen, and H. Wagenaar, 1–28. Abingdon: Routledge.

Waltman, M. 2011. Sweden's prohibition of purchase of sex: The law's reasons, impact, and potential. *Women's Studies International Forum* 34(5), 449–474. https://doi.org/10.1016/j.wsif.2011.06.004

Ward, E., and G. Wylie, eds. 2017. *Feminism, prostitution and the state: The politics of neo-abolitionism*. London: Routledge.

World Health Organization. 2012. *Prevention and treatment of HIV and other sexually transmitted infections for sex workers in low- and middle-income countries: Recommendations for a public health approach*. Geneva, CH: World Health Organization. Available from: http://apps.who.int/iris/bitstream/handle/10665/77745/9789241504744_eng.pdf?sequence=1 [accessed 22 July 2021].

Yttergren, Å., and J. Westerstrand. 2016. The Swedish legal approach to prostitution: Trends and tendencies in the prostitution debate. *NORA* 24(1), 45–55.

6 A cult(ure) of intelligence-led policing

On the international campaigning and convictions of Danish policing

*David Brehm Sausdal**

Introduction

> Danish Police are at the forefront when it comes to analytical-based work…In relation to so-called intelligence-led policing (ILP), Danish police is admired by our neighboring countries. That [w]as something which became clear during [the European Crime Analysis] conference held in Copenhagen this January where researchers and police personnel from outside of Denmark complimented the Danish level of ILP work[.] Danish Police is, in this respect, on its way and a good step ahead of many others.
>
> (Dansk_Politi, 2018).

Intelligence-led policing (ILP) has in many ways become the new 'it' in contemporary policing (Ratcliffe, 2002; 2016; Tilley, 2012; Tilley, 2016; Fyfe et al., 2017; Burcher and Whelan, 2019)—and has been for a while now. Alongside other forms of more analytical and data-driven approaches to police work, such as 'predictive' or 'evidence-based' policing (Williamson, 2008; Bullock and Tilley, 2009; Gundhus, 2012; Perry, 2013; Fleming and Rhodes, 2018; Kaufmann et al., 2019), ILP is hailed by pundits and practitioners alike as a needed remedy to counter a growing globalization and complexity of crime as well as the police's criticized tendency to otherwise rely on experience, or 'gut feeling', in their work.

The gospel of ILP is also sung by the Danish police, being the specific Nordic criminal justice actor focused on in this chapter. As stated in both written and oral reports (cf. Beyer, 2020; Larsson and Skjevrak, 2017; Christensen, 2021), in Denmark there is an officially expressed 'need for a continuing modernization and efficiency-oriented streamlining of Danish Police, including the implementation of analytically-based police approaches ("intelligence-based policing")' (Justitsministeriet, 2017). Yet, the ILP gospel is not only sung. As the introductory words formulated by the *Danish Police Union Magazine*'s chief editor illustrates, ILP is also very much something the Danish police prides itself on, as well as something used to market Danish policing not only nationally but internationally. For example, by hosting the annual European Crime Analysis Conference, aimed specifically at professional crime analysists worldwide, the Danish Police have created a renowned international ILP hub where some the world's foremost

* Research for this chapter is supported by funding from the European Research Council (ERC) under the European Union's Horizon 2020 research and innovation programme (grant agreement CRIMTANG - #725194).

DOI: 10.4324/9781003195504-9

ILP practitioners and academic pundits participate—a knowledge-transfer and networking opportunity often enthusiastically advertized by the Danish police as emblematic of its specific ILP commitment and capability. Indeed, as the introductory words in a rather self-aggrandizing way stipulates: 'Danish police are at the forefront [i]n relation to ILP[.] [It] is admired by neighboring countries [as well as a] good step ahead of many others'. That the Danish police want to be seen as taking ILP particularly seriously is further evidenced by their employment of a dedicated ILP programme manager, Jakob Lindergård-Bentzen—Lindergård-Bentzen who is well-connected to and often fraternize with leading ILP pundits and thereby relay Denmark's aspiration and ability to be a lead in international ILP developments.

Moreover, the branding and self-understanding of Danish policing as an international ILP pioneer is not a spur of the moment. It is a storyline originally introduced by the Danish police's now former National Chief of Police, Jens Henrik Højbjerg. From 2003 to 2006, Højbjerg was the Deputy Director of Europol as Europol expanded its international and intelligence-oriented activities—a commitment which Højbjerg, among others, subsequently introduced as integral to Danish policing as he became Head of the Danish police from 2009 to 2020. During his two decades at the top management level of European and Danish policing respectively, Højbjerg has frequently emphasized the Danish police's readiness to spearhead the international move toward more analytical and evidence-based forms of policing (see Hestehave, 2013: 15). Or, as he personally expressed it to me during a meeting a few years ago,

> Denmark [i.e., the Danish Police] is widely known for our willingness to transform and innovate in the international policing community. People out there often look to us as someone who wants this [i.e., ILP] and who knows how to do it.

This chapter neither seeks to deny nor diminish the potential of ILP, nor the Danish Police's ILP fervor for that matter. The practical ups (and downs) of ILP and similar policing methodologies have already been dissected in many of the publications cited earlier (see also, Egbert and Leese, 2021). Rather, this chapter takes a second look at the convictions that underpins ILP work and the Danish police's international promotion of it. As the more than 45 interviews I have conducted and the approximately 1,000 hours I have spent observing various Danish police officers involved in transnational policing activities have suggested to me, ILP is undeniably passionately promoted as a hallmark of Danish policing. However, paradoxically, this is not the same as ILP being properly understood by its many zealous Danish marketers. Rather, ILP often seems to be something that many in the Danish police have learned to speak of as a particular and marketable entity of Danish policing, yet with very few in the Danish police actually knowing much about its inner workings. In many ways, the Danish police's appreciation and advertising of ILP thereby seems closer to that of a religious belief than that of a fully-developed and vendible work culture. Or to put it in the more mercantile words of Kaneva (2018), one could say that the Danish police ILP campaigning is 'branding without content' (see also Langford and Skilbrei, 2021; Schwöbel-Patel, 2018). The Danish police talk the talk. They speak of their particular ILP exaltations, yet frequently without knowing what they are talking about.

Bearing this paradox in mind, this chapter is more of empirical than theoretical, unfolding as it seeks to describe an elsewise largely overlooked empirical reality. Most existing studies on ILP and similar forms of more analytical approaches to policing have come a long way in discussing new data-driven policing methodologies. Yet, although having produced many vital insights, they appear committed to one central idea about ILP that this chapter puts to the question. Put differently, though at times being critical of ILP's actual worth, most studies seem to have more or less uncritically accepted the notion that ILP *does* exist, somewhere and somehow, as a tangible practice comprised by a dawning yet specific ILP 'work culture' (cf. Chan and Moses, 2019). This is exactly why one of the world's most prominent ILP scholar, Jerry Ratcliffe, has proclaimed that one of the biggest obstacles to the implantation of ILP are 'cultural concerns' (2008)—i.e., the concern that ILP may not come to fruition as a substantial work practice because of how many in the police remain reluctant to take onboard ILP as they prefer their old work culture over this new-fangled one (see also Cope, 2004, Egbert and Leese, 2021).

But what happens, this chapter asks, if there is no real ILP work culture after all, but rather something more 'cult-like' at play? How indeed are we to think about both ILP as well as Nordic criminal justice in broader terms, if its (Danish) international promotion is driven forth by strong convictions more than a considerable knowledge of the practice itself—deified, as Egbert and Leese (2021:166) have briefly pondered, as a 'technoscientific miracle' more than a real method? When it comes to ILP, the Danish police surely sees and sells itself as exceptionally intelligence-led, but what if such 'Nordic exceptionalism' (Pratt and Eriksson, 2014) is in fact more hollow than substantial, more religious than real? These are questions asked and answered in the following pages.

A culture of intelligence-led policing

Before further describing and discussing the Danish police's ILP work, it is worth briefly repeating how not only the police itself but also the existing ILP literature most-often approach the issue. In many ways, the following citation from one of the Danish police's highest-ranking officers captures the essence thereof. It illustrates not only of how ILP is appreciated in and beyond the Danish police, but also the central problems that most practitioners as well as pundits think need to be overcome before ILP can become a fully functional policing practice.

> The challenge we have on our hands is both simple and difficult. In order to get our frontline officers [t]o really understand the use of analytical-based policing and, then, to use the crime analyses we produce, we need to change the work culture. As we all know, we in the police have our old ways of

> doing stuff, which we tenaciously stick to. In other organizations it may be easier to change the work culture and thereby practice, but in the police, this is a difficult task. The guys and girls out there don't like change and they're very skeptical of any kind of change that comes from higher-ups…We need to remember this in our work [t]o implement this [i.e., ILP] and to convince them of its use. That said, they will change, sooner or later…But [w]e have to encourage a faster change in the culture too. Crime is changing and we have to change with it.

While listening to these visionary words in the early summer of 2019, I did my best to jot them down in the notebook I had brought along for the occasion. I was sitting there, just a couple of meters away from the high-ranking officer, as I had been lucky enough to be invited to attend a seminar for the heads of Danish Police. With my knowledge of the policing research literature and, specifically, the literature on 'police culture' and the difficulties of police reform (Cockcroft, 2020; Martin, 2018; Loftus, 2009; Westmarland, 2008), it was not surprising to hear the high-ranking officer speak of the Danish police's struggle to change the frontline officers' work culture to better encompass ILP. Since the birth of police research, this has been a returning subject—a subject most vividly discussed in Loftus's (2009) treatise on how police organizations have largely managed to sustain old-fashioned values and ways even when being subjected to several reforms and otherwise external influences (see also Loader and Mulcahy, 2003; Balvig et al., 2011). In this way, the high-ranking officer seemed acutely aware of the stark conservatism of conventional police work culture as well as the recurrent critiques being raised from academics and activists alike. One may also note that she was in the know about what Reuss-Ianni termed 'the two cultures of policing' (1983), namely that the rank and file are often skeptical towards proposals coming from the police management—a management whom they think more of as embodying a culture of bureaucrats or politicians than 'real police' (ibid).

What is of central interest here, however, is not the problems of changing the old (Danish) police culture in order to implement a culture of ILP as such, but the very framing of the issue as a cultural matter *per se*. In the words of the high-ranking officer, an essential hindrance to the implementation of ILP, and thus for the Danish police to improve their national and internationally oriented move toward ILP, was 'simply' that of exchanging a hoary work culture with a new and better one—an understanding of and solution to the problem in fact shared by many frontline officers who themselves are often well-aware of how they tend to cling on to deep-rooted ways of doing things (see also Loftus, 2009). Indeed, this is the same cultural framing of the problem of implementing ILP that underpins much of the existing ILP literature (Vrist Rønn, 2014; Ratcliffe, 2016; Tilley, 2016; Fyfe et al., 2017; Hestehave, 2017; Gill, 2018; Burcher and Whelan, 2019; Egbert and Leese, 2021). As, for example, expressed by leading ILP scholar Jerry Ratcliffe, one of the main obstacles to properly introducing ILP into the workaday lives of police forces worldwide are the profound 'cultural concerns' that ILP produces (2008: 218). 'The power of [conventional] police culture as an inhibiting influence on change is almost legendary and has the potential to leave an integrated analytical model in a cachectic state' (op. cit.), Ratcliffe asserts—a type of cultural analysis shared by many prominent policing scholars, with for instance Cope downright talking about a potential 'clash of cultures'(!) (2004).

Disregarding whether the challenges of implementing ILP is due to an actual cultural conflict or some more minor complications, what the literature does not seem to question is how ILP amounts to, and is to be analytically gauged as, its own specific work culture—a new kind of work culture that builds on certain substantial principles and practices of its own (Ratcliffe, 2016). Even though frontline officers may not have bought entirely into this new professional concept/culture as of yet, it is widely understood as 'just' being a matter of time before they eventually learn—and thus learn to appreciate what the aforementioned high-ranking Danish officer and many other of her colleagues seemed to have already appreciated about ILP. 'Because', as another part of the Danish police management expressed it to me in an interview,

> there is no other way than forward when it comes to this! We simply need to become more analytical. Basing our work on thorough data analyses is the way to make sure that we pool and use our resources in the right places and better our chances in the fight against future forms of crime. All of us here [i.e., his close colleagues and employees] know this. Now, the task is to make all the others out there understand this too, understanding and adhering to a new intelligence-led policing culture.

In later conversations, the same leading officer reiterated his point, reminding my—and himself—of how

> Denmark has come a long way already, and we are internationally recognized for it. But we still have to develop in order to help not only Danish but also many of our international colleagues understand how this [i.e., ILP and other similar forms of analytical-based policing] is the only way to go.

A cult of intelligence-led policing

But, this chapter asks, do those who so keenly promote the Danish police's turn to ILP, not only internally but also often internationally, themselves always understand this purported ILP policing culture? Or is something else at play?

In observing how many in the Danish police enthusiastically brand(ish) their move toward ILP, one is certainly inclined to think that they know what they are talking about. Why indeed should one second-guess this fact when everyone from the Danish police's top management to its frontline personnel ardently speak of the importance of ILP and the Danish police's international commitment to it? The (former) Danish National Chief has openly celebrated the Danish police's pledge to it. The chief editor of the *Union Magazine* vividly describes how the Danish police is an ILP frontrunner and internationally admired. Through my long-standing ethnographic engagements I have had everything from Danish Europol representatives to rank and file officers explaining to me how ILP 'is something we really focus on Denmark and it is something we are globally known for'. Hearing such statements over and over again, it is no surprise that many scholars of ILP have bought into, if not the prominence, then the growing existence and value of this new methodology to Danish policing (Hartmann et al., 2018; Fyfe et al., 2017; Vrist Rønn and Høffding, 2013; Rønn and Hald, 2013).

However, there may be more to it or, perhaps, less to it than meets the eye. This is what—as many ethnographic insights do—slowly dawned on me during the many hundreds of hours I have spent observing Denmark's daily transnational (and thereby also ILP) police work. Spending considerable time witnessing the police's working day has given me the opportunity to not only research how ILP is promoted and put to practice (see Sausdal, 2018a), but also how ILP is internally discussed and discerned. After a similar beholding of these many praises and promotions of ILP, I nevertheless, slowly but surely, started to also notice how several officers were conveying, directly or more incidentally, an uncertainty about what ILP really entailed—an uncertainty even expressed by individuals otherwise supposed to be in the know. Most often, Danish officers would speak of ILP in dedicated terms, talking about how 'ILP may not only the be future but also a flagship of Danish policing', as one detective did, while, nonetheless, at times quietly airing what may be understood as an ILP illiteracy. 'Between you and I', said the very same detective who had just complimented the Danish police for its ILP leadership, 'then I'm not always sure about what ILP really is. I sort of know, but it's not always completely clear to me'. To be sure, their faith in ILP never truly faltered, but many in the Danish police did, to my growing surprise, also seem fairly insecure about what to do with their newfound faith.

Looking at my fieldnotes, several examples of this exist. In the following, I have tried to pick out some particularly telling ones. The first example illustrates how the managerial level of the Danish police, though strongly promoting Danish ILP efforts, are themselves remarkably uninformed of what ILP actually entails. The second example provided illustrates a similar lack of substantial ILP knowledge as it exists among otherwise proclaimed specialists employed to spearhead the Danish police's marketed move toward ILP. Moreover, the example aims to show how Danish ILP specialists, in trying to describe the workings and worth of ILP, often opt for what appears as more magical than methodical explanations.

Example 1: a yes man(ager)

> 'He's a 'yes man' or, rather 'a yes (man)ager'' a Danish crime analysist told me, celebrating his clever play on words. 'What I mean', he continued, 'is that my boss almost never says no when I present him my ideas– ideas about new data or intelligence we may work with or analyses we could do…Of course, it's my role to be the specialist. But, honestly, I'm not always sure that what I propose is of value. Sometimes I'm floating ideas by him and the other bosses to show them that I'm putting myself to work, doing my best

> and, yes, not only that I'm doing stuff, but that we [i.e., the Danish Police] are being as ingenious as we want to be seen as being, pioneering these analytical-based solutions.

In most cases, this sounds like a professional dream for any employee, having a boss who is automatically supportive. As the analysist also told me, and as echoed by several Danish colleagues of his also working with developing ILP-related crime analyses, 'I shouldn't be complaining, really'. Still, this particular analysist did not seem entirely satisfied with having a 'yes man(ager)' as his superior. The reason for his and other colleagues' dissatisfaction was further explained to me by another analyst employed at an adjacent Danish police unit. 'I pretty much get to do what I want', he said with some pride in his voice. 'And I often go abroad for international conferences, presenting Denmark's particular ILP capabilities, which of course is cool'. 'Yet', he quickly elaborated,

> though it is nice, there's the problem of how many of my analyses are rarely put to use. They often become just another email in some manager's or investigator's inbox, or perhaps part of some unread pile of paper on a crowded desk…Also, when it comes to not only regular cops but the management itself, they most of the time seem to have no clue. They've obviously learned that 'intelligence-led policing', 'crime analyses' and so forth are the way forward. This they've been told by their bosses, who've been told by their bosses, who've been told so when participating in some fancy out of town conference or seminar hosted by, say, Europol. So, yeah, they say 'yes, go ahead', but they do so not so much because they actually seem to understand what this thing is, but, rather because they don't want to appear unknowledgeable. They 'know' [using air quotes to underline the irony] ILP is the way forward, but, really, they don't know much about it. And this goes for not only many in management but for most of us in the police, I would say.

Certainly, one should not base an entire analysis of the Danish police's use and understanding of ILP on a couple of police analysists' individual contemplations. Their thoughts, however, were not extraordinary, but rather a reflection of what not just many other Danish analysists believed but frontline officers and detectives too. During my last eight years of studying and speaking with both Danish and other countries' police officers, including higher-ups, specialists, detectives, and the rank and file, I have indeed continually overheard people admitting to how little they actually knew about what one officer also termed these 'academicizations of police work', ILP included—a lack of substantial ILP knowledge at times noted in the literature, yet often without any substantial theorizing thereof (see Egbert and Leese, 2021).

To provide further documentation of the apparent insubstantiality of ILP, we may also take notice of what a Danish detective reasoned as I was talking to him about what he thought about the Danish police's ILP practices and international promotion:

> The management and specialists keep on pushing for more analyses and for more of our work being based on these analyses. I'd be happy to follow suit if they gave me something I could actually work with. But this rarely happens. And we all report this back up the ladder. But their answer is just that we 'need to do it!'. They think it's because we don't understand their orders and the need of ILP, that we don't do it. Maybe we do. Maybe we don't. But many of us also think it's because they don't understand anything...Thinking of it, I think none of us really understand what's going on!

What is of interest here is not whether Danish detectives are given sufficiently good analyses or not. What remains of interest to this chapter is, on the one hand, the Danish police's widespread marketing of ILP, and thereby themselves, as crucial to modern-day policing and, on the other hand, a widespread lacking understanding of what ILP actually is—a puzzling ILP eagerness *and* ignorance seemingly existing throughout the corps. Frontline personnel do often formally accept the necessity of ILP while not really fathoming what it involves. And the management fervently encourage and campaign for the use of ILP, without themselves truly knowing what they are trying to push. Indeed, as one of the Danish National Police's leading figures conceded during an internal meeting which I was lucky enough to attend:

> There's no denying that we need this [i.e., ILP]. No denying it...But, admittedly, it's also not that easy to really understand what it involves. This I must admit. It's often very abstract. I'm just a policeman who has risen through the ranks and much of this is beyond me—something I think goes for many if not most of us. This is exactly why we hire specialists. For them to know and help us with the process.

Hiring specialists to buttress and advance an organizational change is of course best practice. Still, as the earlier quotes by such very specialists indicated, they sometimes too were not entirely certain about what they were doing. They too were searching for useful feedback and a deeper understanding of their own ILP efforts. Yet, instead of feedback, the specialists often just got a devoted 'yes!' from the management—a management not fully in the know but perhaps, first and foremost, concerned, as known to the policing literature (Reuss-Ianni, 1983; Mawby, 2014; Fleming, 2015), with keeping the organizational hierarchy in place by being unswaying in their communication.

Example 2: knowing because you know

The previous example—alongside other empirical excerpts included in the chapter—is meant to illustrate how ILP is seen as pivotal to and promoted by Danish police as a hallmark of their policing aptitudes, while, ironically, often being poorly grasped by the very people marketing it. The next example is of a somewhat similar kind, yet with a perhaps even more perplexing twist to it. It was given to me by an officer employed at the Danish National Police's National Investigation Centre. The National Investigation Centre (NIC) is the investigational and international flagship of the Danish Police which, as it presents itself online, 'administers the national coordination of criminal investigations in relation to prioritized areas of crime [...] as well as the responsibility of coordinating the Danish Police's international corporation'.[1] As such, as a trusted NIC employee, this particular officer and specialist was presented to me as a 'leading ILP expert both in and beyond Denmark'.

I was put in contact with him to discuss the Danish police's intelligence-led work specifically in relation to issues of transnational crime and its policing. As part of the interview, and in order to illustrate the first-rate ILP work of the Danish police, he had brought along one of their newer crime analyses—an analysis, he told me, which had in fact also been 'complimented by other European colleagues'. The report included numbers, trends, and descriptions of typical transnational crime MOs. Listening attentively to his presentation, I ended the interview by asking him how 'the Danish police can be sure that the accounts included and conclusions drawn in this report are in fact accurate?' I was not trying to goad him. I merely asked the question, knowing how the much of the available research literature concludes that the available data and analyses of transnational crime are somewhat lacking in scientific quality (Sheptycki, 2004; Manning, 2008; Safjański and James, 2020). As one sociologist and Europol employee even admitted to me during an interview in 2015:

> In terms of proper science, our data wouldn't always be considered of a good enough quality...For example, it's much up to the individual countries what they report back to us. Some, like Denmark, report a lot and do a pretty decent job. Some don't. Also, it's often some individual 'expert' in the individual countries' police forces who, based on a mix between real knowledge and personal hunches, report not only statistical but qualitative data back to us, describing how *they* [emphasizing 'they'] understand their country's criminal issues...I'm not saying the reports we produce aren't useful, but calling it 'Data' with a capital D would be a bit of a stretch.

It was such considerations about the veracity of the data and conclusions produced in transnational crime analyses that led me push the NIC officer to say a bit more about the report he was showing me. Giving my question some thought, while not looking all too pleased with what he saw as unwarranted nosiness, he eventually responded: 'Listen, we *know* it's true [emphasizing 'know'], because the report's conclusions are based on an in-depth analysis of data. That's how we know. We did the analysis and this is what came out. That's how we know it's true'.

As already stated, the interest of this chapter is not whether the police are right or wrong in relation to their ILP work and products, or, for that matter, what the potential practical issues of it are (see instead Sausdal, 2018a). The NIC officer appeared well-informed and the report may have been of great worth. What nevertheless struck me here—and what has struck me on several other occasions

(Sausdal, 2018b)—was that he exuded such a steadfast belief in the ILP report he had brought along. Rather than being in the business of producing 'guestimates', as otherwise seems be what most ILP crime analyses of transnational crimes are able to do (Ruggiero, 2014; Bruinsma, 2015), the NIC officer represented the report and its findings as largely incontestable. One explanation to such incontestability may of course be (much like the earlier mentioned 'yes manager') that he saw it as part of his job to communicate in clear and committed terms, especially to an outsider like me. Still, this did not seem to be the only explanation of why he and others in the Danish police so frequently appear disproportionately confident in the work and worth of ILP. Rather than simply performing certainty, he and many others officers I have come across have appeared not falsely but fundamentally convinced. And not just that. What has specifically struck me is the way such certainty is conceived. Indeed, as this Danish NIC officer enigmatically explained it me, a given ILP outcome was 'true...because...we know it's true'. They had '[done] the analysis' and, having done the analysis, they had produced an incontrovertible piece of knowledge.

Contrary to conventional analytical work in social science (or any kind of science for that matter) where the conclusion is only as good as the analysis allows for, and the analysis only as good as the data or empirical material it is based on, in Danish policing, ILP analyses often come to represent more of a conviction than a systematic conclusion. Or, to paraphrase the aforementioned NIC officer's own words, the Danish police 'knew it was veracious because they knew'—thus displaying a kind of fetishization of ILP work as a reified means unto itself (see also Sausdal, 2021). To be sure, this was not the first time during my ethnographic studies that I witnessed Danish police officers—managers as well as frontline officers—talk about ILP and other forms of more analytical-based police work as intangible yet consequential entities in their own right. As a lower-level manager and police detective tellingly said it:

> Even though we do not always altogether understand how these reports and results are being produced, not always knowing what they are all about, we simply have to assume that they speak the truth, that they work. That's the only way to make it work.

What does such an 'assumptive approach' to the verity and value of ILP tell us? Remarkably, although officially branded by both the Danish police and pundits worldwide as the very antidote to old and more haphazard ways of doing police work, it exemplifies how the Danish police's ways of understanding ILP practices often come to embody many of the same mystical characteristics. What have indeed often caught my eye, and what the above examples are illustrations of, is the Danish police's tendency to represent their ILP work in much the same way as they represent what Gundhus (2013) has termed the conventional 'experience-based ways' of policing. Similar to how research has noticed how orthodox police concepts such as 'gut feelings' or 'police noses' often include supernatural and largely inexplicable capacities which, nevertheless, are believed to work (Ferguson, 2016; Foley, 2009; Sausdal, 2018a), what I have found is that the Danish police's ILP work are regularly exemplified in a comparable quasi-religious light. Contrary to the purported evidence-based rationality and scientism of such new policing methodologies, its (Danish police) advocates—sometimes at least—thus appear more like devotees than knowledgeable doyens. They 'simply have to assume that they speak the truth, that they work', they say. Rather than being able to methodically demonstrate and discuss the inner workings of what they do, the police often-times simply 'know' that it works—feeling it more than thinking it, willing it more than explaining it. Perhaps this was also why an individual belonging to the Danish police's upper management pondered the following, as him and I were discussing the Danish police's efforts in becoming an internationally renowned analytically driven police force:

> Seriously, sometimes it does feel like some kind of cult-like thing, this. I've been in this business for quite a while now. And every now and then a new trend comes a long and we all jump onboard. No time for questions. Still, I'm not saying ILP is not the way to go. It is. That I'm sure of. This is what is needed and what we in the Danish police are becoming increasingly known for.

Strong but empty words

Intelligence-led policing, alongside similar forms of more data-driven police work, have arguably become the new 'it' in modern-day policing. This is at least true in a Danish context with the Danish Police actively articulating the need for, and their special capability in leaving behind longstanding experienced-based models of policing. Danish police and their actions, the story goes, should increasingly be guided not by 'police noses' or 'gut feelings' but by evidence and a rigorous consideration of data and intel—by astute police deciphering rather than old-school 'police discretion' (Davis, 1975; Holmberg, 2000). Such as shift in professional attitudes and practice is, the police themselves say, needed to make policing more efficient and to combat evermore complex and peripatetic forms of criminality in a globalized and digitalized world. ILP is 'the future of policing!'—and a future which the Danish police not only wishes to take an active part in, but where Danish police sees and speaks of itself as an international frontrunner.

This chapter supports this motion. Too much police work, now and then, has been left in the hands of individual officers and managers who, presumably doing their best, have made choices based on what their own personal and shared experience have told them without the corroborating aid of substantiating evidence and analyses. The fundamental potential of ILP and similar approaches are, thus, to provide such substantiation—a potential, or failing, that has been cleverly discussed in many of the already available ILP publications previously cited in this chapter. A fresh and first-rate exposition of the work and worth of ILP and similar forms of analytical and data-driven approaches to policing worth mentioning is, for example, Egbert and Leese's *Criminal Futures: Predictive Policing and Everyday Police Work* (2021)—a major ethnographic contribution to the field which, as Danish policing researcher and ILP scholar, Kira Vrist Rønn has rightly noted, finely illustrates that

> the promise and expectation that predictive policing [e.g. ILP] will reshape policing practices in radical ways seems to be overstated…[Instead] it should be seen as just another tool, one that at best adjusts practice rather than revolutionising it.
>
> (Vrist Rønn, 2021)

However, while such both constructive and critical expositions of ILP are of great worth, they also come with a blind sport. This, in short, is the blind sport here considered and exemplified—a blind spot that, principally, has to do with the difference between seeing ILP as a perhaps revolutionizing yet still real-world supplement to contemporary police work culture *or* seeing and thus analyzing it as a strong yet largely unsubstantiated vocational belief—as a 'work cult' more than a work culture. Indeed, existing research does discuss implementation issues and the foot-dragging that ILP is met with among frontline officers (Ratcliffe, 2002; Sheptycki, 2004; Hestehave, 2017; Burcher and Whelan, 2019; Egbert and Leese, 2021). Research does also consider the political and economic problems of a move toward ILP, pointing to how a fear and data-driven police future may spills into the hands of political and private interests (Egbert, 2019; Kaufmann et al., 2019). And research expertly questions the moral and human rights issues involved when policing increasingly comes to rely on intelligence and data as an unbiased source of insight and action (Rowe and Søgaard, 2019; Gill, 2018; Fyfe et al., 2017; Vrist Rønn, 2014; Maguire, 2000). Yet, for all its worth, and for all the vital questions asked, existing research *does not* truly question whether ILP is in fact an actual cultural reality in contemporary policing, Danish policing included. ILP practices and plans are criticized. Yes. But prevailing criticisms all tend to include and automatic acceptance that there in the police organization exists, at least somehow or somewhere, a thought-out plan—i.e., that the not only in Denmark but in many places marketed move toward ILP is effectively supported by a deeper and detailed understanding of what ILP entails.

The ultimate aim of this chapter has been to question this underlying hypothesis. Through my ethnographic studies, what I found most curious was how ILP was stalwartly promoted and appreciated by many in the Danish police yet with much the same people habitually exhibiting a scarce understanding of its inner mechanisms. Many if not most believe in its promise and the Danish police's positioning as an international ILP precursor. They say 'yes' to ILP, but they remain largely unaware of what they are agreeing to. This, therefore, is not only a matter of the Danish police 'talking the talk but not walking the walk', as already discussed in the ILP literature; it is also a matter of the Danish police not fully understanding the words that are coming out of their own mouths.

Hence, if asked to concludingly describe ILP in the current state and context of Danish policing, I would be inclined to describe it as more of a persuasion than a practice, a cult more than culture or, for that matter, something closer to religion than reality. Much like the young person who takes a random phone sales job to earn some pocket money, and who then goes on to learn just enough to know how to sell whatever the company sells, the preferment of ILP by the Danish police seem—sometimes at least—to rest less on a substantial appreciation of what ILP entails and more on individual disciples having learned to routinely speak of its splendors. This is not to say that ILP is not of worth, that it cannot be the future of policing worldwide, and that the Danish police will not be a central part of this; it is only to say that, as of now, the Danish police's promotion of ILP is perhaps mostly just that, i.e., a passionate promotion without any deep acuity. As Lacan might have said it, the police have learned to speak of ILP using 'empty words' (Lacan et al., 2020), i.e., words without much if any inherent meaning to them. Or, as Kaneva (2018) have discussed in her work on how nations brand themselves, one may say that the Danish ILP promotion is, to some extent, 'branding without content'.

Conclusion

This chapter has pointed to an ostensible paradox. One the one hand, the Danish police eagerly promote the need, and their international proficiency of, ILP. On the other hand, the Danish police's belief in ILP seems to be just that, a belief more than a thought-out work practice. Before bringing the chapter to its conclusion, I would have loved to go even further into the different questions that a more contentless or even cultish understanding of ILP and its advertisement provoke. Unfortunately, because of space limitations, but mainly because of how ILP (as well as policing more generally) has only narrowly been studied in these terms, this is a theoretical task for the future. In pursing this task one may find inspiration in Reiner's writings about 'police fetishism' (2010) and Martin's (2018) exploration of how policing (just as other spheres of life) are governed by larger sociocultural beliefs that often remain beyond reproach, or, for example, in the recurrent yet rarely analytically pursued observation that many police forces across the world have a lot of faith in 'technoscientific miracle fix[es]' (see Egbert and Leese, 2021: 166)—hoping that the next methodological or technological devlopment will be that which finally puts policing at the forefront of things. Though looking at ILP through what may also be seen as a sociology of religion lense (Wach, 2019) is both exciting and novel, this chapter has first of all been written to be able to ask such questions altogther. As research of contemporary (Nordic) corporations have already succesfully shown, many adhere to procedures and discourses which may indeed be better understood as magical or, indeed, cult-ish rather than purely rational or functional (Löfgren et al., 2005; Tracey, 2012). So why not also police organizations? To be sure, if ILP and similar analytical-based policing perspectives have come alive in policing more as religion than reality, then what does this tell us about these phenomena and their future? And what does such police religiosity tell us about policing in broader terms?

Moreover, recalling the specific focus of the book to which this chapter belongs, one particular question appears particularly prevalent: what does a more cultish-cum-religious understanding of ILP mean in terms of Nordic criminal justice in a global context? For example, which new criminological analyses may be developed if we are not only to critically question Nordic criminal justice's otherwise self-purported and internationally promoted qualities (Langford and Skilbrei, 2021), but if we also have to start acknowledging that what we in the North are selling are not only not always first-class criminal justice quality (see also Sausdal, 2021). Indeed, what would it mean if the Nordic countries' otherwise trademarked 'Nordic exceptionalism' (Pratt and Eriksson, 2014) is not just exceptional but, at least sometimes, ethereal? Though it is obvious that Nordic criminal justice policy makers and practitioners do market thought-out and effectual methods, what this chapter has exemplified is that not all criminal justice promotion rests on a similarly solid base of practice and know-how. Sometimes it may be 'branding without content' (Kaneva, 2018). At least, when it comes to ILP, one does sometimes get the sense that many in the Danish police are primarily in the business of peddling beliefs, unconscious as it may be. Here, the Danish police are therefore not just typical '(transnational) moral entrepreneurs' as otherwise suggested in the literature (Becker, 1995; Nadelmann, 2010; Sausdal, 2021), i.e., local agents of criminal justice trying to sell and force upon international others their own deeply felt and carefully considered worldviews. The Danish police do believe in it. They do brand themselves as ILP vanguards. They think of themselves as admired and want to be so. Undoubtedly. But, contrary to many other moral entrepreneurs discussed in the criminological literature, the Danish police do not always know *what* it is they believe in; not knowing what their trade really includes. In a global criminal justice world increasingly known for its campaigning and commerciality (Schwöbel-Patel, 2021), this seems important for (Nordic) criminological researchers to remember: that what is being marketed, by police forces or others, may not always be fully developed criminal justice competences and commodities but (also) convictions.

Note

1 https://politi.dk/virksomheden/rigspolitiet/organisationen.

References

Balvig F, Holmberg L and Nielsen MPH (2011) *Verdens bedste politi*. København: Djøf.

Becker HS (1995) Moral entrepreneurs: The creation and enforcement of deviant categories. In: Herman N (ed.), *Deviance: A symbolic interactionist approach*. Lanham, MD: General Hall, pp. 169–178.

Beyer L (2020) *Predictive policing i dansk politi*. Master's Thesis. Aalborg: Aalborg University.

Bruinsma G (2015) *Histories of transnational crime*. New York: Springer.

Bullock K and Tilley N (2009) Evidence-based policing and crime reduction. *Policing: A Journal of Policy and Practice* 3(4): 381–387.

Burcher M and Whelan C (2019) Intelligence-led policing in practice: Reflections from intelligence analysts. *Police Quarterly* 22(2): 139–160.

Chan J and Moses LB (2019) Can 'big data' analytics predict policing practice? In: Hannem S, Sanders C, Schneider C, Doyle A and Christensen T (eds.), *Security and risk technologies in criminal justice: Critical perspectives*, Toronto: Canadian Scholars, pp. 41–82.

Christensen MJ (2021) Battles to define the Danish police. In: Mbuba J (ed.), *Global perspectives on policing and law enforcement*, Lanham: Lexington Books, pp. 61–82.

Cockcroft T (2020) *Police culture: Research and practice*. Bristol: Policy Press.

Cope N (2004) 'Intelligence led policing or policing led intelligence?' Integrating volume crime analysis into policing. *British Journal of Criminology* 44(2): 188–203.

Dansk_Politi. (2018). *Redaktionens fokus - DANSK POLITI – flot og fjernt*. Available at: https://dansk-politi.dk/nyheder/redaktionens-fokus-dansk-politi-flot-fjernt. (accessed 15 August 2022).

Davis KC (1975) *Police discretion*. Eagan, MN: West Group.

Egbert S (2019) Predictive policing and the platformization of police work. *Surveillance and Society* 17(1/2): 83–88.

Egbert S and Leese M (2021) *Criminal futures: Predictive policing and everyday police work*. Milton Park: Taylor & Francis.

Ferguson AG (2016) Policing predictive policing. *Washington University Law Review* 94: 1109.

Fleming J (2015) *Police leadership: Rising to the top*. Oxford: Oxford University Press.

Fleming J and Rhodes R (2018) Can experience be evidence? Craft knowledge and evidence-based policing. *Policy and Politics* 46(1): 3–26.

Foley BJ (2009) Policing from the gut: Anti-intellectualism in American criminal procedure. *Maryland Law Review* 69: 261–343.

Fyfe N, Gundhus HO and Rønn KV (2017) *Moral issues in intelligence-led policing*. Abingdon, Oxon: Routledge.

Gill P (2018) *Rounding up the usual suspects?: Developments in contemporary law enforcement intelligence: Developments in contemporary law enforcement intelligence*. Abingdon, Oxon: Routledge.

Gundhus HI (2012) Experience or knowledge? Perspectives on new knowledge regimes and control of police professionalism. *Policing: A Journal of Policy and Practice* 7(2): 178–194.

Gundhus HI (2013) Experience or knowledge? Perspectives on new knowledge regimes and control of police professionalism. *Policing: A Journal of Policy and Practice* 7(2): 178–194.

Hartmann MRK, Hestehave NK, Høgh L and Rønn KV (2018) Knowing from within. *Nordisk Politiforskning* 5(1): 7–27.

Hestehave NK (2013) *Proaktiv kriminalitetsbekæmpelse*. København: Samfundslitteratur.

Hestehave NK (2017) Predicting crime?: On challenges to the police in becoming knowledgeable organizations. In: Fyfe N, Gundhus H and Rønn K (eds.), *Moral issues in intelligence-led policing*. Abingdon. Oxon: Routledge, pp. 62–80.

Holmberg L (2000) Discretionary leniency and typological guilt: Results from a Danish study of police discretion. *Journal of Scandinavian Studies in Criminology and Crime Prevention* 1(2): 179–194.

Justitsministeriet (2017) *Nyt analyseværktøj skal styrke politiets kamp mod kriminelle*. Available at: https://www.justitsministeriet.dk/pressemeddelelse/nyt-analysevaerktoej-skal-styrke-politiets-kamp-mod-kriminelle/ (accessed May 18).

Kaneva N (2018) Simulation nations: Nation brands and Baudrillard's theory of media. *European Journal of Cultural Studies* 21(5): 631–648.

Kaufmann M, Egbert S and Leese M (2019) Predictive policing and the politics of patterns. *The British Journal of Criminology* 59(3): 674–692.

Lacan J, Sheridan A and Bowie M (2020) The function and field of speech and language in psychoanalysis. In: Lacan J, Sheridan A and Bowie M (eds.), *Écrits*. Abingdon, Oxon: Routledge, pp. 33–125.

Langford M and Skilbrei M-L (2021) Branding the Nordic model of prostitution policy. In: Byrkjeflot H, Mjøset L, Mordhorst M and Petersen K (eds.), *The making and circulation of Nordic models, ideas and images*. Abingdon, Oxon: Routledge, pp. 165–191.

Larsson P and Skjevrak P (2017) Nordic Police Research Seminar: Proceedings-Oslo 8th–9th September 2016.

Loader I and Mulcahy A (2003) *Policing and the condition of England: Memory, politics and culture*. Oxford: Oxford University Press.

Löfgren O, Willim R, O'Dell T, et al. (2005) *Magic, culture and the new economy*. Oxford: Berg Publishers.

Loftus B (2009) *Police culture in a changing world*. Oxford: Oxford University Press.

Maguire M (2000) Policing by risks and targets: Some dimensions and implications of intelligence-led crime control. *Policing and Society: An International Journal* 9(4): 315–336.

Manning PK (2008) *The technology of policing: Crime mapping, information technology, and the rationality of crime control*. New York: New York University Press.

Martin JT (2018) Police culture: What it is, what it does, and what we should do with it. In: Karpiak, Kevin & Garriott, Kevin (eds.), *The anthropology of police*. Milton Park: Taylor and Francis, pp. 34–53.

Mawby RC (2014) The presentation of police in everyday life: Police–press relations, impression management and the Leveson Inquiry. *Crime, Media, Culture* 10(3): 239–257.

Nadelmann EA (2010) *Cops across borders: The internationalization of US criminal law enforcement*. University Park, PA: Penn State University Press.

Perry WL (2013) *Predictive policing: The role of crime forecasting in law enforcement operations*. Santa Monica, CA: Rand Corporation.

Pratt J and Eriksson A (2014) *Contrasts in punishment: An explanation of anglophone excess and Nordic exceptionalism*. London: Routledge.

Ratcliffe J (2002) Intelligence-led policing and the problems of turning rhetoric into practice. *Policing and Society* 12(1): 53–66.

Ratcliffe JH (2008) Knowledge management challenges in the development of intelligence-led policing. In: Williamson T (ed.), *The Handbook of knowledge-based policing: Current conceptions and future directions*. Chichester: John Wiley and Sons, pp. 205–220.

Ratcliffe JH (2016) *Intelligence-led policing*. Abingdon, Oxon: Routledge.

Reiner R (2010) *The politics of the police*. Oxford: Oxford University Press.

Reuss-Ianni E (1983) *Two cultures of policing: Street cops and management cops*. Piscataway, NJ: Transaction Publishers.

Rønn KV (2021). Debugging the Techno-Utopian Myth of Predictive Policing: Book Review of Criminal Futures: Predictive Policing and Everyday Police Work by Simon Egbert and Matthias Leese. *Journal of Extreme Anthropology*, 5(1), 130–134.

Rønn KV and Hald C (2013) *Om at opdage: metodiske refleksioner over politiets undersøgelsespraksis*. Copenhagen: Samfundslitteratur.

Rowe M and Søgaard TF (2019) 'Playing the man, not the ball': Targeting organised criminals, intelligence and the problems with pulling levers. *Policing and Society*, 30(2), 120–135.

Ruggiero V (2014) Organised and transnational crime in Europe. In: Body-Gendrot S, Hough M, Kerezsi K, Lévy R and Snacken S (eds.), *The Routledge handbook of European criminology*. Abingdon, Oxon: Routledge, pp. 154–167.

Safjański T and James A (2020) Europol's crime analysis system—Practical determinants of its success. *Policing: A Journal of Policy and Practice* 14(2): 469–478.

Sausdal D (2018a) Everyday deficiencies of police surveillance: A quotidian approach to surveillance studies. *Policing and Society*. https://doi.org/10.1080/10439463.2018.1557659.

Sausdal D (2018b) *The last policeman: On the globalisation of local policing*. Stockholm: Department of Criminology, Stockholm University.

Sausdal D (2021) A fighting fetish: On transnational police and their warlike presentation of self. *Theoretical Criminology* 25(3): 400–418. https://doi.org/ 13624806211009487.

Schwöbel-Patel C (2018) The rule of law as a marketing tool: The international criminal court and the branding of global justice. In: May, Christopher & Winchester, Adam (eds.), *Handbook on the rule of law*. Cheltenham: Edward Elgar Publishing, pp. 434–452.

Schwöbel-Patel C (2021) *Marketing global justice: The political economy of international criminal law*. Cambridge: Cambridge University Press.

Sheptycki J (2004) Organizational pathologies in police intelligence systems some contributions to the lexicon of intelligence-led policing. *European Journal of Criminology* 1(3): 307–332.

Tilley N (2012) Modern approaches to policing: Community, problem-oriented and intelligence-led. In: Newburn T (ed.), *Handbook of policing*. Willan, London: Routledge, pp. 401–431.

Tilley N (2016) Intelligence-led policing and disruption of organised crime: Motifs, methods, and morals. In: Delpeuch T and Ross J (eds.), *Comparing the democratic governance of police intelligence: New models of participation and expertise in the United States and Europe*. Cheltenham: Edward Elgar Publishing, p. 153.

Tracey P (2012) Religion and organization: A critical review of current trends and future directions. *Academy of Management Annals* 6(1): 87–134.

Vrist Rønn K (2014) (Mis-) informed decisions? On epistemic reasonability of intelligence claims. *International Journal of Intelligence and Counterintelligence* 27(2): 351–367.

Vrist Rønn K and Høffding S (2013) The epistemic status of intelligence: An epistemological contribution to the understanding of intelligence. *Intelligence and National Security* 28(5): 694–716.

Wach J (2019) *Sociology of religion*. Abingdon, Oxon: Routledge.

Westmarland L (2008) Police cultures. *Handbook of Policing* 2: 253–281.

Williamson T (2008) *The handbook of knowledge-based policing: Current conceptions and future directions*. Hoboken, NJ: John Wiley & Sons.

7 Nordic penal humanitarianism

Status-building, brand alignment, and penal power

Kjersti Lohne

Introduction

The image of Rolf Einar Fife filled the overhead mounted in the World Forum Theatre in The Hague, hosting the annual diplomatic meeting of member states to the global and permanent International Criminal Court (ICC). It was 2013, and the politics of international criminal law was seeping into the otherwise technocratic diplomatic Assembly of State Parties meeting to the ICC: the African Union had requested a special segment in the general debate on the 'Indictment of sitting Heads of State and Government and its consequences on peace and stability and reconciliation'. The background was the ICC's indictment against Kenya's heads of state, who had successfully mobilized against the ICC after they stepped into power, charging the ICC with imperialist and neo-colonial rule. The project of international liberal legalism was at stake.

Fife, who represented Norway in the Rome negotiations for the ICC's statutes, had been video-called in as a panellist on the special segment: 'The Rome negotiations in 1998 establishing the International Criminal Court was a historic turning of a page', he began.

> We were united in a common development, of mutual respect, of commonality of purpose. We rallied behind a key Nuremberg principle—unanimously endorsed—that the position of the person can never become a shield of impunity for the worst international crimes.

'At the same time', he continued through the screen:

> The Statute is built around other principles too: the presumption of innocence, procedural safeguards. And how about the dignity for the office, and not the state? To ensure good state cooperation, we might have to consider practical arrangements, and to distinguish between immunity and dignity of the highest representative of the state involved. Our display of respect for the state concerned must be combined by respect by states for independence. Peace and reconciliation are values that are not contrary to justice, or vice versa. But there is a need for mutual respect, and to listen. Together we can

DOI: 10.4324/9781003195504-10

> prove that the international community is actually moving forward. It is proof of genuine willingness to carry out dialogue.

As he wished the assembly a fruitful exchange and success, the World Forum Theatre overflowed with applause. As an example of Norway's prominent role in international criminal justice, Fife's performance animates questions of criminal justice as a politics of *branding* in international relations. How is the image of Nordic penality 'at home' put to use and connected with Nordic foreign policy abroad? What and who constitutes 'good punishers' in international politics?

While the study of punishment is overwhelmingly set side by side with the study of the national, this chapter aims to open up the study of the 'penal state' with attention to its *external* logics and practises. As such, the chapter is based on an analysis of Norway's engagement in international criminal justice—the normative and material system of international criminal laws and tribunals established to ensure individual criminal accountability for extreme forms of violence referred to as core international crimes: war crimes, crimes against humanity, genocide, and the crime of aggression. The chapter argues that 'Nordic penal exceptionalism' has become part of a politics of branding the Nordics as particularly 'good punishers'—both by competence and virtue—and as such, of particular value for international export. This raises several questions about the logics of penal power and the study of penality under the global condition, and of Nordic penality in particular.

The chapter proceeds in four parts. Following a contextualization of Nordic penal exceptionalism and Norway's engagement with international criminal justice, the chapter proposes three incremental processes through which Norway's positioning as 'good punishers' can be understood. To conceptualize how Norway positions itself in the international order based on a claim to moral authority, the first section introduces status-building theories in International Relations (Wohlforth et al., 2018). Second, the image of Nordic penal exceptionalism is connected with other Nordic 'brands' in Norway's foreign policy. I conceptualize this process as brand alignment, in which incremental moral authority across transnational fields are claimed by Norway in its foreign policy engagements. Third, I draw on the notion of penal humanitarianism to describe how humanitarian logic is put to use in moving criminal justice beyond the territorially bounded nation state (Bosworth, 2017; Lohne, 2018). As such, it sets out an interpretation of Nordic criminal justice as a form of Nordic penal humanitarianism, enabling penal power to be put to use as a form of soft power and positioning in the international order. The chapter concludes by discussing the viability of Nordic penal humanitarianism in an increasingly volatile international order.

Background

The debate and scholarship on 'Nordic penal exceptionalism' has been the analytic prism for studies of Nordic penality for well over a decade (see Ugelvik and Dullum, 2011; Barker, 2012). According to the thesis developed by John

Pratt in a two-part article series in British Journal of Criminology (2008a, 2008b), and since developed further in his monography with Pratt and Eriksson (2014), Nordic criminal justice systems are relatively 'humane' as far as prison conditions and imprisonment rates go, and whose success is demonstrated by subsequent low rates of recidivism (Skardhamar and Telle, 2012). Against the background of an expansive 'culture of control' (Garland, 2001) in western liberal democracies, with accelerating rates of imprisonment and populist retributive sensibilities, explanations for Nordic 'humaneness' in punishing are predominantly found in its political economy (see Cavadino and Dignan, 2006), characterized as 'inclusive', 'welfare-oriented', and 'social-democratic' nation-state societies. However, the conceptual pairing of Nordic penality with welfarism reflects an idealized image of the relation between state and citizen. To explain the power to punish with a view to include and rehabilitate citizens gives but a partial view of the actors, discourses, policies, and practices that motivate the power to punish under the global condition. Analysis of criminalization processes at the global level emphasize the significance of transnational power networks, such as human rights organizations, lawyers, and police networks (Christensen and Levi, 2017; Lohne, 2019a). These processes have been particularly conspicuous in the field of international criminal justice where the power to punish is driven by a humanitarian impetus to 'put an end to impunity' for crimes that 'shock the conscience of humanity' (Rome Statute Preamble): war crimes, crimes against humanity, and genocide.

The creation of the international military tribunals in Nuremberg and Tokyo following the Second World War marked the birth of the international criminal justice system. Since then, another seven international criminal courts have been established, including the International Criminal Tribunal for the Former Yugoslavia (ICTY) and the International Criminal Tribunal for Rwanda (ICTR) set up by the United Nations (UN) in 1993 and 1994, respectively (for an empirical overview, see Smeulers et al., 2013). In 2002, the Rome Statute entered into effect after a necessary 60 state ratifications, which established the permanent ICC. The Court is based in The Hague in The Netherlands. Today, 122 are members of the Court, and has thus subjected their territories and citizens to the jurisdiction of the Court over war crimes, crimes against humanity and genocide.[1] The Court has so far opened 26 cases—all against African nationals—in eleven situations under investigation. Until now, there has been three convictions and three acquittals. Most of the defendants remain at large, or have had their charges vacated, withdrawn, or not confirmed by the Pre-Trial Chambers because of, among other things, lack of access to evidence or due to their passing.

Previously the domain of international legal and relations scholars, international criminal justice has attracted growing attention by criminologists this past decade. This body of scholarship is interchangeably referred to as 'supranational criminology' (Smeulers and Haveman, 2008) and the 'criminology of international crimes' (Parmentier and Weitekamp, 2007). Thematically, it overlaps with criminological approaches to genocide (Hagan and Rymond-Richmond, 2009), transitional justice (McEvoy, 2007), state crime (Cohen, 2001), and international criminal court practices (Hoyle and Ullrich, 2014; Houge, 2015). Generally, however, criminology and the sociology of punishment has primarily been concerned with state punishment and national society on the conceptual, empirical, and analytical levels (see Simon and Sparks, 2012). Without undermining the contribution of this scholarship, nor the role of punishment as embedded in nation state formation, this chapter inscribes itself within a growing body of criminological work concerned with conceptualizing how questions of criminal law and justice are increasingly disembedding from their associations with national justice (Franko, 2017). Elsewhere, and by examining the role of human rights NGOs in international criminal justice, I have probed the characteristics of penality when it is analytically and empirically detached from the nation state (Lohne, 2018; Lohne, 2019a). Here, however, I am interested in exploring penality as part of nation-states' foreign policy toolbox, thus directed outwards horizontally towards other states in the international order (and/or outwards vertically towards citizens of foreign states). Disrupting the truism in political theory that the power to punish is the prerogative of the nation state over its citizens (Zedner, 2016), the chapter aims to contribute to the emerging criminological scholarship on how contemporary penal power is changing, at least partially, in its effects and justifications (Bosworth, 2012).

Norway has an extensive and long-standing political engagement with international criminal justice, and the support and development of the international liberal legalist order generally. The unifying role attributed to Fife at the ASP meeting in 2013 was not accidental. Fife led the Norwegian delegation to the ICC treaty negotiations in Rome in 1998. During the final hours of the six-week long diplomatic meeting, the US delegation proposed to open the 'package', to which Norway proposed to accept as a whole, which was what states ended up doing. Norway is since accredited a role in ensuring the creation of the ICC (Benedetti and Washburn, 1999; see also Fife, 2000). Following the treaty-making conference, another eminent Norwegian international criminal law persona, Morten Bergsmo, was put in charge of the preparatory committee for the establishment of the Court's office of the prosecutor. Bergsmo had represented the ICTY in the ICC treaty negotiations and had vast experience in investigating international crimes. In the preparatory committee, he also drew on his Norwegian network, with several of the sections put together by Norwegian legal experts, such as Tor Aksel Busch and Gunnar Ekeløve-Slydal. Bergsmo has continued to liaise with Norwegian Ministry of Foreign Affairs, whose cooperation were also behind the instrumental work of the Norwegian Centre for Human Rights at the University of Oslo setting up of an open access law database for the ICC, the ICC Legal Tools Program.

Norway has since continued a strong presence and engagement with the ICC. For example, the Norwegian embassy in The Hague holds a specific office with an international justice portfolio. Apart from Ambassadors with particular interests for international justice, such as Annika Kruse and the Martin Sørby, this tailored office has enabled an active participatory role on international criminal justice in The Hague. Norway has recently lead many of the diplomatic working groups among State Parties to the ICC, such as those on issues of state cooperation, complementarity, victims and witness protection. As will be returned to in the next section, Norway is also one of the main funders of the Trust Fund for Victims (alongside Sweden and the UK), which is a semi-independent fund established by the Assembly of States Parties to provide assistance to victims of international crimes. Besides diplomatic work 'outside', most notably in The Hague and in New York, Norway has also taken several steps 'inside' to demonstrate their engagement with international criminal justice. Besides ratifying and implementing the Rome Statute (Ingadóttir, 2017), they have established sentencing transfer agreements with the ICC, whereby those sentenced by the ICC can be transferred to serve out their sentences in Norway. This agreement is a continuation from Norway's sentencing transfer agreements with the ICTY, through which Norway received 5 prisoners from the ICTY (Holá and van Wijk, 2014).

According to Norwegian diplomats, 'international criminal justice is a pillar in Norwegian foreign policy'.[2] It is part of their support and work for an international liberal legal order. This must also be seen in conjunction with the government's focus on human rights as its 'overarching foreign policy doctrine',[3] which is said to guide the government's general approach to development aid and foreign policy. As part of this, the ICC is perceived as 'an important contribution to democratization and peace-building worldwide'. Thus, through its political investment in the ICC, Norwegian authorities express support and contribution to a global social order where, 'human rights, democracy and the rule of law are intimately connected and mutually dependent on one another'.[4]

However, human rights, democracy, rule of law—these are values as much as they are expressions of the liberal world order, its force and its power; this makes their export and expansion a cultural and political project too, which means that they need to be manifested in concrete social practices, political discourses, and institutional logics. While the government recognizes pushback against the ICC especially and the liberal legal world order generally, their perspective is, according to one of their representatives, everlasting.[5] They see international criminal justice as constituted by and of a global norm development, in spite of current pushback.

In what follows I propose three analytic layers of making sense of Norway's role in international criminal justice. To theorize the complexity of penal policy-making in a way that connects the internal and external logics of the state, the first part draws on status theories in International Relations (Renshon, 2017) and in particular those concerned with the relational positioning of middle-size powers and normative authority (Wohlforth et al., 2018). Contributions to the strengthening of the international liberal order, through peace operations or rule of law promotion, is an indicator of what it means to be a 'good' state, in the sense of doing good while behaving well vis-à-vis more powerful states in the international order. Second, to unpack the image of the Nordics as 'good punishers', by competence and virtue, I recognize the alignment with other Nordic brands—humanitarianism, development aid, peace building—through which the Nordics position themselves in international politics (Browning, 2007). Third, I apply and develop the criminological notion of 'penal humanitarianism' (Bosworth, 2017; Lohne, 2018; 2019b) to describe how humanitarian reason enable penal power to move beyond the nation state. I argue that these three analytical layers operate in tandem to create a politics of branding for Norway's foreign policy on international criminal justice.

Methods

As a case study, the chapter draws on data from official documents, interviews, and observations of Norway's foreign policy across the domains of international criminal justice, peace-building, human rights, humanitarianism, and (gender) development as collected through various previous and on-going research projects throughout the past decade.[6] The analysis includes observations of Norway's diplomatic engagement with international criminal justice in the Netherlands and at the annual Assembly of States Parties meetings on the ICC throughout the past decade. Semi-structured interviews and documents were mostly coded and analysed in Nvivo, a qualitative analysis software. To theorize the *external* dimensions of the penal state, the analysis works in the 'in-between' areas of Criminology and International Relations (see Bhabha, 2004), and combines constructivist International Relations theory on 'branding' and 'status-theory' with emerging criminological scholarship on the transnationalization of penal power.

Analysis

International status-building

As mentioned above, 122 states are currently States Parties members to the Rome Statute system of justice, that is, the ICC. For an international treaty, the ICC ratification rate is relatively unprecedented. The ICC's widespread acceptance through state ratifications are held as an example of what international relations scholar Sikkink has referred to as a 'justice cascade'—'a shift in the legitimacy of the norm of individual criminal accountability for human rights violations and an increase in criminal prosecutions on behalf of that norm' (2011: 5). However, the states that have chosen to remain outside the Court and its jurisdiction include some of the world's most powerful and populous states—the United States, China, India, and Russia. One may therefore ask to what extent a ratification rate that excludes these states constitutes a global norm, or, indeed, a 'justice cascade'.

While constructivist approaches within IR emphasize the constitutive role of norms in international society (see e.g. Adler, 2002), and indeed the normative role that the ICC has in spite of the big power's lack of signatures, realist approaches emphasize states' functional and strategic approach to international law. According to this view, states' approach and use of international law will differ according to their relative strength and size. Whereas small and middle size states have a relatively larger tendency to embrace international law in lieu of access to politics by other means, big powers will not need the protection of international law given their substantial power position in international politics. From a realist perspective, hard power—military power—trumps all.

However, sociologically abreast international relations theory point to the interlinkages between norms and power in international politics, where not only power matters but relative positioning. While most scholarship of international relations focuses on big power politics, this relational approach is particularly useful for understanding the politics of small and medium size states. It can be conceptualized as part of power-struggles in international politics: a 'survival strategy in a world of great powers or as a way of increasing status and thus making it possible to realize national interest' (Leira, 2015: 339). In contrast to big powers, small and medium-size states are more concerned with *status* as a differentiating feature in the international system. Status is maintained or increased by showing oneself *useful* to the big powers and the contemporary international order. To accept responsibility and contribute to the sustainment of international law and order, for example through contributions to international peace operations, is therefore viewed as an indicator of what it means to be a 'good' state; understood in the dual sense of doing good while behaving well vis-à-vis the more powerful states in the contemporary international order. This conceptualization of strategic positioning in the international order can contribute to explain Norway's role as a 'peace nation', 'moral' and 'humanitarian superpower'. It may also explain its prevalent position in international criminal justice.

However, status-work only works if one knows who to work for. Questions of how contemporary changes in the geopolitical landscape may play into Norway's status-seeking behavior as a small state is worth exploring further both here and elsewhere. Following a period of relatively widespread support and enthusiasm for the ICC to end impunity for 'the most serious crimes of international concern' (the Rome Statute's Preamble), the Court has been subject to increasing criticism for a while now (e.g. Drumbl, 2007; Nouwen and Werner, 2010; Mégret, 2016). The most potent point of critique has been accusations of the ICC 'targeting Africa', which culminated in the threat of a mass exodus of African member states from the Court in late 2016. However, the legitimacy crisis for the Court, charged as it is with colonialism and imperialism (Clarke et al., 2016), must be seen alongside a changing geopolitical landscape, where the 'transformationist rhetoric about "post-Westphalia"' (Hurrell, 2007: 9) is losing traction in the face of the emergence of a multipolar world order, that is, 'a world of renewed sovereignty, resurgent religion, globalized markets, and the stagnation or rollback of universal norms about human rights' (Hopgood, 2013: 166). At the 'end of history', as Fukuyama (1989) aptly described the end of the Cold War, there was only one ideology left in town—establishing the hegemony of the liberal world order. In this context, the universal travelled smoothly, freed from the conflict and contrariety of an alternative political future. Now, however, the 1990s—the golden age of international law-making—are long gone. Pluralism is back in the game, as expressed by the turn to regionalism and the pushback against international law (as global law) as such. The pushback against international criminal justice is thus embroiled in broader geopolitical developments. International liberal legalism is experiencing friction, and the power dynamics in international politics are much more volatile than they have been since the end of the Cold War.

This lack of geopolitical stability—and order—complicates status-work in international politics. In the next section, I suggest that a manner in which Norway engages in status-work is through 'brand-alignment', asserting moral authority across multiple international domains to leverage political influence.

International brand alignment

The 'humane' appearance of the Nordic region reflects its representation in international engagements. As 'natural born friends of peace' (Leira, 2013) and 'moral superpowers' (Dahl, 2006), the Nordic countries have been recognized (by President Barack Obama) as 'punching above their weight'[7] through their considerable international engagements, including especially (gender) development, humanitarianism, and peace-building. Despite the recent prominence of studies of Nordic brands and models,[8] there is less attention given to how these representations of the Nordics merge and coalesce; especially in ways that enable penal power to move beyond the territorial nation state.

In his seminal article on 'branding Nordicity', Browning (2007) writes about 'Nordic exceptionalism' as being different from and better than the norm. While the notion of Nordic *penal* exceptionalism is far from uncontested (see generally Ugelvik and Dullum, 2011), it is the alignment or coupling of this 'brand' with Norway's status as a moral superpower in international politics that I suggest contributes to its moral authority as a 'good punisher' in international criminal justice. Multiple brands are at play, where Norway's representation of 'humane exceptionalism' is put forward across these different sectors, being human rights, peacebuilding, development, gender welfarism, and humanitarian policy generally.

Human Rights as overarching foreign policy value

First, human rights are defined as a main pillar of Norway's foreign policy and development aid.[9] As a language liberated from the politics of the nation state, the discursive embeddedness of human rights in Norway's foreign policy illustrates how embroiled human rights have become in nation-state politics. Mindful of temporal shifts, it can be useful to note the extent to which 'human rights' and 'development aid' have been linguistically recognized (and leveraged) as part of Norway's organization of foreign relations. In 1984, an independent Ministry for Development Aid was separated out from the Norwegian Ministry of Foreign Affairs (MFA). Although this ministry was closed five years later, later governments have continued to keep a minister of development aid, albeit as part of the Ministry of Foreign Affairs. In 2013, this post was discontinued, and revived again in 2018. The names of these minister posts and ministries have also changed, as can be seen to reflect broader societal change. From 1997–2000, Hilde Fraford Johnson was the minister for *development aid and human rights affairs*. From 2001–2005, human rights issues were transferred to the MFA; Johnsen remained minister of *development aid*. In 2005, these portfolios were again administratively mixed, although with two different ministers still, in the Ministry of Development

Aid and Foreign Affairs. Noticeably, human rights 'peaked' in government recognition in the late 1990s.

Global peacebuilders

Second, another related policy theme is about the perception of Norway as a peaceful nation and global peace mediator (Leira, 2013), including in such cases as in Guatemala, Israel and Palestine, Sri Lanka, and Sudan. However, Norway's role in peace processes is also contested. In concerns Sri Lanka, for instance, Höglund and Svensson (2011) discuss dilemmas arising from combining the role of 'peacemaker' with mediating peace through humanitarian action provided by NGOs (Kelleher and Taulbee 2006). Another stream of research on Norway's peace-building activities also focuses on the importance of humanitarian mine action as a prerequisite for building peace and development (Harpviken and Skåra, 2003). As part of this, Norway took a particularly prominent role initiating the Convention on Cluster Munition in 2008 (van Woudenberg and Wormgoor, 2008).

The Norwegian development aid model

Third, there is branding of a particular 'Nordic model' in 'doing' development aid, which revolves around being a 'good donor'. The 'Norwegian model' refers to a high level of cooperation between the Norwegian state and civil society, most notably non-governmental organizations (NGOs). In policy documents, it is emphasized that the model also implies a clear division of roles; however, it is not specified *how* this division is upheld. In a report to the Storting (no. 49, 2008–2009), the model is further defined: it is founded upon internationally accepted principles for humanitarian action and international humanitarian law, an active multilateral engagement, and a close relationship with the Red Crescent Movement and the other non-state humanitarian organizations. Developing and improving the model is put forward as a goal for the Norwegian Government. Moreover, it is worth noting that the 'Norwegian model' is seen as emanating from Norwegian and Nordic identity, or culture, as civil society engagement is considered part of how Norway is governed also internally. At the same time, the model is represented as effective, particularly in reaching affected populations. According to policy documents, the Nordic model has contributed to the success of Norway as a donor country, *and* to that of Norwegian NGOs, enabling them to be leading development aid and humanitarian organizations in their respective fields. Indeed, the Norwegian model is considered to have made Norway a 'vigorous, flexible and respected partner in the international humanitarian system'.

Women's rights and gender mainstreaming

Fourth, the policy documents assert that Norway has taken a particularly active role in working for gender mainstreaming (including in Norwegian humanitarian

NGOs) and the strengthening of women's rights globally. It is clear that women's rights are one of the issues that Norway wants to focus on globally. The policy documents state that Norway was a driving force for the adoption of UNSC Resolution 1325 on women, peace, and security, and that this resolution asserts that women shall participate on equal terms in deliberative processes, and that women and girls shall be protected against sexual violence. While Resolution 1325 is indeed an important document for gender mainstreaming and especially the right to participation, the document does not deal with the right to protection (Houge and Lohne, 2017).

The Democratic Republic of Congo (DRC) has become particularly infamous for widespread sexual violence and rape as a weapon of war-narrative, to the extent that it has been labeled the 'rape capital of the world' and the 'world's worst place to be woman' (e.g., BBC News, 2010; *The Guardian*, 2011). Thus, DRC is the central hotspot for humanitarian action against sexual violence. Here, Norway funds efforts that aim to protect against sexual violence, empower and increase women's rights and participation, and prevent the occurrence of sexual violence through attitude change and criminal prosecutions. Notably, work against impunity for sexual violence is legitimized as preventative work. In other words, criminal prosecution of these crimes are presumed to have a deterrent effect, albeit this is not dealt with in detail.[10] However, it is unclear whose duty it is to prosecute sexual violence, or 'end impunity', as illustrated by sentences such as: 'sexual violence may constitute war crimes or crimes against humanity and shall be prosecuted, but so far there is too few punished for such acts'.[11]

The International Criminal Court has a Victims Trust Fund for victims of international crimes, to which Norway is one of the largest donors. Interestingly, Norway has earmarked funds to female victims of sexual violence in DRC, as part of these donations (Lohne, 2019a), a result of having leftover funds from one humanitarian budget that can be used on another budget. Indeed, NOK 110 million were earmarked efforts to increase women's rights and equality, included here the fight against sexual violence in humanitarian situations. Norway has a framework agreement with the Norwegian Church Aid (NCA) in eastern DRC, focusing particularly on the protection, participation and prevention of sexual violence in the region. In 2012 for instance, NCA received ten million NOK to its work in eastern DRC.[12] It is stressed that to end the occurrence of sexual violence in DRC, work at the *structural* level needs to be done. There are also several examples of what can be conceptualized as 'gender accountability'. For instance, the Norwegian government has looked into how the Norwegian humanitarian NGOs attend to and operationalize gender mainstreaming through their work, with varying results.[13] Further, Norway has contributed, through GenCap, to a UN coding system for how gender perspectives are handled in humanitarian appeals, including so-called 'gender marks' as a tool to measure the extent to which a humanitarian project fulfil the needs of women, men, girls, and boys, and whether the project actively promotes equality.[14]Among other activities, Norway has also hosted international conferences on the topic, for instance in 2017 where it declared a donation of one billion NOK earmarked sexual violence (countering its concept note warning of earmarked contributions).

Norwegian humanitarian policy

Finally, there is Norway's humanitarian policy. The Norwegian Government's humanitarian efforts are based on the two Norwegian white papers; namely the white papers' Norwegian policy on the prevention of humanitarian crises (Stortingsmelding no. 9, 2007–2008) and the Norwegian Humanitarian Policy (Stortingsmelding No. 40 [2008–2009]). While the mere existence of a humanitarian strategy and subsequent humanitarian policy documents indicates the field's significance to the Norwegian Government, the documents also explicitly articulate a vision of Norway as a leading political and financial partner in the humanitarian field. In the policy documents, Norway's humanitarian engagement is framed as a result of the 'particular Norwegian'.[15] It is emphasized that the Norwegian populace significantly supports humanitarian principles and the imperative to pursue significant humanitarian engagement as a result of being a political and economic surplus nation. It is claimed that 'we' have 'long traditions' and broad civil society participation for solidarity with repressed and poor fellow humans; refugees and internally displaced are drawn particular attention to.[16] The tradition of 'nestekjærlighet' (love for one's neighbour) is firmly embedded within the Norwegian population.[17] This observation parallels the literature on Norwegian 'foreign policy of peace [as] rooted in an historical self-understanding of Norway and Norwegians as particularly peaceful' (Leira, 2013: 338). Such invocation of historical references can be interpreted as part of Norway's missionary, as opposed to colonial, histories. However, at the same time, humanitarian principles are legitimized as 'global universals'—in the sanctity of all human lives, dignity, and rights. Norway's rationale for its 'humanitarian engagement' is, at the same time particularly Norwegian *and* universal. Thus, in the policy documents, there is a tension between elevating humanitarian values as universal and acknowledging that this is *Norwegian foreign policy*. This tension might be worth exploring further for how it plays out in the constitution of the 'Norwegian model' but also in larger debates on the shrinking of 'humanitarian space'—it becomes increasingly difficult to defend a space situated 'above' the politics of place. Importantly, the emphasis on 'humanitarian values' as 'innate' to Norway's and Norwegian identity and therefore guiding of policies and politics can be understood as part of a turn where humanitarianism, or 'humanitarian reason' has become a powerful political discourse (Fassin, 2011).

These different Nordic models or brands work incrementally across fields to yield moral authority to Norway as a 'good punisher'. Representing an image of 'good punishers' as competence and virtue, the Nordic states' penal exports—policies, practices, personnel, and other resources to increase criminal justice capacity abroad—parallel other Nordic brands—humanitarianism, development aid, peace building—through which the Nordics position themselves in international politics (Browning, 2007). In what follows, I turn to the final analytical layer of this positioning, namely how humanitarianism is put to work in moving penal power beyond the territorial nation state.

Penal humanitarianism

Humanitarianism is many things to many people. Humanitarianism is 'an ethos, a cluster of sentiments, a set of laws, a moral imperative to intervene, and a form of government' (Ticktin, 2014). The study of humanitarian sentiments in criminology has mainly focused on how these sensibilities have 'humanized' or 'civilized' punishment (Elias, 1978 [1939]). As such, the notion of humanism in the study of crime, punishment, and justice is associated with human rights implementation in penal practices and with a normative bulwark against penal populism (Simon and Sparks, 2012); indeed, with a 'softening' of penal power. Scholarship on 'penal humanitarianism' (Bosworth, 2017; Lohne, 2018; 2019b) takes a slightly different approach, as it explores how humanitarianism is put to work on and for penal power. In doing so, it connects with critical scholarship generally on how muscular forms of power—expulsion, punishment, war—are justified and extended through the invocation of humanitarian reason (see Lohne, 2019b).

Moving beyond nation-state borders and into the 'international', 'global', and 'cosmopolitan', I have previously written on how the power to punish is particularly driven by humanitarian reasoning when punishment is delinked from its association with the nation state altogether (Lohne, 2018). I delve into the field of international criminal justice and show how it is animated by a humanitarian impetus to 'do something' about the suffering of distant others, and how, in particular, the human rights movement has been central to the fight against impunity for international crimes (Engle et al., 2016). Through the articulation of moral outrage, humanitarian sensibilities have found their expression in a call for criminal punishment to end impunity for violence against distant others. However, building on an ethnographic study of international criminal justice (Lohne, 2019a), I demonstrate how penal power remains deeply embedded in structural relations of (global) power, and that it functions to expand and consolidate these global inequalities further. Removed from the checks and balances of democratic institutions, I suggest that penal policies may be more reliant on categorical representations of good and evil, civilization and barbarity, humanity and *in*humanity, as such representational dichotomies seem particularly apt to delineate the boundaries of cosmopolitan society (Sagan, 2010). This seems especially the case regarding the fight against sexual violence in conflict (Houge and Lohne, 2017). While attention towards conflict-related sexual violence is critically important, there is an overwhelming dominance of criminal law solutions on academic, policy, and activist agendas, as the fight against conflict-related sexual violence has become the fight against impunity. The combination of a victim-oriented justification for international justice and graphic reproductions of the violence victims suffer, are central in the advocacy and policy fields responding to this particular type of violence. Indeed, it epitomizes how humanitarianism facilitates the expansion of penal power (Houge and Lohne, 2017; Lohne and Houge, 2019).

For example, when Norway strengthened its contribution to penal aid, the then-Minister of Justice announced that Norwegian justice personnel are 'good Norwegian export goods' (Hansen, 2006) indicating a merger of the nation's brand as a 'humanitarian' superpower (de Carvalho and Neumann, 2015) and 'humane' penal state (Pratt, 2008a)—a good, in the word's dual sense, punisher. In exploring how 'humanitarianism allows penal power to move beyond the nation state' (Bosworth, 2017: 40), there is a need to (re)consider the direction of movement, and to what extent one can talk about 'penal import states' and 'penal export states'. While the nation state continues to operate as an essential territorial site of punishment, the power to punish has become increasingly complex.

Discussion

The analysis put forward in this chapter challenges the truism in criminology and political science that penal power exclusively concerns the relation between the sovereign and its citizen. Instead, and despite its legitimation through humanitarian reason, penal power is also part of states' foreign policy—another tool by which states strive to position themselves in the international order. As concerns Norway, the analysis has shown how it positions itself as a 'good punisher'—both by behaving well *vis-à-vis* the more powerful states in the international order, and by virtue, leveraging penal exports upon other Norwegian brands in international politics—peacebuilding, gender, development aid. However, to what extent does this analysis hold true for the Nordic region generally? And to what extent does this analysis differ from the one being applied to Canada, for instance, which traditionally has pursued a similar line of foreign policy interest as that of Norway.

The Nordic penal exceptionalism thesis derivate from 'the outside'—it caught on as a denominated case under the gaze of John Pratt, a New Zealander's perspective on how Nordic societies and its criminal justice systems deviated from the norm; the norm in criminology being defined by the US and the UK. Viewed from the outside, Nordic countries may appear more homogenous than is the case from 'the inside'. For example, Norway, Sweden, and Finland have a more similar foreign policy profile than with Denmark, which to a larger extent engages in 'negative' branding. Moreover, Norway's craving for moral recognition may also be seen in tandem with its behaviour in other international domains, where it stands for a hazardous export of oil and gas that has not only made it affluent but has also, perhaps, invoked a global form of *noblesse oblige*. Another explanation may be found in the simple fact that Norway, as the only Nordic country that stands outside the EU, has more to gain from engaging with other multilateral organizations than the other Nordic countries.

Notwithstanding, status-building only works as long as one knows who to work for. With the liberal world order currently in crisis, it remains to be seen how Norway and the Nordics will continue to navigate ideas of Nordic societies as 'inclusive', 'humanitarian', and 'social liberal' in a time when they are increasingly stacked up against a variety of populist and realpolitik considerations of 'walling the welfare state' (Barker, 2017). These developments are not isolated events, but are part of a changing geopolitical order with heightened instability. The liberal world order is losing traction in the face of resurgent nationalism, geopolitical instability and pushback against notions of welfarism, humanitarianism, and international liberalism—ideas that have not only characterized Nordic identity construction internally but also provided the Nordic states with a role internationally. Will the Nordics retract inwards, or continue to promote and defend the cosmopolitan normative foundations of the liberal legalist world order, and as such, maintain the resiliency of humanitarian reason as a politics of penal power?

Conclusion

This chapter has attempted to connect the internal and external logic of the penal state by inquiring into how Norway's brand as a 'good punisher' and penal humanitarian is constituted both within and beyond the nation state. As such, it suggests a theoretical approach to criminology and sociology of punishment scholarship that transgresses the national–international divide, and views issues of crime and punishment across these scales as interconnected. This illustrates the need for a transnationalization of the sociology of punishment, not least because penal power should always raise these awkward questions of legitimacy (Garland, 1990)—and perhaps even more so when it is applied to external subjects that, at least theoretically, are outside the limits of the state social contract.

Notes

1 Since 17 July 2018, the ICC has also had jurisdiction over the crime of aggression for states members that have opted in for this crime also (see Kreß, 2018).
2 Norwegian diplomat, meeting with MFA and the Penality Research Group, 2017.
3 Report No. 10 to the Storting (2014–2015), Opportunities for All: Human Rights in Norway's Foreign Policy and Development Cooperation—Meld. St. 10 (2014–2015). (white paper).
4 Report No. 10 to the Storting (2014–2015), Opportunities for All: Human Rights in Norway's Foreign Policy and Development Cooperation—Meld. St. 10 (2014–2015). (white paper).
5 Meeting with MFA and the Penality Research Group, 2017.
6 These research projects cover the fields of international criminal justice (Lohne, 2018; 2019a), humanitarianism (Sandvik and Lohne, 2014; Lohne and Sandvik, 2017), and gender and crime in international relations (Houge et al., 2015; Houge and Lohne, 2017), in addition to joint projects on 'Nordic Branding' (University of Oslo), 'Nordic exceptionalism in international criminal justice' (funded by a NOH-S grant), and AidInCrisis (PRIO, funded by a NRC grant). The research includes interviews and observations of Norwegian diplomatic engagement with international criminal justice for the past decade, in Norway and in the Netherlands. Norwegian foreign policy research also includes thematic analysis of all Norwegian policy documents on humanitarian policy, consisting of four white papers, one humanitarian policy strategy document (recent one missing from analysis), and seven annual reports.

7 https://eu.usatoday.com/story/news/politics/2016/05/13/obama-nordic-leaders-summit-punch-above-their-weight/84330852.
8 See for example, Browning, C. (2007). 'Branding Nordicity: Models, Identity and the Decline of Exceptionalism'. Cooperation and Conflict 42: 27–51; Dinnie, K. (2008). Nation Branding: Concepts, Issues, Practice. Oxford, Elsevier; Bailliet, C. (2016). 'A Nordic Approach to Promoting Women's Rights within International Law: Internal v. External Perspectives', forthcoming, *Nordic Journal of International Law* 2016; Christoffersen, J. and Madsen, M.R. (2011). 'The End of Virtue? Denmark and the Internationalisation of Human Rights'. *Nordic Journal of International Law*, 80(3), pp. 257–277; Magnus, J. (2016). 'International branding of the Nordic region'. *Place Branding and Public Diplomacy*, *12*(2–3): 195–200; Marklund, C. (2016). The Nordic Model on the Global Market of Ideas: The Welfare State as Scandinavia's Best Brand. *Geopolitics*: 1–17; Tryggestad, T. (2014). 'State feminism going global: Norway on the United Nations Peacebuilding'.
9 Report No. 10 to the Storting (2014–2015), Opportunities for All: Human Rights in Norway's Foreign Policy and Development Cooperation—Meld. St. 10 (2014–2015), (white paper).
10 See Report No. 9 to the Storting (2007–2008), Norwegian Policy on the prevention of humanitarian crises (white paper).
11 Report No. 40 to the Storting (2008–2009), Norway's Humanitarian Policy (white paper), page 26.
12 Annual Report [Årsrapport] 2012.
13 Annual Report [Årsrapport] 2009.
14 Annual Report [Årsrapport] 2010.

References

Adler E. (2002) Constructivism and International Relations. In: Carlsnaes W, Risse-Kappen T and Simmons BA (eds.), *Handbook of International Relations*, London: SAGE Publications, 112–144.

Barker V. (2013) Nordic Exceptionalism Revisited: Explaining the Paradox of a Janus-Faced Penal Regime. *Theoretical Criminology* 17(1): 5–25. 1362480612468935.

Barker V. (2017) *Nordic Nationalism and Penal Order: Walling the Welfare State*. London: Routledge.

BBC News. (2010) *UN Official Calls DR Congo 'Rape Capital of the World' BBC News*, BBC.

Benedetti F and Washburn JL. (1999) Drafting the International Criminal Court treaty: Two years to Rome and an afterword on the Rome diplomatic conference. *Global Governance* 5(1): 1–37.

Bhabha Homi K. (2004) Statement for the Critical Inquiry Symposium. *Critical Inquiry* 30(2): 342–349.

Bosworth M. (2012) Subjectivity and Identity in Detention: Punishment and Society in a Global Age. *Theoretical Criminology* 16(2): 123–140.

Bosworth M. (2017) Penal Humanitarianism? Sovereign Power in an Era of Mass Migration. *New Criminal Law Review: An International and Interdisciplinary Journal* 20(1): 39–65.

Browning CS. (2007) Branding Nordicity Models, Identity and the Decline of Exceptionalism. *Cooperation and Conflict* 42(1): 27–51.

Cavadino M and Dignan J. (2006) Penal Policy and Political Economy. *Criminology and Criminal Justice* 6(4): 435–456.

Christensen MJ and Levi R. (2017) *International Practices of Criminal Justice: Social and Legal Perspectives*, Routledge.

Clarke KM, Knottnerus AS and De Volder E. (2016) *Africa and the ICC*, Cambridge: Cambridge University Press.

Cohen S. (2001) *States of Denial: Knowing about Atrocities and Suffering*, Cambridge: Polity.

Dahl A-S. (2006) Sweden: Once a Moral Superpower, Always a Moral Superpower? *International Journal* 61(4): 895–908.

de Carvalho B and Neumann IB. (2015) *Small States and Status Seeking: Norway's Quest for International Standing*, London and New York: Routledge.

Drumbl MA. (2007) *Atrocity, Punishment and International Law*, Cambridge: Cambridge University Press.

Elias N (1978 [1939]) *The Civilizing Process*, Oxford: Basil Blackwell.

Engle K, Miller Z and Davis DM. (2016) *Anti-Impunity and the Human Rights Agenda*, Cambridge: Cambridge University Press.

Fassin D. (2011) *Humanitarian Reason: A Moral History of the Present*. California: Univ of California Press.

Fife RE. (2000) Elements of Nordic Practice 1999: Norway and the International Criminal Tribunals 1994–2000. *Nordic Journal of International Law* 69: 359.

Franko K. (2017) Criminology, Punishment, and the State in a Globalized Society. In: Liebling A, Maruna S and McAra L (eds.), *The Oxford Handbook of Criminology*, Oxford: Oxford University Press, 353.

Fukuyama F. (1989) The End of History? *The National Interest* 16: 3–18.

Garland D. (1990) Frameworks of Inquiry in the Sociology of Punishment. *British Journal of Sociology* 41(1): 1–15.

Garland D. (2001) *The Culture of Control: Crime and Social Order in Contemporary Society*, Chicago, IL: University of Chicago Press.

Hagan J and Rymond-Richmond W. (2009) *Darfur and the Crime of Genocide*, Cambridge: Cambridge University Press.

Hansen ID. (2006) Norske jurister rykker ut i verden. *Aftenposten*. Available at: https://www.aftenposten.no/norge/i/APzan/Norske-jurister-rykker-ut-i-verden

Harpviken KB and Skåra BA. (2003) Humanitarian Mine Action and Peace Building: Exploring the Relationship. *Third World Quarterly* 24(5): 809–822.

Höglund K and Svensson I. (2011) Schizophrenic Soothers: The International Community and Contrast Strategies for Peace-Making in Sri Lanka. *Cooperation and Conflict* 46(2): 166–184.

Holá B and van Wijk J. (2014) Life after Conviction at International Criminal Tribunals: An Empirical Overview. *Journal of International Criminal Justice* 12(1): 109–132.

Hopgood S. (2013) *The Endtimes of Human Rights*. Ithaca, NY: Cornell University Press.

Houge AB. (2015) Re-Presentations of Defendant Perpetrators in Sexual War Violence Cases Before International and Military Criminal Courts. *British Journal of Criminology* 56(3): 419–437.

Houge AB and Lohne K. (2017) End Impunity! Reducing Conflict-Related Sexual Violence to a Problem of Law. *Law and Society Review* 51(4): 755–789.

Houge AB, Lohne K and Skilbrei M-L. (2015) Gender and Crime Revisited: Criminological Gender Research on International and Transnational Crime and Crime Control. *Journal of Scandinavian Studies in Criminology and Crime Prevention* 16(2): 1–15.

Hoyle C and Ullrich L. (2014) New Court, New Justice?: The Evolution of 'Justice for Victims' at Domestic Courts and at the International Criminal Court. *Journal of International Criminal Justice* 12(4): 681–703.

Hurrell A. (2007) *On Global Order: Power, Values, and the Constitution of International Society*, Oxford: Oxford Universisty Press.

Ingadóttir T. (2017) The Implementation of the Rome Statute of the International Criminal Court in the Nordic Countries: A New Comprehensive Criminalization of Serious Crimes. In *Nordic Approaches to International Law*, Brill: Nijhoff, 115–146.

Kelleher A and Taulbee JL. (2006) Bridging the Gap: Building Peace Norwegian Style. *Peace & Change* 31(4): 479–505.

Kreß C. (2018) On the Activation of ICC Jurisdiction over the Crime of Aggression. *Journal of International Criminal Justice* 16(1): 1–17.

Leira H. (2013) 'Our Entire People are Natural Born Friends of Peace': The Norwegian Foreign Policy of Peace. *Swiss Political Science Review* 19(3): 338–356.

Leira H. (2015) The Formative Years: Norway as an Obsessive Status-Seeker. In: De Carvalho B and Neumann IB (eds.), *Small States and Status Seeking: Norway's Quest for International Standing*, London: Routledge, 22–41.

Lohne K. (2018/2020) Penal Humanitarianism Beyond the Nation State: An Analysis of International Criminal Justice. *Theoretical Criminology*. online first, 24(2): 145–162.

Lohne K. (2019a) *Advocates of Humanity: Human Rights NGOs in International Criminal Justice*, Oxford: Oxford University Press.

Lohne K. (2019b). Introducing the New Themed Series on Penal Humanitarianism. In: Lohne K (ed.), *Border Criminologies*, University of Oxford. Available at: https://blogs.law.ox.ac.uk/research-subject-groups/centre-criminology/centreborder-criminologies/blog/2019/03/introducing-new

Lohne K and Houge AB. (2019) The Fight Against Impunity for Sexual Violence in Conflict: Penal Humanitarianism Par Excellence? In: Lohne K (ed.), *Criminologies, Border*, Oxford: Oxford University Press. Available at: https://blogs.law.ox.ac.uk/research-subject-groups/centre-criminology/centreborder-criminologies/blog/2019/03/fight-against

Lohne K and Sandvik KB. (2017) Bringing Law into the Political Sociology of Humanitarianism. *Oslo Law Review* 4(1): 4–27.

McEvoy K. (2007) Beyond Legalism: Towards a Thicker Understanding of Transitional Justice. *Journal of Law and in Society* 34(4): 411–440.

Mégret F. (2016) The Anxieties of International Criminal Justice. *Leiden Journal of International Law* 29(1): 197–221.

Nouwen SMH and Werner WG. (2010) Doing Justice to the Political: The International Criminal Court in Uganda And Sudan. *European Journal of International Law* 21(4): 941–965.

Parmentier S and Weitekamp E. (2007) Political Crimes and Serious Violations of Human Rights: Towards a Criminology of International Crimes. *Crime and Human Rights, Series in Sociology of Crime, Law and Deviance* 9: 109–144.

Pratt J. (2008a) Scandinavian Exceptionalism in an Era of Penal Excess: Part I: The Nature and Roots of Scandinavian Exceptionalism. *British Journal of Criminology* 48(2): 119–137.

Pratt J. (2008b) Scandinavian Exceptionalism in an Era of Penal Excess: Part II: Does Scandinavian Exceptionalism Have a Future? *British Journal of Criminology* 48(3): 275–292.

Pratt J and Eriksson A. (2014) *Contrasts in Punishment: An Explanation of Anglophone Excess and Nordic Exceptionalism*. London and New York: Routledge.

Renshon J. (2017) *Fighting for Status: Hierarchy and Conflict in World Politics*, Princeton, NJ: Princeton University Press.

Sagan A. (2010) African Criminals/African Victims: The Institutionalised Production of Cultural Narratives in International Criminal Law. *Millennium: Journal of International Studies* 39(1): 3–21.

Sandvik KB and Lohne K. (2014) The Rise of the Humanitarian Drone: Giving Content to an Emerging Concept. *Millennium: Journal of International Studies* 43(1): 145–164.

Sikkink K. (2011) *The Justice Cascade: How Human Rights Prosecutions are Changing World Politics*, New York: W. W. Norton and Company.

Simon J and Sparks R. (2012) *The SAGE Handbook of Punishment and Society*, Los Angeles, CA: Sage.

Skardhamar T and Telle K. (2012). Post-Release Employment and Recidivism in Norway. *Journal of Quantitative Criminology* 28: 629–649.

Smeulers A and Haveman R. (2008) *Supranational Criminology: Towards a Criminology of International Crimes*, Antwerp: Intersentia.

Smeulers A, Hola B and van den Berg T. (2013) Sixty-Five Years of International Criminal Justice: The Facts and Figures. *International Criminal Law Review* 13(1): 7–41.

The Guardian. (2011) The Worst Places in the World for Women: Congo. *The Guardian*, Guardian News and Media Limited.

Ticktin M. (2014) Transnational Humanitarianism. *Annual Review of Anthropology* 43: 273–289.

Ugelvik T and Dullum J. (2011) *Penal Exceptionalism?: Nordic Prison Policy and Practice*, Abingdon: Routledge.

van Woudenberg N and Wormgoor W. (2008) The Cluster Munitions Convention: Around the World in One Year. *Yearbook of International Humanitarian Law* 11: 391–404.

Wohlforth WC, De Carvalho B, Leira H and Neumann IB. (2018) Moral Authority and Status in International Relations: Good States and the Social Dimension of Status Seeking. *Review of International Studies* 44(3): 526–546.

Zedner L. (2016) Penal Subversions: When is a Punishment Not Punishment, Who Decides and on What Grounds? *Theoretical Criminology* 20(1): 3–20.

8 From model to problem

The demise of Sweden's anti-torture brand

Johan Karlsson Schaffer and Axel Tengwall

Introduction

Why are international human rights treaty bodies increasingly criticizing Sweden's efforts to counteract torture? Sweden used to be a norm entrepreneur in placing the fight against torture on the global agenda, being the key sponsor of the United Nations Convention against Torture (Vik and Østberg 2021), and was internationally renowned for its allegedly uniquely humane penal regime (Nilsson 2011). Scholars have sought to locate the roots of both Sweden's international activism and its penal reformism in the supposedly solidarist, egalitarian values of the welfare state (Barker 2012).

Yet in their periodic reviews, international anti-torture committees, which initially praised Sweden as a model for other countries to emulate, seem to have grown frustrated with Sweden's unwillingness to reform its domestic practices, such as the widespread use of isolation in remand prisons or the reluctance to criminalize torture in national law (Langford et al. 2017). What does this increasing criticism mean? It could indicate that Swedish practices have deteriorated, that the committees are becoming harsher in their scrutiny, that the government is providing more information on its transgressions (Eck and Fariss 2018), that the standards have shifted, and/or that the understanding of torture has changed.

Addressing some of these issues, this chapter analyzes the evolving contestation over Sweden's anti-torture policies in the periodic reviews by two key monitoring bodies: the UN Committee against Torture (CAT) and the Council of Europe's Committee for the Prevention of Torture (CPT). We analyze committee reports and state responses from the late 1980s through the 2010s to identify how the problematization of torture develops in exchanges between the committees and the state. We find that the CAT widens its notion of torture from a criminal and penal law problem to a societal one, in effect expanding the state's responsibilities but also its opportunities to assert its 'do-gooder' brand, whereas the CPT, due to its different mandate, rather deepens the problem and consequently increases the dissonance with the government's view that 'the system' in Sweden works as intended.

The chapter makes empirical and analytical contributions: first, by comparing how the problem of torture has been construed in dialogues between Sweden

DOI: 10.4324/9781003195504-11

and two international torture committees, we show that whereas the two committees cast the problem of torture in terms of providing adequate safeguards for individuals, Sweden trusts the professionalism and law-abiding practice of its public authorities. Second, our case study of torture contributes to understanding the resilience of Sweden's humanitarian brand (de Bengy Puyvallée and Bjørkdahl 2021). Foreign policy human rights activism and penal humanitarian exports helped nurture both a national self-identity and an international reputation, yet the progressive domestication of human rights has challenged the doctrine of dualism on which the Nordic 'politics of international virtue' rested (cf. Christoffersen and Madsen 2011; Schaffer 2020). Thus, the problem of torture is indicative of a more profound test of the resilience of Swedish claims to exceptionalism.

The chapter is structured as follows: first, we account for how Sweden gained its reputation of being a pioneer in combating torture through domestic and foreign policy activism from the 1960s to the 1980s. Next, we introduce our analytical framework for identifying discursive struggles in human rights treaty body reviews of Sweden. The following two sections analyze reviews by the CAT and the CPT, respectively, and state party reports and responses, from the 1990s through the 2010s. The last section discusses the emerging results, before we conclude.

Sweden's anti-torture activism, 1960s–1980s

Since the 1960s, if not earlier, Sweden has enjoyed a strong reputation as an international champion against torture and a model of humane penal policies, setting a standard for other states through both its external activism and domestic progressivism. Sweden sponsored initiatives to hold repressive regimes accountable for torture and to criminalize torture in international law, while domestic reformers sought to transform the penal system from punishment to rehabilitation of the criminal.

In the 1960s, fighting torture became a key cause in Sweden's increasingly activist foreign policy, alongside its support for decolonization and the struggle against apartheid. Already in the 1950s, public outrage against torture in Algeria had prompted the government to support Algerian independence and Sweden had pursued the international abolition of the peacetime death penalty (Vik and Østberg 2021). In 1967, the so-called 'Greek Case' cast Sweden in the role of a daring critic. Following the military coup in Greece in 1967, Sweden—together with Denmark, Norway, and the Netherlands—filed an inter-state complaint against Greece with the European Commission on Human Rights (Demker 2005; Schaffer 2020). The Greek Case has been praised as a cosmopolitan breakthrough in the international criminalization of torture, since the plaintiffs innovatively used an inter-state complaint to protect the rights of the citizens of another state against its government (Sikkink 1993, p. 149f) and the Commission's report was the first instance ever of an international human rights body establishing that a state had practiced torture, although Greece had then already left the Council of Europe. In

1982, Sweden participated in a similar coordinated inter-state complaint against Turkey, which eventually resulted in a friendly settlement (Leckie 1988).

From the 1970s, Sweden also helped raise torture on the agenda of multilateral organizations. Collaborating with Amnesty International and the government of the Netherlands, Sweden's legal diplomats contributed to swaying the UN first to adopt a resolution and declaration against torture and then, in 1977, to start drafting a convention (Clark 2001, p. 136; Vik and Østberg 2021). Meanwhile, as it became clear that the UN convention would not include a preventive mechanism, the Council of Europe initiated a regional prevention system authorized to inspect places of detention (Cassese 1989). Later, Sweden also played a leading part in the protracted drafting of the Optional Protocol to the Convention against Torture, adopted in 2002, which established an *in-situ* inspection system modeled on the European preventive mechanism (Evans and Haenni-Dale 2004).

Beyond foreign policy activism against torture, Sweden also gained an international reputation as an exemplar of penal progressivism in the mid-20th century. Partly, this image reflected successive Social Democratic governments' efforts to reform the penal system. Up into the mid-1970s, successive criminal and penal policy reforms served to implement the treatment model, transforming prison from punishment to rehabilitation of the criminal. Partly, Sweden's reputation for penal progressivism was also created through active international marketing by government officials, especially to United States audiences since the 1940s, promoting the Swedish prison system as a model to inspire reforms elsewhere (Nilsson 2011). This penal exceptionalism resonated with dominant beliefs among elites that Sweden, by virtue of its welfare state achievements, was both entitled and obligated to guide other nations (cf. Schaffer 2021). And while criminologists and radical critics in the 1970s increasingly disputed the treatment model as both ineffective and humiliating for the prisoners, the international brand lived on—and seems to have persisted despite successive shifts in criminal and penal discourse, such as the rise of victims-of-crime perspectives or tough-on-crime policies since the 1980s (Barker 2012; Nilsson 2011; Scharff Smith and Ugelvik 2017).

In the late 1980s, political elites took pride in Sweden being first to ratify the United Nations Conventions against Torture and being one of the states whose ratification brought the Committee for the Prevention of Torture and Inhuman or Degrading Treatment or Punishment into force. In the 1970s, government and courts had reasserted the doctrine of dualism, according to which international law regulations apply in national law only by way of an active measure, which allowed Sweden to ratify IHRL conventions on the presumption that national legislation satisfied international obligations (Schaffer 2020). Consequently, the ratification of the Convention against Torture impelled no change of domestic laws to conform with the convention and government framed the decision as a continuation of Sweden's international activism against torture (Utrikesdepartementet 1985). The ratification of the convention prompted minor legislative changes to grant the committee access to places of detention and immunity (Utrikesdepartementet 1988). Meanwhile, government allocated funds to rehabilitation centres treating refugees suffering post-traumatic stress due to torture.

Thus, Sweden used to enjoy an exceptionally strong brand as a penal do-gooder, abroad as at home. Notably, though, external human rights activism and penal reformism were distinct discourses: while compliance with the ECHR prompted limited reforms of administrative detention practices (Schaffer 2020, p. 48), debates about Swedish penal reformism before the 1990s were hardly ever framed in terms of compliance with international human rights norms. This discursive division also reflected the doctrine of dualism, which allowed government to control the domestic effect of its international commitment to human rights (cf. Christoffersen and Madsen 2011; Schaffer 2020; cf. Vik and Østberg 2018). The human rights angle would enter domestic criminal and penal debate partly because of the scrutiny by the CAT and CPT and, more generally, the international human rights regime's stronger focus on domestic implementation since the 1990s. Yet distinct as they were, Sweden's anti-torture activism and penal policy marketing directed to the international domain were both helped by the overall brand of the Swedish welfare state as a model to the world (cf. Browning 2007).

However, the actual penal regime in Sweden was also more double-faced than the brand admits (Barker 2012): relatively low rates of imprisonment and generally humane prison conditions have coexisted with repressive penal practices, such as single-cell isolation as the norm well into the mid-twentieth century; the widespread use of restrictions in pre-trial detention; the detention of asylum seekers, including children; and the imprisonment of drug users. As we shall see, this dual nature of Sweden's penal model has increasingly puzzled the international anti-torture bodies Sweden once helped bring about.

Analytical framework: what's the problem with torture?

In the international human rights regime, the report-and-review mechanisms of treaty bodies play a central part. The Convention against Torture, which entered into force in 1987, established the Committee against Torture (CAT), which, like other UN human rights treaty bodies, is mandated to receive and examine periodic reports by state parties on their implementation of the convention and, based on these reports, issue recommendations, so-called Concluding Observations (COs). It can also hear individual and inter-state complaints on alleged treaty violations, undertake investigations of serious or systematic abuse, and issue so-called general comments clarifying its interpretations of treaty provisions. Consisting of ten independent experts, elected by the state parties, the CAT engages in a 'constructive dialogue' with the reviewee state.

The Convention for the Prevention of Torture entered into force in 1987. Unlike UN treaty bodies, the monitoring body established by this convention does not process individual complaints or serve other quasi-judicial functions: its mandate is to visit all places of detention—such as prisons, immigration detention facilities, and psychiatric hospitals—to see how public authorities treat persons deprived of their liberty. During its country visits, the CPT interviews detainees, and consults with management, staff, and others who can provide information, such as non-governmental organizations (NGOs).[1] After its visit, the CPT sends a report to the state and requests a detailed response.

Previous research on periodic human rights review procedures (for overviews, see Carraro 2019; Creamer and Simmons 2019) have found, for instance, that while states' participation in self-reporting is conditioned on the practices of neighbouring countries and the state's commitment to human rights (Creamer and Simmons 2015), self-reporting seems to contribute to state compliance by providing NGOs, mass media, and parliamentary actors an opportunity to challenge governmental practices and mobilize stakeholders (Creamer and Simmons 2019). Moreover, participants in treaty body review processes believe reviews can promote compliance by providing learning opportunities and an accurate overview of the compliance challenges a state faces, and by delivering recommendations, although participants find the treaty bodies sometimes to set unattainable standards (Carraro 2019). Analyzing the substantive exchanges between committees and states, previous studies have found, for instance, that even high-profiled states such as the Netherlands, New Zealand, and Finland routinely disregard most recommendations by the treaty bodies (Krommendijk 2015); that Scandinavian states were persistently unresponsive to calls from the CAT to address the problem of solitary confinement (Langford et al. 2017); and that Nordic governments deny or disagree with criticisms of the CPT about as often as they accept it (Lappi-Seppälä and Koskenniemi 2018).

For this paper, we draw on the 'What's the problem represented to be?' (WPR) approach (Bacchi 1999, 2012) to analyze how representations of the problem of torture in anti-torture treaty body reviews and state reports on Sweden have evolved over time. The WPR approach analyzes how problems are constructed and represented in policy discourse. Rather than regarding policy problems as exogenous to policymaking, it treats them as problematizations emerging from social practices. By analyzing how actors involved in policymaking explicitly and implicitly frame central issues, the approach works to expose the rationale of a broader problem conception. Our analytical focus has been to trace how the periodic report-and-review cycles on Sweden gradually rearticulate the problem of torture. The WPR approach allowed us to map the general contents of the material, while also interrogating the underlying rationales in how the problem of torture is presented. Not strictly speaking policy documents, the reports and reviews form a dialogue where the state, the committee, and other participants present contrastive understandings of what the problem of torture is.

We have analyzed CAT state party reports and COs from 1988 through 2018, as well as CPT Reports and Government Interim Reports from 1991 until 2021. This comparative research design allows us to analyze how two international bodies, different in their mandates and institutional designs, have evolved in their understanding of the Swedish problem of torture during a period of significant change in both domestic politics and the global order. Our analytical strategy was to map what concerns and criticisms the CAT and CPT raise in their reports, compile these concerns into overall themes and trends, and thus conceptualize the concerns as problem representations. Our strategy was largely identical in analyzing Swedish state party reports and government interim reports, primarily focusing on government replies on contentious issues.

The Committee against Torture: expanding the problem of torture

When the Committee against Torture reviewed Sweden for the first time in 1989, its COs represented the peak manifestation of the international discourse of Swedish exceptionalism. Throughout, the CAT seemed pleased with Sweden and found the report to reflect Sweden's 'pioneering role in the field of human rights' (CAT 1993). In its next report, the committee concluded that Sweden's 'legal and administrative regimes [...] were models to which most other countries should aspire' (CAT 1993). However, the report also revealed concerns. For instance, other states questioned the lack of an actual torture legislation in Swedish law, and many members viewed the Swedish dualist approach to international law as potentially problematic (CAT 1993).

Initially, the committee framed the problem of torture as relating to the uneven power relationship between the state and the individual. Some committee members raised concerns about whether Swedish police officers could be adequately prosecuted for crimes resembling severe torture, since Swedish law did not criminalize torture per se (CAT 1993). Sweden replied that specific torture legislation was not needed in such cases, as they would be handled according to existing laws on severe abuse and maltreatment (Government of Sweden 1992a).

In this early phase, Sweden's state party reports were rather short, asserted Swedish excellence, and construed the problem of torture narrowly. The initial state party report defined torture by referring to the Swedish constitution, claiming that the domestic legal framework did not consider isolation as a potential type of torture—only direct physical mistreatments were understood as torture (Government of Sweden 1988). Likewise, the subsequent state party report was short and assertive of Swedish excellence (Government of Sweden 1992a).

In its early CAT reporting, Sweden cited the first CPT inspections of Swedish detention facilities in 1991. For instance, in 1992 the Swedish state party report accurately stated that the CPT had found no evidence of torture during its visit—yet omitted mentioning the concerns that the CPT brought up regarding the imposition of prisoner restrictions, treatment of foreign nationals, and the material conditions of prison facilities, etc. (Government of Sweden 1992a). In 1996, Sweden again cited the CPT report, this time acknowledging some recommendations, comments and requests for information, yet downplaying or omitting the CPT's concerns and failing to mention the ad-hoc CPT report from 1994 (Government of Sweden 1996a). Swedish reports tended to construe the problem of torture narrowly as merely physical abuse, conceptually unrelated to social isolation of, for instance, remand prisoners—a major concern in the CPT reports, as we'll show in the next section. Describing its work against torture, the government almost exclusively referred to Sweden's efforts in the international context. The report extensively documents Sweden's commitments to rehabilitating refugees who had been victims of torture in their countries of origin (Government of Sweden 1996a), in effect framing the problem of torture as chiefly happening outside of Sweden.

Over time, the CAT dialogue changed: it stated the subjects of concern more explicitly, while also articulating new concerns regarding police misconduct and restrictions on remand prisoners. Already in 1997, the committee raised concerns about the integrity of Swedish law enforcement and its penal system, such as instances of ill-treatment by the Swedish police and the wide-spread use of isolating restrictions on pre-trial remand prisoners (CAT 1997). The CAT also demonstrated concern about the police forces' crowd-control strategies, particularly the use of riot dogs (CAT 1997). Yet the report also gave Sweden praise for its treatment and rehabilitation of refugees who had been subject to torture before coming to Sweden (CAT 1997). The problem of torture remained delimited to the state–individual relation, but criticisms against Sweden were becoming more focused.

In its next response, Sweden for the first time addressed the committee's concerns regarding restrictions on remand prisoners, and explained that following a recent reform, prosecutors now had to present a case for restrictions to a court before imposing them (Government of Sweden 2000). (Before 1994, prosecutors could decide more independently whether restrictions were necessary or not, which the CPT was early to criticize [see later in this chapter].) As for the use of riot dogs, the reply simply stated that the use of crowd-control measures was always ruled by the proportionality principle (Government of Sweden 2000).

Compared to the earlier focused criticism, the next CAT COs represent an explosion of criticisms. First, the committee raised severe concerns about how the police handled the riots during the European Union (EU) summit in Gothenburg in 2001, where the committee's earlier concerns about Swedish crowd-control methods came to fruition. Additionally, the committee expressed concerns over what it perceived as a trend of cases of 'the excessive use of force by police personnel and prison guards, leading to the death of the persons concerned' (CAT 2002). Furthermore, the committee questioned whether a new law, the so-called Anti-Terrorism Act, was in keeping with the Convention, since it allowed Sweden to expel foreigners suspected of terrorism under a procedure with no provision for appeal. Overall, the CAT COs of 2002 offer an interesting example of how external events, reflecting global developments, highlight critical aspects of Swedish practices.

Replying, Sweden had to address this intensified criticism and seems to have found itself more on the defensive than before. Whereas previous state party reports were a mere 7–8 pages, the 2006 response amounted to 24 pages. Much of the document was dedicated to presenting different human rights advocacy programmes within the police force, presumably to assure the international community that Sweden had taken adequate measures after the 2001 EU summit riots (Government of Sweden 2006). In 2008 and 2014, the committee largely reiterated its concerns and criticisms, seemingly growing frustrated in several areas (CAT 2008). The committee continued to be 'seriously concerned' about the lack of safeguards against ill-treatment, the lack of explicit torture legislation, widespread isolation of pre-trial remand prisoners, under-dimensioned recreational facilities in prison, and the detention of foreign nationals in remand prisons under the Aliens Act (CAT 2008).

However, in these years the committee also began expanding its view of the social situations in which the problem of torture manifests itself, and consequently, expanded the responsibility it ascribes to the state. In 2008, the committee remarked on issues regarding violence against women and children, honour crime, and hate crimes. For the first time, the committee expressed concern over the situation facing Swedish Roma persons and their vulnerability to discrimination and hate crimes. More generally, the CAT was concerned about the 'persistence of violence against women and children, including domestic violence and crimes committed against women and children in the name of honour,' and urged the state to act more resolutely (CAT 2008).

While the CAT previously focused on issues related to the state's intervention and repression in individual lives, its later reports effectively broadened the problem of torture to include situations where torture or ill-treatment might occur between individuals, and where the state fails to intervene both preventively and reactively. In 2014, the CAT again widened the scope of criticism. When issues of hate crime and discrimination re-appeared, it now included concerns over the situation of 'other vulnerable groups in Sweden, including Muslims, Afro-Swedes, Roma and Jews, as well as persons belonging to the lesbian, gay, bisexual and transgender community' (CAT 2014).

In the subsequent Swedish state party replies, Sweden responded quite dismissively to the repeated criticisms of lacking legislation and adequate safeguards against ill-treatment. The government mostly argued that there was no need for legislative reform regarding various concerns about formalized safeguards against ill-treatment. Sweden continually argued that further safeguards against the arbitrary use of restrictions on remand prisoners were unnecessary due to reforms that were introduced in the 1990s (Government of Sweden 2006, 2013, 2018). Likewise, it argued that specific torture legislation was unnecessary because existing laws were seen as compliant with the convention (in line with Sweden's dualist approach), and because Sweden had incorporated the ECHR which includes Article 3—another provision prohibiting torture (Government of Sweden 1996b). The Swedish position on these issues hardly changed over the years.

Compared to the late 1980s and early 1990s, Sweden increasingly found itself in a defensive position. In the later replies, Sweden tried to handle the broadening of the torture problem, by explaining its general human rights work in various domains, including efforts to change norms and attitudes in the police forces, but also issues that are only distantly related to the traditional torture problem.

The Committee for the Prevention of Torture: growing frustrations with Sweden's reluctance to reform

Let us turn to the themes that emerge and evolve in exchanges between the CPT and the Swedish government. Overall, the CPT acknowledges the generally humane conditions in Swedish prisons and its penal system. Its first visit to Sweden in 1991 included on-site inspections of police stations, remand prisons, prisons, psychiatric homes, and refugee detention centres. The first report praised Sweden's legal and administrative system and stated—as would all subsequent reports—that the risk of being subject to torture or ill-treatment by police or detention staff was very low. Yet the committee has also raised several concerns about the Swedish system. In this section, we'll analyze interchanges on three such concerns: restrictions and conditions in remand prisons; the expulsion of foreign nationals; and police misconduct.

Restrictions and conditions in remand prisons

A top theme in the CPT reports on Sweden is the situation in remand prisons and prisons more generally. Already in its first report, the committee criticized the highly arbitrary use of restrictions on remand prisoners, who were subject to excessive isolation in their cells, with little or no contact with the outside world. The committee found the Swedish system too reliant on its public prosecutors, who could issue restrictions without consulting a court, and therefore applied restrictions 'too liberally' (CPT 1992). Disputing the image of exceptionally humane prisons, the CPT also criticized the 'impoverished' access to services such as a productive rehabilitative regime, sanitary facilities, and outdoor exercise areas. Discovering that the exercise yard in a Stockholm remand prison it inspected consisted of 'a series of small cages perched on the roof of the establishment', the committee required immediate action to remedy the situation (CPT 1992).

The first CPT report established a pattern of critique where restrictions, regimes and material conditions in remand prisons would grow into the most prominent problem. In 1994, continued allegations about sub-standard remand prisons compelled the CPT to conduct an *ad hoc* visit. Whilst acknowledging modest improvements in facilities and remand regimes, the committee found that 'the vast majority of prisoners spend almost all their time locked in their cells, subject to a regime 'more akin to that of a police station than of a prison establishment' (CPT 1995). In its following periodic visits, the CPT largely iterated its concerns and recommendations regarding restrictions and material facilities in remand. The committee also noted that while its earlier critique had prompted a procedural law reform requiring prosecutors to present their case to a judge before imposing restrictions, such decisions were still too dependent on the prosecutor's argument, as the judge rarely had time to assess independently the case for restrictions and thus tended to accept the prosecutor's arguments (CPT 1999, 2004).

Having visited a remand prison in the Gothenburg area, the CPT wondered whether restrictions were the norm rather than a tool for exceptional circumstances (CPT 2004). Later, the CPT also raised concerns about prison conditions more generally, such as the understaffing of medical staff in some cases, the lack of toilets in remand prison cells, instances of unofficial collective punishment, and the excessive use of high-security restrictions without legal grounds (CPT 2016).

In its latest report, the CPT introduced new concerns about overcrowding in both remand and regular prisons (CPT 2021).

In its successive responses, the Swedish government initially tended to concede and reaffirm the criticism of material conditions in prison and remand facilities. The first response grasped on to the positive aspects, quoted all the praise Sweden received, and argued that in most areas Swedish law and practice sufficed to maintain the rights and dignity of prisoners (Government of Sweden 1992b). Seemingly agreeing with the committee's concerns, government pointed to efforts to renovate outdated or inappropriate facilities (Government of Sweden 1992b) and improve practical and material arrangements, such as prisoner healthcare and recreation (Government of Sweden 1993, cf. 1999). Conceding the factual circumstances, the responses also brought up financial constraints as a reason for the state's inability to renovate and relocate remand prisons according to the CPT's recommendations (Government of Sweden 1995, 1999).

However, overall, Sweden was reluctant to admit any systematic, fundamental flaws, seeking to evade or even deny the problems. One line of defence was to justify the excessive use of restrictions by explaining Swedish criminal and procedural law. Repeatedly, the government stated that the extensive use of restrictions was caused by Swedish criminal procedure relying exclusively on the information supplied by the accused and others in the main hearing when establishing a conviction (Government of Sweden 1992b, 1995, 1999, 2010). Consequently, the numbers of remand prisoners placed under restrictions 'may be expected to be greater in Sweden than in countries with different procedural rules' (Government of Sweden 1995).

Sweden did acknowledge the risks of 'routine action' when prosecutors decide whether to impose restrictions or not (Government of Sweden 1992b) and the 1994 reform (requiring prosecutors to present their case for restrictions before a court) entailed a concession to CPT concerns. The government emphasized the formal rights of the detainee and the practical routines prosecutors had to adhere to, and argued the new procedure implied 'courts make a 'proportionality' assessment of the reasonableness of the restrictions' (Government of Sweden 1995). As the reform failed to impress the CPT, the government responded to concerns about the arbitrary imposition of restrictions on remand prisoners by extensively describing laws and practices. Yet it avoided addressing the CPT's concerns about judges lacking time to appropriately review restriction cases (Government of Sweden 2004) and rehashed its arguments from the 1990s about the importance of the main hearing in Swedish criminal procedure (Government of Sweden 2010).

Later exchanges evidence how the CPT and Sweden hold contrasting understandings of what a remand prison ought to be. A case in point is the issue of out-of-cell time for remand prisoners, where the CPT argued that prisoners (including remand prisoners) should get at least eight hours of productive, educational, or recreational time outside of the cell per day (CPT 1999, 2016). Responding, Sweden seemed unwilling to accept this standard, pointing to substantial improvements in prisoner regimes and out-of-cell activities, while avoiding binding itself to any specific out-of-cell time standard (Government of Sweden 1999). Later, Sweden explicitly rejected the eight-hour standard as unrealistic for practical reasons, and instead cited the standard of ill-treatment set by the Istanbul Declaration, which defines isolation as being locked in a cell more than 22 hours a day (Government of Sweden 2016)—in effect, substituting the more demanding standard with a minimal one.

Expulsion of foreign nationals

Another continual issue of frustration in CPT–Sweden interactions is the treatment of foreigners under the Aliens Act (*Utlänningslagen*). Already in its first report, the CPT expressed concern that foreign nationals might run the risk of being expelled to countries where they could be subject to ill-treatment or torture (CPT 1992). The committee had received information indicating that Sweden might violate the principle of non-refoulement. Yet the Swedish response flatly denied the circumstances: describing at length Swedish law and practice on the matter, the response concludes that Sweden would not deport aliens to places where they run any significant risks because 'the authorities responsible for examination are organizationally structured so as to achieve the greatest possible competence on the part of officials regarding circumstances in various countries' (Government of Sweden 1992b). This pattern—the CPT expressing concern about risks for ill-treatment of foreign nationals and Sweden instead averring the professionalism of its authorities—would repeat in subsequent exchanges.

Apparently, the CPT would not take at face value Sweden's assertions about the professionalism of its authorities in implementing expulsions under the Aliens Act. The CPT did acknowledge some positive aspects of the Act, for instance that individuals subject to potential expulsion had some opportunities for appeal, but requested increased provision of legal aid (CPT 1999). Yet it also found many grounds for concern: having consulted with refugee support groups, the CPT doubted that Swedish authorities were as well informed as suggested on the dangers of expelling foreigners to certain countries (CPT 1999). Later, CPT frustrations grew as Sweden continued to hold some individuals subject to expulsion in remand prisons (CPT 2009).

Responding, Sweden would either deny or seek to evade the criticism. Reiterating its explanations of how Swedish legislation and public authorities work, the government denied any systematic risks in implementing expulsion of foreign nationals under the Aliens Act. It pointed to its rigorous information gathering, in dialogue with regional and international bodies, yet also admitted it rarely monitored how expellees fared after their expulsion (Government of Sweden 1999). And when the CPT recommended always providing foreigners detained under the Aliens Act with a public counsel, the government rejoined that for short-term detention, the costs would be disproportionate to the benefit to the detainee (Government of Sweden 2016).

Police misconduct

A third recurring theme that illustrates different constructions of the problem of torture concerns the investigatory process regarding cases of ill-treatment by law enforcement. Starting in the late 1990s, the CPT began voicing concerns about whether Sweden properly prosecuted crimes and misconduct committed by police officers. The CPT argued that the lack of an independent authority investigating the police created serious and well-grounded mistrust for the state's capability of holding police officers accountable for alleged instances of ill-treatment and misconduct (CPT 1999). The EU summit riots in Gothenburg seemingly amplified such concerns and recommendations. After *in situ* inspections in the Gothenburg area, the delegation 'found that complaints against police officers are still being investigated by serving police officers, on occasion with little or no effective supervision by public prosecutors' (CPT 2004). Unconvinced by the government's earlier accounts, the committee urged Sweden to install a demonstrably independent body that could deal with complaints directed towards the police (CPT 2004).

As with remand restrictions and the expulsion of aliens, Sweden responded to the CPT's concerns by seeking to explain Swedish law and practice. Addressing the criticism Sweden lacked an independent institution investigating police misconduct, the government argued there already was one: the prosecutor authority (Government of Sweden 1999). Of course, the criticism of the CPT was rather that police officers usually administer the early stages of a potential investigation (CPT 1999). Yet Sweden claimed to have established an internal mechanism within the police, designed to take complaints of police misconduct virtually automatically to a prosecutor. Furthermore, Sweden referenced two public inquiry commissions that had found no reason to suspect any flaws in these procedures or in the professionalism of the investigative staff (Government of Sweden 1999). Later, Sweden argued that the already existing mutual independence of different police departments and the professional autonomy of public officials were a *de facto* guarantee for adequate handling of cases that involve mistreatment by police officers—indeed, this system, government implied, is a model as good as the one advocated by the CPT (Government of Sweden 2004).

Besides the professionalism of its mutually independent agencies, government also cited its work to reinforce human rights values in the police force. For instance, without going into much detail on the EU summit riots, government ensured the CPT that 'ethical reminders' had been sent out to all state actors involved in the incidents (Government of Sweden 2004). Furthermore, government stressed the long-term work with norms and values in all police departments and underscored that to reflect a multicultural society, efforts 'are made with a view to increasing the multitude within the police services' (Government of Sweden 2004).

Eventually, however, Sweden seems to have taken some impression of the criticism. The establishment of a new internal investigation department allayed most of the committee's concerns. Yet since the department was still part of the police authority, the committee reiterated its recommendation to set up a demonstrably independent agency that the public would regard as impartial (CPT 2016).

Discussion

What are some overall patterns in how the CAT and CPT reporting on Sweden represents the problem of torture? First, throughout the CAT and CPT documents, concerns tend to grow over time, but in different directions: whereas the CAT expands the problematization of torture, the CPT deepens it. In the early reports, both committees construed the problem of torture as confined to the state–individual relationship, i.e., the domain of criminal and penal law. Eventually, however, the CAT has widened its focus to a societal domain, to include ill-treatment by non-state actors, such as honor killings, and other phenomena, such as ethnic discrimination. By contrast, the CPT consistently construes torture as occurring in the domain of coercion and detention by public authorities, but it has added to the list of concerns in this domain over time, and its criticism has grown increasingly detailed. For both committees, the early 2000s represent a turning point: their concerns increased, and the CAT's reporting began expanding the conception of torture.

What can account for this shift? The committees' changing notions of torture may reflect how the discourse on torture has evolved in response to political events. Early on, reviews focused on the state's implementation of its treaty obligations within the state. However, after 2001 committee reviews increasingly place the state's implementation efforts in a global perspective. Certainly, the committees had expressed concerns at the police force's crowd control techniques or the expulsion of foreign nationals before. Yet the police brutality during the 2001 EU summit in Gothenburg and—far more pervasively—the 'war on terror' following the September 11 terrorist attacks in the US, and the Swedish Government's participation in CIA rendition flights of terrorist suspects to places where they risked torture, placed Sweden's efforts to combat torture in a new light. It could no longer live off its old merits of having helped to establish the anti-torture regime.

However, the way in which the two committees elaborate their concerns in different directions might also reflect their institutional designs, which differ in important respects. First, the CPT's mandate expressly focuses on public authorities, ruling out ill-treatment or deprivation of liberty by non-state actors, whereas the CAT, whose quasi-judicial functions include the authority to interpret its own treaty, in 2008 expanded state obligations to prevent acts of torture committed by non-state actors, as well as to protect individuals and groups made vulnerable by discrimination (Gaer 2008). Second, while the CAT's review is based on reports submitted by the state party and additional information provided by UN bodies and third parties, the CPT review is also based on information the committee gathers itself during its periodic and ad hoc visits. This provides for a different dynamic, where the CAT review model informally grants NGOs a more crucial role in providing parallel reporting yet also grants the state more control of its own narrative, compared to the CPT. Over time, Swedish NGOs have learned to exploit the review process of the CAT to name and shame their government with a view to changing domestic practices and enhancing compliance. The CPT, by contrast, gathers its own information and presumably provides fewer opportunities for civil society initiatives.

A second notable pattern is how Sweden, when responding to criticism, tends to be selective in its deference to the committees. On the one hand, during the 1990s and 2000s, Sweden expressed its general goodwill and dedication to humane conditions in detention by accommodating CPT concerns over material conditions in prisons, claiming to take concerns into consideration, and pointing to ongoing reform processes, etc. On the other hand, when the committee questions Swedish law, practices, or institutions, Sweden rather seeks to evade the critique by explaining how 'the Swedish system' works. For instance, when criticized for the use of restrictions on remand prisoners, Sweden points to its unique criminal investigation model, which 'naturally' puts more prisoners under restrictions. Sweden also initially strictly denies the need for an independent body investigating police misconduct by referring to the presumed independence of public prosecutors. Over time, Sweden's responses to these issues become more concessionary, as some reforms are implemented, but the government still responds on the presumption that 'the system' works as intended according to its guiding norms—a response that repeatedly fails to sway the CPT.

Swedish replies to the CAT COs follow a similar trajectory—with the crucial difference that Sweden doesn't have to answer to specific, place-bound criticism. This allows Sweden to be less specific in its responses and refer to its relative decency in global comparison. After 2001, however, Sweden finds itself in a more defensive position, as CAT criticizes the lack of safeguards against ill-treatment and the excessive use of force during the 2001 EU summit. Conceding the outcomes were suboptimal, Sweden lifts new and old efforts to promote human rights norms and change attitudes within the police force. When the CAT expands its conceptualization of torture, it also introduces a host of new concerns. While this expansion opens several new fronts on which to question Sweden's claims to exceptionalism and broadens the state's responsibilities, it also allows the state to showcase its efforts in a broader range of policy areas, such as preventive measures against honor crime and violence against women and children.

Overall, the analysis reveals how the CAT and CPT, on the one hand, and Sweden on the other construe the problem of torture in contrastive ways: for the committees, preventing torture and ill-treatment requires ensuring anti-torture rights are effective, enforceable, and justiciable—i.e., seeing to that the rights-bearers, who are in a poor position to assert their rights, can nevertheless do so. Sweden, by contrast, trusts the professionalism and law-abiding practice of its public authorities to deliver humane outcomes for individuals, rejecting formalized safeguards against torture and ill-treatment. The Swedish approach reflects established worldviews among government and legal elites, for instance the predominant constitutional doctrine that fundamental rights and liberties serve as instructions to the legislator, rather than as legal entitlements citizens can claim against authorities. As the committees reiterate their concerns and criticisms, however, the state's logic seems increasingly circular, repeatedly describing the supposed strengths of Swedish legal-administrative practices, with little consideration for the recurring specific (often empirically grounded) concerns of the CPT and CAT about those very practices.

Lastly, how does the increasing concerns raised by the committees affect Sweden's self-image and brand as a pioneer in the global struggle against torture? Over time, the two committees provide diverging opportunities: when the CAT widens its conception of torture, it opens a new space for Sweden to promote its brand, writing extensively in its responses about its various measures to address the amorphous societal problem of torture and ill treatment. The CPT, by contrast, pokes ever deeper in the practices of public authorities, exposing how Sweden, unable or unwilling to reform its supposedly unique system, grows increasingly weary with the repeated criticism.

Perhaps Swedish policymakers are also growing ambivalent to maintaining the notion of Sweden as a humane model to the world. The international anti-torture activism and domestic penal reformism of a previous era rested on a consensus among key elites, which has since likely eroded. As public discourse in Sweden has shifted towards more repressive criminal and penal policies, and more restrictive migration policies, being framed as 'tough on crime' or 'tough on migration' needn't be a bad thing. The demise of Sweden's anti-torture brand might thus be part of a broader end to 'the politics of international virtue' (cf. Christoffersen and Madsen 2011).

However, when treaty bodies question Swedish penal practices, their critique may also, paradoxically, serve to reinforce the do-gooder brand. Chris Browning has argued that the 'good state' brand of the Nordics is resilient partly because it 'has become embedded with fantasized notions of Nordic identity', and therefore 'even dissonant experiences and practices tend to be managed in ways that reinforce fantasized conceptions of a Nordic ideal' (Browning 2021). Thus, while challenges to the Swedish anti-torture brand may be embarrassing and unsettling for policymakers and publics that have invested in it, embracing such shame may also regenerate the affective influence of the do-gooder brand on both Swedish elites and citizens, and external audiences.

Conclusion

This chapter has analyzed how notions of torture have evolved in periodic reviews of Sweden by the Committee against Torture and the Committee for the Prevention of Torture. Drawing on the 'what's the problem represented to be?' approach, we analyzed committee reports and state responses from the late 1980s through the 2010s. Our results suggest that the committees have increasingly called into question Sweden's brand as a pioneer for penal humanitarianism, especially after 2001. Over time, both the CAT and the CPT grow frustrated with Sweden's reluctance to implement legislative and institutional reforms. Yet their critique grows in different directions: the CAT widens its definition of torture to include also non-state abuse, such as honour crimes, discrimination, and violence against women, whereas the CPT, mandated to do *in-situ* inspections of places of detention, rather intensifies its scrutiny of public authorities, which prompts Sweden to respond with increasingly detailed accounts of its domestic practices and routines, and the principles and good intentions supposedly governing 'the system' in Sweden.

Thus, the demise of Sweden's anti-torture brand partly reflects conjectural changes in world affairs. Sweden's domestic penal progressivism and international anti-torture activism helped foster its image as 'different but better' during the Cold War era (cf. Waever 1992). Yet once the bodies Sweden had helped to establish turned their critical gaze on its domestic practices, assisted by domestic groups increasingly apt at learning how to place their concerns on the committees' agendas, they have increasingly chipped away at the notion of Sweden as a model to the world to identify instead a Swedish problem of torture.

Note

1 https://www.coe.int/en/web/cpt/faqs#what-is-the-cpt.

References

Bacchi C. 2012. Why study problematizations? Making politics visible. *Open J. Polit. Sci.* 2(1):1–8.

Bacchi CL. 1999. *Women, policy and politics: The construction of policy problems*, SAGE, London.

Barker V. 2012. Nordic exceptionalism revisited: Explaining the paradox of a Janus-faced penal regime. *Theor. Criminol.* 17(1):5–25.

Browning CS. 2007. Branding Nordicity: Models, identity and the decline of exceptionalism. *Coop. Confl.* 42(1):27–51.

Browning CS. 2021. Fantasy, distinction, shame: The stickiness of the Nordic 'good state' brand. In: *Do-gooders at the end of aid: Scandinavian humanitarianism in the twenty-first century*, eds. A de Bengy Puyvallée, K Bjørkdahl, Cambridge University Press, Cambridge, 14–37.

Carraro V. 2019. Promoting compliance with human rights: The performance of the United Nations' universal periodic review and treaty bodies. *Int. Stud. Q.* 63(4):1079–1093.

Cassese A. 1989. A new approach to human rights: The European convention for the prevention of torture. *Am. J. Int. Law* 83(1):128–153.

CAT. 1993. Report of the Committee against Torture. *A/48/44(SUPP)*, United Nations, New York.

CAT. 1997. Report of the Committee against *A/52/44*, United Nations, New York.

CAT. 2002. Concluding observation and recommendations of the Committee against Torture. *CAT/C/CR/28/6*, United Nations, New York.

CAT. 2008. Concluding observations of the Committee against Torture. *CAT/C/SWE/CO/5*, United Nations, New York.

CAT. 2014. Concluding observations on the sixth and seventh periodic reports of Sweden. *CAT/C/SWE/CO/6-7*, United Nations, New York.

Christoffersen J, Madsen MR. 2011. The end of virtue? Denmark and the internationalisation of human rights. *Nord. J. Int. Law* 80(3):257–277.

Clark AM. 2001. *Diplomacy of conscience: Amnesty international and changing human rights norms*, Princeton University Press, Princeton, NJ.

CPT. 1992. Report to the Swedish government on the visit to Sweden carried out by the European Committee for the Prevention of Torture and Inhuman or Degrading Treatment or Punishment (CPT) from 5 to 14 May 1991. *CPT/Inf (92) 4*, Council of Europe, Strasbourg.

CPT. 1995. Report to the Swedish government on the visit to Sweden carried out by the [CPT] from 23 to 26 August 1994. *CPT/Inf (95) 5*, Council of Europe, Strasbourg.

CPT. 1999. Report to the Swedish government on the visit to Sweden carried out by the [CPT] from 15 to 25 February 1998. *CPT/Inf (99) 4 [Part 1]*, Council of Europe, Strasbourg.

CPT. 2004. Report to the Swedish government on the visit to Sweden carried out by the [CPT] from 27 January to 5 February 2003. *CPT/Inf (2004) 32*, Council of Europe, Strasbourg.

CPT. 2009. Report to the Swedish government on the visit to Sweden carried out by the [CPT] from 9 to 18 June 2009. *CPT/Inf (2009) 34*, Council of Europe, Strasbourg.

CPT. 2016. Report to the Swedish government on the visit to Sweden carried out by the [CPT] from 18 to 28 May 2015. *CPT/Inf (2016) 1*, Council of Europe, Strasbourg.

CPT. 2021. Report to the Swedish government on the visit to Sweden carried out by the [CPT] from 18 to 29 January 2021. *CPT/Inf (2021) 20*, Council of Europe, Strasbourg.

Creamer CD, Simmons BA. 2015. Ratification, reporting, and rights: Quality of participation in the Convention against Torture. *Hum. Rights Q.* 37(3):579–608.

Creamer CD, Simmons BA. 2019. Do self-reporting regimes matter? Evidence from the Convention against Torture. *Int. Stud. Q.* 63(4):1051–1064.

de Bengy Puyvallée A, Bjørkdahl K. 2021. On the resilience of the scandinavian humanitarian brand. In: *Do-gooders at the end of aid: Scandinavian humanitarianism in the twenty-first century*, eds. A de Bengy Puyvallée, K Bjørkdahl, Cambridge University Press, Cambridge, 1–13.

Demker M. 2005. Dans på slak lina: Sverige och den grekiska diktaturen 1967–1974. *Forskningsprogrammet Sverige under kalla kriget*. Statsvetenskapliga institutionen, Göteborgs universitet, Göteborg.

Eck K, Fariss CJ. 2018. Ill treatment and torture in Sweden: A critique of cross-case comparisons. *Hum. Rights Q.* 40(3):591–604.

Evans MD, Haenni-Dale C. 2004. Preventing torture - The development of the optional protocol to the UN convention against torture. *Hum. Rights Law Rev.* 4(1):19–56.

Gaer FD. 2008. Opening remarks: General comment No. 2. *CUNY Law Rev.* 11(2):187.

Government of Sweden. 1988. Considerations of reports submitted by states parties under article 19 of the convention: Sweden. *CAT/C/5/ADD.1*, United Nations, New York.

Government of Sweden. 1992a. Consideration of reports submitted by states parties under article 19 of the convention: Sweden. *CAT/C/17/Add.9*, Committee Against Torture, United Nations, New York.

Government of Sweden. 1992b. Response of the Swedish government to the reports of the European Committee for the Prevention of Torture and Inhuman or Degrading Treatment or Punishment (CPT) on its visit to Sweden from 5 to 14 May 1991. *CPT/Inf (92) 6*, Council of Europe, Strasbourg.

Government of Sweden. 1993. Follow-up report from the Swedish government in response to the report of the European committee for the prevention of torture and inhuman or degrading treatment or punishment [CPT] on its visit to Sweden from 5 to 14 May 1991. *CPT/Inf (93) 7*, Council of Europe, Strasbourg.

Government of Sweden. 1995. Response of the Swedish government to the report of the European committee for the prevention of torture and inhuman or degrading treatment or punishment [CPT] on its visit to Sweden from 23 to 26 August 1994. *CPT/Inf (95) 12*, Council of Europe, Strasbourg.

Government of Sweden. 1996a. Third periodic reports of states parties due in 1996, addendum: Sweden. *CAT/C/34/Add.4*, Committee Against Torture.

Government of Sweden. 1996b. Third periodic reports of states parties du in 1996: Sweden. *CAT/C/55/Add.3*, United Nations, New York.

Government of Sweden. 1999. Interim report of the Swedish government in response to the report of the European committee for the prevention torture and inhuman or degrading treatment or punishment [CPT] on it visit to Sweden from 15 to 25 February 1998. *CPT/Inf (99) 4 part 2*, Council of Europe, Strasbourg.

Government of Sweden. 2000. Fourth periodic reports of states parties due in 2000: Sweden. *CAT/C/55/Add.3*, United Nations, New York.

Government of Sweden. 2004. Response of the Swedish government to the report of the European committee for the prevention of torture and inhuman or degrading treatment or punishment [CPT] on its visit to Sweden from 27 January to 5 February 2003. *CPT/ Inf (2004) 33*, Council of Europe, Strasbourg.

Government of Sweden. 2006. Fifth periodic reports of states parties due in 2004 - Addendum: Sweden. *CAT/C/SWE/5*, United Nations, New York.

Government of Sweden. 2010. Response of the Swedish government to the report of the European committee for the prevention of torture and inhuman or degrading treatment or punishment [CPT] on its visit to Sweden from 9 to 18 June 2009. *CPT/Inf (2010) 18*, Council of Europe, Strasbourg.

Government of Sweden. 2013. Combined sixth and seventh periodic reports of State parties due in 2012: Sweden. *CAT7C/SWE/6-7*, United Nations, New York.

Government of Sweden. 2016. Response of the Swedish government to the report of the European committee for the prevention of torture and inhuman or degrading treatment or punishment [CPT] on its visit to Sweden from 18 to 28 May 2015. *CPT/Inf (2016) 20*, Council of Europe, Strasbourg.

Government of Sweden. 2018. Eighth periodic report submitted by Sweden under article 19 of the Convention pursuant to the optional reporting procedure, due in 2018. *CAT/C/ SWE/8*, United Nations, New York.

Krommendijk J. 2015. The (in)effectiveness of UN human rights treaty body recommendations. *Neth. Q. Hum. Rights* 33(2):194–223.

Langford M, Fisher AD, Schaffer JK, Pareus F. 2017. The view from elsewhere: Scandinavian penal practices and international critique. In: *Scandinavian penal history, culture and prison practice*: Embraced by the welfare state?, eds. P Scharff Smith, T Ugelvik, Palgrave Macmillan, London, 451–479.

Lappi-Seppälä T, Koskenniemi L. 2018. National and regional instruments in securing the rule of law and human rights in the Nordic prisons. *Crime Law Soc. Change* 70(1):135–159.

Leckie S. 1988. The inter-state complaint procedure in international human rights law: Hopeful prospects or wishful thinking? *Hum..Rights Q.* 10(2):249–303.

Nilsson R. 2011. 'The most progressive, effective correctional system in the world': The Swedish prison system in the 1960s and 1970s. In: *Penal exceptionalism?* Nordic prison policy and practice, eds. T Ugelvik, J Dullum, Routledge, Abingdon.

Schaffer JK. 2020. The self-exempting activist: Sweden and the international human rights regime. *Nord. J. Hum. Rights* 38(1):40–60.

Schaffer JK. 2021. How democracy promotion became a key aim of Sweden's development aid policy. In: *Do-gooders at the end of aid: Scandinavian humanitarianism in the twenty-first century*, eds. A de Bengy Puyvallée, K Bjørkdahl, Cambridge University Press, Cambridge, 143–170.

Scharff Smith P, Ugelvik T. 2017. Punishment, welfare and prison history in Scandinavia. In: *Scandinavian penal history, culture and prison practice: Embraced by the welfare state?*, eds. P Scharff Smith, T Ugelvik, Palgrave, London, 3–31.

Sikkink K. 1993. The power of principled ideas: Human rights policies in the United States and Western Europe. In: *Ideas and foreign policy: Beliefs, institutions, and political change*, eds. J Goldstein, RO Keohane, Cornell University Press, New York, pp. 139–170.

Utrikesdepartementet. 1985. *Om godkännande av FN-konventionen mot tortyr och annan grym, omänsklig eller förnedrande behandling eller bestraffning*. Prop. 1985/6:17.

Utrikesdepartementet. 1988. *Sveriges tillträde till den europeiska konventionen till förhindrande av tortyr m.m.* Prop. 1987/88:133, Sveriges riksdag.

Vik HH, Østberg SA. 2018. Deploying the engagement policy: The significance of legal dualism in Norway's support for human rights treaties from the late 1970s. *Nord. J. Hum. Rights* 36(3):304–321.

Vik HH, Østberg SA. 2021. Sweden, Amnesty International and legal entrepreneurs in global anti-torture politics, 1967–1977. *Int. Hist. Rev.* 44(3): 633–652.

Waever O. 1992. Nordic nostalgia: Northern Europe after the Cold War. *Int. Aff. R. Inst. Int. Aff. 1944-*. 68(1):77–102.

9 Through Scandinavia, darkly

A criminological critique of Nordic noir[1]

Keith Hayward and Steve Hall

Introduction

Nordic noir is a cultural juggernaut. Renowned for its gloomy atmosphere, psychologically complex characters, unpretentious narrative form, and 'social criticism', it has mushroomed from regional niche-market to international phenomenon in little over a decade. This remarkable success owes much to the fact that, while Nordic noir exhibits many of the classic elements associated with 'genre work' (Frow, 2015), it does so not in a static or one-dimensional sense, but by merging together various mutually reinforcing strands of cultural production. For example, many people's first exposure to the genre came via compelling TV drama series such as *Forbrydelsen* (*The Killing*) (2007–2012), *Wallander* (2005–2010), and *Broen* (*The Bridge*) (2011–present). But before this Viking conquest of our television schedules, Scandinavian crime-fiction authors like Henning Mankell, Karin Fossum, Jo Nesbo, Liza Marklund, and most famously, Stieg Larsson, had paved the way by colonizing bestseller lists the world over. Beloved by critics and fans alike, interest in Nordic—or sometimes 'Scandi'—noir shows no sign of diminishing. Thanks to its capacity to mutate and migrate 'from one location to another, where it may be received and understood in different ways' (Hill and Turnbull, 2017), the genre is now being adapted and co-opted even by countries far removed from the rugged Scandinavian peninsula (Garcia Avis, 2015; Hedberg, 2017: 19–22).

The term 'Nordic noir' (NN) was purportedly coined by *The Guardian* TV critic, Sam Wollaston (Peacock, 2014), in a 2012 review of the Swedish police procedural *Sebastian Bergman* (2010–present). In stressing the 'bleak' mood and 'wonderful character-led' nature of Nordic detective drama, Wollaston recognized the genre's essential stylistic appeal. But Wollaston's review was also important because of its timing. Knowingly or not, he had tapped into a trend already very much alive among bourgeois tastemakers: the popularity outside Scandinavia for all things Scandinavian (Kingsley, 2012). This tendency, sometimes referred to as 'Scandi love' or 'Nordientalism' (Hague, 2003), typically folds NN in with other fashionable elements of Scandinavian culture, including mid-century furniture design, minimalist architecture, 'New Nordic cuisine', ecological sustainability, and the Danish 'Hygge' aesthetic. Such global popularity elevated

DOI: 10.4324/9781003195504-12

Nordic Noir to a lofty cultural perch, from where it could challenge the perception of the Scandinavian welfare and criminal justice systems as the pinnacle of modernity and the model for others to follow. Yet, alongside its exposure of the systems' flaws, the genre also displayed a tendency to represent the major institutions that structured the Scandinavian way of life as redeemable if only the specific human errors, operational imperfections and regressive cultural forces that undermined them could be exposed, addressed, and remedied. Rather than a requiem for the Scandinavian ideal, Nordic Noir began its ascendancy at the end of the twentieth century as a plea for it to do better.

So goes the standard interpretation of NN: a genre 'associated with a region (Scandinavia), with a mood (gloomy and bleak), with a look (dark and grim), and with strong characters and a compelling narrative' (Hill and Turnbull, 2017); and typically consumed by middle class, liberal audiences who appreciate the region's progressive politics, replete with high levels of governmental trust and transparency. On the face of it, everything appears straightforward, but there is something far more important in these popular cultural expressions than this conventional framing would suggest. More specifically, underneath the surface of NN's defining themes something hidden and more sociologically profound is being worked out/on. It is this opaque, possibly even subconscious, dimension of NN that interests us. For it is here, we will argue, in the genre's subterranean recesses, that many of Scandinavian society's all-too-real, yet largely repressed (Norman, 2018), social problems can be glimpsed.

Our critique of NN recruits two approaches from criminological theory. With its focus on subculture, space, emotion, and especially 'the politics of meaning' (Ferrell, 2007), cultural criminology is an obvious choice, especially its work on the crime–media nexus (Hayward and Presdee, 2010). For cultural criminologists, mediated representations conceal the reality of events but can also script them beforehand. In today's mediascape, this process takes place at unprecedented speed via what cultural criminologists call mediated 'loops' and 'spirals', a dual 'ongoing process by which everyday life recreates itself in its own image' (Ferrell et al, 2015:155). This approach will be of use in unearthing the symbolic motifs and meanings that often underpin NN.

The ghosts of signification are also important in ultra-realism, a criminological approach that uncovers the deep-rooted human drives and actions that constitute and reproduce the social order. Influenced by transcendental materialism and Lacanian psychoanalysis, ultra-realism challenges the fundamental domain assumptions of both right-realist and left-liberal criminology: both these positions, ultra-realists argue, overstate the autonomy and efficacy of individual agency and ignore the role of the unconscious in shaping subjectivity. Ultra-realists focus instead on the deep structures and processes that drive everything from normalized forms of harm to popular cultural expressions of violence or hyper individualism.

Cultural criminologists and ultra-realists have occasionally disagreed about aspects of their respective approaches, principally around the crucial issue of whether resistance to the dominant order is organic and constantly active or dormant until it finds symbolic coherence. However, more recently something of a rapprochement has occurred, and there is now some cross-pollination taking place between the two schools (e.g., Smith and Raymen, 2018: Hayward and Smith, 2017; Hayward and Turner, 2019). In what follows, we combine both approaches to undertake: a) a close reading of NN that outlines the genre's defining narrative, aesthetic tropes, and socio-political foundations; and b) a 'drive-oriented' interpretation of these same themes that highlights their (unarticulated) role within the prevailing symbolic order. By undertaking this dual critique of NN we hope to add greater symbolic depth to the cultural criminological maxim that 'the screen scripts the street, and the street scripts the screen' and thus further expand criminological knowledge on the interplay between the fictional/virtual and the real.

Nordic noir: a review of definitive themes and cultural origins

The Nordic region has a rich tradition of storytelling. From Scandinavian folklore and Viking mythology to Icelandic Sagas and Old Norse *skáldic* and Eddaic poetry, much of the region's cultural self-image and historical identity is bound up with these epic, mystical, pre-Christian tales. More recently, NN's phenomenal international success has added a new page to Scandinavia's storytelling tradition; only this time, rather than shaping regional culture, the 21st century iteration has projected Nordic values and motifs outward to a global audience, (re)shaping the way the region is understood and imagined.

Three main themes define the genre. First, is what we might collectively refer to as landscape, atmosphere, and Scandinavian imagery. Irrespective of medium, NN has a certain aesthetic feel to it, mainly due to the relationship between location and affect—especially the way landscape is used to evoke emptiness, mournfulness and the uncanny. This nexus of 'matter and memory' is nicely captured by Christopher James (2020) when he writes,

> If setting is important and unites these works, it is as more than just because of the aptness of Nordic society for plumbing depths and secrets. It is a place whose geography is poignant in allowing the memory of characters to be established, reconsidered and changed.

The use of space and atmosphere to elicit a sense (often at the same time) of melancholy and menace is consistent across urban and rural settings. You are as likely to encounter this geography of disconsolation in a dimly-lit Copenhagen business park as you are in the idyllic, close-knit Swedish coastal town of Ystad, setting for the hugely popular *Wallander* novels. NN's bleak spatial aesthetic is further enhanced by another consistently deployed signifier—the Scandinavian climate. Known for its dreary winters, midsummer light, and (in the North) an abundance of snow and frozen tundra, the region's climate also features prominently as both a plot device in-and-of-itself (as in case of the Icelandic TV series *Trapped* (2015) and most famously in Peter Høeg's 1992 novel, *Miss Smilla's*

Feeling for Snow), and as one of the genre's quintessential stylistic trademarks. For some commentators, the combination of bleak landscape and frigid climate embodies an ideal of Northern purity (Davidson, 2005), of sterile, remote worlds where culture is frozen in time and outsiders are matter out of place. This same atmosphere of nostalgia and purity is also present in the discreet modernistic style of Scandinavian design and interior settings (Waade, 2011). By visually referencing the 1950s and 1960s, contemporary NN is exhibiting nostalgia for a lost 'Scandinavian utopia', a simpler, more ordered society now eclipsed by global currents and 'social ambivalence' (Brodén, 2011). These sombre interiors, when combined with colour-palette manipulation and dissonant musical scoring, create what Anne Marit Waade (2011:18) calls 'a guilty landscape'—settings with almost human or emotional characteristics.

A second defining theme within NN is its use of emotionally complex or psychologically troubled lead characters. Two archetypes stand out: the morose male detective and the resourceful, but emotionally distant, heroine. Most of NN's key elements were foreshadowed in Maj Sjöwall and Per Wahlöö's ten-book series *Novel of a Crime* ['Roman om ett brott'] (1965–1975) (Forshaw, 2013a; Stougaard-Nielsen, 2017). The central character is the jaded Stockholm police detective Martin Beck. Trapped in a loveless marriage, plagued by health problems and personal crises, and disillusioned to the point of reclusiveness, Beck established the blueprint for 'the morose Scandinavian detective'. Since Beck, a laundry list of personal problems has become the default backstory for one troubled male Scandinavian fictional detective after another, including Mankell's Kurt Wallander, Nesbo's Harry Hole, Adler-Olsen's Carl Mørck, Staalesen's Varg Veum, Martin Rohde in seasons one and two of *The Bridge,* and Andri Olafsson from *Trapped.* This type of emotional framing even extends to the 'feminization' of male protagonists (Waade (2017:384), whereby established masculine anti-hero traits are replaced with emotional concerns about family and estranged relationships.

Female counterparts are frequently portrayed in even less favourable terms—at best socially awkward, at worst psychologically traumatized or suffering from clinical personality disorders. Such emotional complexity has added to the genre's appeal. The never-smiling, workaholic, heroines of NN—Sarah Lund, Saga Nøren, Annika Bengtzon—are today not just popular, but iconic, with at least one commentator describing Lisbeth Salander, the Goth hacker-hero of Stieg Larsson's *Millennium* trilogy, as 'possibly the single most distinctive female character in modern crime fiction' (Forshaw, 2013a:38). Tattooed, hyper-violent, and displaying psychopathic tendencies, Salander is viewed by many readers as a feminist hero.[2] It is also clear that Larsson intended Salander's story arc—in childhood she was raped by state-employed staff charged with her care; in adulthood she dedicates herself to exposing and punishing corrupt state officials and politicians—to be read as a forthright critique of Swedish society. Thus, in this sense she clearly embodies the final defining feature of NN.

The third frequently highlighted theme is the genre's robust critique of the Scandinavian welfare state model (Nestingen, 2008; Brodén, 2011; Tapper, 2011;

Robbins, 2017). While many perceive Scandinavia as a 'near-perfect society' characterized by cultural homogeneity, political trust, and a 'cradle-to-grave' welfare system, the reality is darker and more complex. NN allows consumers to glimpse the 'gritty reality' of Scandinavian society, including its crumbling welfare regime and its pivot towards neo-liberalism. Slavoj Žižek (2003), for example, believes the Henning Mankell novels articulate 'the long and painful decay of the Swedish welfare state', while for Daniel Brodén '[t]he ever-present violence and corruption in the welfare state is a central theme in the contemporary Swedish crime film' (2011:96). In the spectacularly successful crime novels of Stieg Larsson this motif is foundational; a point made by the journalist Ian MacDougall in a review article evocatively entitled 'The man who blew up the welfare state':

> To read the 1,802 pages of the Swedish crime novelist Stieg Larsson's *Millennium* trilogy is to be told that, for all their perceived virtue, the institutions of social democracy are a farce. In Larsson's books… [readers will] find a country they didn't expect. In this Sweden, the country's well-polished façade belies a broken apparatus of government whose rusty flywheels are little more than the playthings of crooks. The doctors are crooked. The bureaucrats are crooked. The newspapermen are crooked. The industrialists and businessmen, laid bare by merciless transparency laws, are nevertheless crooked. The police and the prosecutors are crooked. And the criminals, of course, are crooked, though not always: it's often the case that criminal acts… are the only means by which to overcome the comprehensive failure of the world's most comprehensive welfare system.

Taken together, these three features constitute the standard interpretation of NN. This explanatory consistency even extends to more sophisticated accounts that go one step further in their analysis and trace the socio-cultural genealogies of these themes. For example, NN's deployment of a bleak mood and naturalistic *mise-en-scène* as a metaphor for the hidden aspects of social life is commonly traced back to late-19th and early-20th century Scandinavian painting (Waade and Jensen, 2013:192; Waade, 2017:382). Most obviously, the poignant interior scenes of Vilhelm Hammershøi (1864–1916) or the psychologically charged landscapes of Edvard Munch (1863–1944). Similarly, the despondency and emotional complexity associated with NN's central protagonists are viewed as an extension of the tradition of 'Nordic Melancholy' (Creeber, 2015; Waade, 2013);[3] a thematic element of Scandinavian art, culture, and philosophy that is evident in everything from the disquieting realism of Ibsen's plays and Sibelius' symphonies, to 20th-century work by filmmaker Ingmar Bergman and dramatist Lars Norén. However, rather than explore cultural continuity, the more common critical approach is to stress instead a narrative of disjuncture based on the third theme—the putative 'crisis of legitimacy' in the Scandinavian welfare state model, the focal point of our own particular critical criminological analysis.

Trouble in paradise: Nordic noir's political conscience

To understand NN, one needs to be familiar with the Swedish concept of the 'people's home' (*Folkhemmet/Folkhem*) (Hentilä, 1978). From the 1920s, the goal of social democratic Sweden was a functioning welfare society based on 'social citizenship' and 'modelled on the synecdoche of the "good home", with its foundation in equality and mutual understanding: a home that would not be divided by social classes, but based on consideration, cooperation and helpfulness' (Stougaard-Nielsen, 2017).[4] Such progressive ideals were common in the early 20th century, but only in Scandinavia did they actually come to fruition (see Esping-Anderson and Korpi, 1987). Underpinned by Keynesian economics, close relationships between trade unions and corporations, and a general willingness to subordinate individual interests in favor of common economic and political goals, Sweden and its Nordic neighbours made good on the *Folkhemmet* ideal, creating egalitarian societies characterized by encompassing welfare regimes and socio-cultural homogeneity (Edling, 2019). Between the 1950s and the 1970s, the Scandinavian countries established an entirely new 'social democratic' welfare state model that balanced the requirements of the free market with high levels of public planning and regulation across most aspects of everyday life (Esping-Anderson, 1990). It was a welfare model that flourished without challenge until the end of the 1970s, by which time Scandinavia was viewed by many social policy scholars as the blueprint for liberal democracies everywhere.

However, in the 1980s, a series of cracks started to appear in the walls of the 'people's home' (Marklund, 1988). Despite its generally favourable labour relations, Sweden started the decade with a general strike in 1980, and this was followed soon after by cuts to benefits and pensions. For the first time in years, many Scandinavian countries were facing up to the reality of big spending deficits and contracting living standards. Problems continued in the early 1990s, when Sweden experienced its highest rate of unemployment since the 1930s, along with a run on its currency that briefly forced interest rates up to 500%. These incidents were, of course, harbingers of a wider neo-liberal transformation already reshaping economic governance in the region and establishing 'a different ideological approach to the role of the state in the everyday life of its citizens '(Pratt, 2008: 278). By the end of the 1990s, the nurturing *Folkhem* ideal had been beaten back by a less socially democratic successor — the corporatist, neo-liberal mode of political governance (Hänninen et al, 2019).

It is against this context that most commentators make sense of NN's rise; arguing that the genre is both a critical rejoinder to, and a means of making sense of, the many changes wrought by this economic and political transformation. It is a narrative that arcs across the work of the genre's defining authors, and thus in this section we trace the political conscience at work within NN.

Scandinavian crime fiction first appears in 1893 with Frederik Lindholm's book *Stockholmsdetekiven* (*The Stockholm Detective*) and flourished in the mid-20th century with small-town 'whodunit'; mysteries by *inter alia* Dagmar Maria Lang and R. K. Ronblom. However, things changed dramatically in the 1960s when, buttressed by the radical politics of the era, crime writers rejected the 'bourgeois accoutrements' of early Scandinavian crime fiction (Forshaw, 2013a:14), and engaged instead in a searing internal critique of the inequality and corruption that they believed lay behind the façade of the *Folkhem* model. Most notably, the aforementioned Sjöwall and Wahlöö used their successful 'police procedural' series as a vehicle to expose crime, disorder, and venality in urban Stockholm. Unabashed Marxists, Sjöwall and Wahlöö's critical position was similar to that of contemporaneous British 'realist cinema'; that welfare states reproduced capitalism by neutralizing the class struggle.

Sjöwall and Wahlöö's critique, like most Scandinavian art and cultural production of the 1960s, remained distinctly modernist, but this changed as the region was exposed to globalizing forces, including various immigration pulses from the 1980s onwards. At this point, rather than view crime as a national problem linked to fractures in the welfare state, as had been the case in the Sjöwall and Wahlöö novels, crime started to be perceived as a consequence of cultural heterogeneity and the region's inability to stem the flow of globalization. These sentiments were concretized in the Scandinavian psyche by a series of unprecedented events, including the unsolved assassination of the Swedish Prime Minister Olof Palme in downtown Stockholm in February 1986; the Chernobyl nuclear disaster just a few months later that saw radioactive caesium-137 particles drift into Scandinavian airspace from across the Baltic Sea; and the deep economic recession of the early 1990s. These incidents, along with a major drop in real GDP across the Nordic region in the late-1980s/early-1990s (Honkaphoja, 2009) became known as 'the end of Scandinavian innocence' (Norman, 2018).

This sense that the state could no longer protect its citizens from the dangers of globalization is precisely what drives Henning Mankell's Kurt Wallander novels and TV dramas (Waade, 2013). Like Sjöwall and Wahlöö, Mankell is keen to excavate the deep divisions at the heart of Sweden and the wider region, only this time his beleaguered and conflicted NN detective is given a broader investigative canvas. Or, as Nestingen puts it, Mankell extends Wallander's remit to the question of how (social) 'solidarity might figure in transnational political-economic and cultural-social formations' (2008:228). Consequently, 'Mankell evokes all the traumatic topics which give rise to the New Right populism: the flow of illegal immigrants, soaring crime and violence, growing unemployment and social insecurity, the disintegration of social solidarity' (Žižek, 2003). But rather than wilt in the face of moral decline, xenophobia, and sexism, Wallander instead serves as an unlikely defender of the *Folkhemmet* ideal. In many ways Wallander, along with *Forbrydelsen's* Sarah Lund and *Broen*'s Saga Norén, symbolically personifies the Scandinavian welfare state (Robbins, 2017)—bowed certainly, but not yet entirely broken.

This weary stoicism is absent in Stieg Larsson's *Millennium* trilogy, the books that set the table for NN's worldwide domination of 21st century crime fiction. Instead, Larsson's central character, Lisbeth Salander is an avenging angel, hell bent on punishing the state-appointed guardians who abused her as a girl. However, she quickly moves on to target other irredeemably evil male figures who embody the type of racism, sexism, corporatism, and avaricious neo-liberalism that for Larsson were endemic in *fin de siècle* Sweden. A former investigative journalist, Larsson was a passionate feminist and a brave opponent of the far right, but as a novelist his critique of Scandinavia's moral decline in the *Millennium* trilogy is not only implausible and conspiratorial, but also gratuitous.

In the work of Mankell and Larsson we see a clear rebuttal of modernism, a tendency that has grown stronger in subsequent NN offerings (see e.g., the novels of Jo Nesbo or TV series like *Borderliner* [2017] and *The Protectors* [*Livvagterne*] [2009–2010]). In today's NN, the consensus, or 'unified point of view', has now virtually disappeared, replaced by a pronounced postmodern emotionality and a fixation on fashionable identity politics. Despite this transparent narrative shift, two standard readings persist: first, the assertion that NN represents a form of melancholic 'longing' for a by-gone Scandinavian golden age of welfarism and social homogeneity; and second, the common perception of NN as a 'gritty' narrative form that allows consumers to peel back the veneer of 'perfect Scandinavia' to reveal the dark realities that lie beneath. No doubt these interpretations are useful in explaining both the form and appeal of NN, but do they tell the whole story? We don't believe they do, and thus in the next section we offer an alternative criminological elucidation.

'A nightmare that can make us happy': a criminological re-examination of NN[5]

Here we make the claim that, because of pronounced cognitive dissonance between its much-vaunted 'realism' and the actual, on-the-ground realities of social life in the region, the genre is no longer capable of accurately interpreting the shifting cultural and political landscape of Scandinavia and the broader (neo) liberal economic order. Expressed differently, in its contemporary form, NN has strayed so far from its earlier 'gritty' roots, it now exists largely in the realm of fantasy—and by doing so, has far less interpretive value.

This loosening of NN's grip on reality is most evident in two tropes that have become increasingly prominent features of the genre:

1. *A Retreatist trope*: a discernible shift in scene-setting from urbanscape to more idealized, nostalgic, close-knit rural locations, 'where almost all traces of globalization and threats from an external world are absent' (Bergman, 2014:103); a return to the 'neo-romantic conventions' associated with earlier 'whodunit' forms of fiction. Examples here include the works of Karin Fossum, Johan Theorin's *Echoes from the Dead*, Vidar Sundstøl's The *Devil's Wedding Ring*, Ragnar Jonasson's *Snowblind*, and Mari Jungsted's *Gotland* novels.
2. *A Sensationalist trope*: a shift from realism to melodrama in a bid to sustain viewership; the frequent evocation of lurid, conspiratorial or sensational plot themes, including Nazi conspiracies (the Millennium Trilogy), off-book secret government agencies, bomb plots and sniper attacks (*Broen*),

paedophile rings and sadomasochistic murders, and serial killers (*Darne Ahl* [2015]; *Those Who Kill* [*Den som dræber*] (2011–present).[6] Other examples here include the TV series *Johan Falk* (1999–2015) and the highly derivative Finnish police drama *Bordertown* (2016–2020); the novels of Jo Nesbo and 'Lars Kepler'; and cross-European TV productions such as *Fortitude* (2015–present) and *Midnight Sun* (2016).

By retreating to the local/traditional context, NN writers and cultural producers are (consciously or unconsciously) constructing what Catherine Phelps has described as a 'psychic corral' (cited in Hansen and Waade, 2017:108) against the assaults of globalization. As Scandinavian society is forced to confront the demise of its traditional state-centered institutions of control and community solidarity, we witness a wave of nostalgic melancholia much in evidence in the lurch to the right in Scandinavian politics with the emergence of right-wing populist parties like Sweden Democrats (Elgenius and Rydgren, 2017; Teitelbaum, 2019), the Finns Party (Arter, 2020), and the Danish People's Party (Rydgren, 2004).

Similar and related processes also fuel the growth of the second trope—the drift towards *sensationalism*. While sensationalism is often a normal consequence of a mature genre striving to maintain audience share, in this case it highlights something deeper. As we will discuss in the following paragraphs, the underlying contemporary political problem in many parts of the region is the Scandinavian social democratic left's inability to accept that their ideology and welfare-based institutions are now, to use Adrian Johnston's (2008) term, *de-aptative*.[7] This sense of loss is now heightened by a seeming inability to either recover that past or take it further forward in the new globalized context. Both regressive recovery and progressive adaptation seem, and probably are, impossible. In other words, not only are Scandinavians unable to mourn the loss they cannot fully accept but, because of the political and cultural limitations they have imposed on themselves, they now feel incapable of explaining or acting upon their structural predicament. Quietly but inexorably, the politicians of the new right and the cultural producers of the liberal left have driven themselves into a psycho-cultural *cul-de-sac*, and as a result, we are seeing a rapid deflection into sensationalist fantasy.

What the standard analyses of NN are struggling to articulate is the death of the Scandinavian social democratic 'big Other', and the subsequent inevitable decline into symbolic inefficiency. To understand exactly what we mean by this, it is necessary at this point to undertake a brief review of Jacques Lacan's 'three orders of the psyche' (see e.g., Lacan, 1964),[8] as this is the framework that we use to offer our alternative interpretation of NN.

A starting point for Lacan's revision of Freud is the common philosophical trope of the 'state of nature' in which human beings exist without culture or language and thus lack the cognitive processes required to comprehend themselves and their experiences. In this natural, raw state, devoid of any complex structure through which we might grasp the essence of our being, we exist in what Lacan describes as *The Order of the Real*. Here, our raw, pre-symbolic experiences are so disturbing, so inexplicable, that they become almost impossible to bear, forcing the subject to escape in a bid to constitute the self elsewhere, initially, into the 'madness' of *The Imaginary*, a realm of loss and profound negativity and misrecognition; and then, in a bid to escape such subjective chaos, into *The Symbolic Order*, a constructed 'state of culture'—a mythic world of meanings that we use to explain and systematize the subjective experience of the world around us, the purview of which includes religion, language, tradition, law, and any other shared system that allows the creation of social life to take place within a structure of communicable meanings and committed relations.

Now, the self (*cogito*) is no longer in a vacuum, but in a space in which it can build relationships, commitments, and social identities. However, for Lacan, existing in this space comes at an existential cost—the cost of accepting and submitting to the 'rule' of the *big Other*. Crudely put, the *big Other* is the 'truth' that supposedly underpins the collective identities, the communal network of social institutions, and the traditional values, customs, and laws of our shared cultural life. The problem, of course, is that the *big Other* is a nothing more than the mythical embodiment of the *Symbolic Order*. It is essential therefore, if we are to maintain a reasonably civil social order/space, that we all act *as if* the *big Other* really exists and determines the things in which we should believe. If, for any reason, we decide that the *big Other*'s symbolic efficiency is simply an ideological illusion, then we are forced to face the terror of unexplained stimuli that invade our psyche (Hall, 2012a). By refusing to accept the rule of the *big Other* and its *Symbolic Order*, we are denied access to its meanings and drift perilously close to the *Real*, the deep void of conflicting and inarticulate drives and stimuli that forever underlies the subject. This, we suspect, is postmodern society's ultimate destination.

For Žižek (1999), liberal-postmodernism has actively sought to attack and debase the common meanings of modernity's *Symbolic Order* by exposing the falsities or political manipulations behind modernist truths. Archetypal postmodernists challenge everything from the concept of nationhood (a cultural myth) to the rule of law (a system structured around enshrined privilege and a partial conception of morality). Even the objectivity of post-Enlightenment science is traduced, dismissed as merely a social construction of status hierarchies that organize truth claims. This relentless abstraction, relativity and denunciation has stripped away the modernist order of meaning without offering anything else in its place. The result of all this destruction (or as the postmodernists prefer by adding a mitigating syllable, deconstruction) is that many liberal societies are now relinquishing the very things that enabled their citizens to live a reasonably civil and organized life. To be clear, we are not suggesting this situation is anywhere near as pronounced in Scandinavia as it is in, say, the UK or the US. Mercifully, Nordic society still maintains certain precious core economic principles and cultural values that continue to insulate the region from the worst excesses of facile postmodern relativity. However, the rule of the Scandinavian *big Other* is under threat, a danger apparent in the declining symbolic efficiency that courses though contemporary NN.

Consider again the two tropes mentioned before. From a Lacanian/ultra-realist perspective, the first tendency—*retreatism*—perfectly illustrates dwindling symbolic efficiency. Because postmodernism is now incapable of—and indeed averse to—producing new truths that explain new realities, NN creatives have progressively fewer collective forms of belief to deploy. Hence the rather unimaginative return to the remote rural or claustrophobic island setting. Although the issues of globalization and multiculturalism do feature—for instance, worthy but entirely one-dimensional people trafficking storylines in *Wallander* and *Trapped*—but these ham-fisted attempts to globalize the local should be understood as a trace of initial realism, an unexplained 'foreign body' to be misrecognized by *The Imaginary*. The psycho-cultural effect of this is to intensify and indefinitely reproduce 'objectless anxiety' (Hall, 2012b), the enduring feeling that something quite serious but imperceptible is wrong in the social order. This in turn creates an epistemologically insecure space in which ideological scapegoats such as immigrants can (ironically) be constructed. Anxiety can be transformed into fear and active interventions when an object is located, but of course it is crucial that the object has real causal properties, otherwise the subject remains trapped in *The Imaginary*. The reduction of cultural and political life to an eternal battle of misrecognitions, the manufactured epistemological defeatism that Foucault misdiagnosed as epistemic 'regimes of truth', is the true macro-regression facilitated by the cultural turn and its post-structural framework.

The *sensationalist* trope in turn can be understood as an expression of the distinction between the natural *Real* and the political *Real*[9]—that which by its elusive nature is difficult to symbolize, and that which has been blocked from symbolism by the prevailing neoliberal ideology. In other words, the political *Real* has diverted efficient symbolization of the Nordic countries' gathering political and social predicament, confining Scandinavian culture to *The Imaginary*. This explains the genre's quickening descent into fantasy, replete with sensationalist tropes, such as the frequent but seldom commented upon deployment of conspiratorial narratives—the most famous example being the various ungrounded plots (Nazi-corporate-underground-serial killing networks, rogue security agencies, etc.) that pepper Larsson's *Millennium* novels. In order to escape the torment of a world that makes less and less sense, we rely instead on conspiratorial narratives to (re)construct the semblance of a *big Other*, or more accurately what Žižek (following Lacan) calls *the Other of the Other*.

In the absence of an efficient *Symbolic Order*, the only alternative escape route from the terror of *the Real*, the unexplained drives and stimuli that hide in the noumenal darkness,[10] are the fantastic misrecognitions of *the Imaginary*, which, as always, are effortlessly recruited by modernity's vigilant and powerful engines of mythology—TV, film, and popular fiction.

Paradise lost?: Nordic noir's political amnesia

The dual positions outlined above illustrate the extent to which the possibility of democratic socialism has been virtually erased from Nordic popular culture. Likewise, progressive left-wing values are largely ejected from political and intellectual life, and principled socialist figures marginalized. Political principles once active in political economy have been replaced by a pragmatic acceptance of the global market economy. The fundamental Scandinavian ambitions of fairness, equality, and social reorganization are increasingly now being played out on the cultural battlefield of identity politics, based around individuality, heterogeneity, sexuality, ethnicity, and transnationalism as 'dimensions of belonging'. Such 'intersectional' cultural antagonisms, of course, are no longer embedded in political economy and can thus be effortlessly co-opted by the lifestyle calibrations of market capitalism (Hayward and Schuilenburg, 2014; Winlow et al., 2017). Where, as we have seen, media and literary figures once *encouraged* left-wing disclosures of neoliberalism's destruction of working-class communities, today such disclosures are anathema. Indeed, serious problems such as the unprecedented recent spate of bomb attacks in Sweden (Henley, 2019), or the 23-hour lockdown regime in certain Copenhagen prisons due to rising levels of violence, are dismissed by both neoliberal manager-politicians and the identitarian left alike as 'temporary events' or 'alarmist' scaremongering. In the liberal-postmodern cultural imagination, it's better to cover up serious problems because, within its truncated political parameters, no comprehensive solutions are possible.

But the population no longer needs the mass media to induce fear. Where media sensationalism once acted culturally upon a rather quiet and comfortable social democratic landscape to stir up the fear required to justify authoritarian policies, fearful events now occur more frequently in proximal reality. The hand grenade in the street in Malmo (Barry and Anderson, 2018; Clayton and Hanrahan, 2018), or the new 'Ghetto' housing zones for immigrants in Copenhagen (Barry and Sorensen, 2018), are clearly symbolic of this relocation of fearful stimuli and a general ideological failure. The dream of socialism in its traditional structurally embedded form has gone; while the new twenty-first century 'lite' form of social democracy has never been able to penetrate the structural depths of socio-economic reality with telling and enduring interventions. Neoliberalism is failing all around us; a situation that has already revived the fortunes of nationalist and populist political parties across the region (Teitelbaum, 2019)—and there, lurking in the shadows, is the inevitable rise of Scandinavia's violent extremist right (Kølvraa, 2019; Sedgwick, 2013; Ravndal, 2018).

Rather than confront this troubling politico-economic situation, the liberal left push these problems outside the realm even of the *Imaginary*. Instead, their political ideology machine is fixated on the usual cultural signifiers of equal opportunity and victimhood as imagined and championed by metropolitan elites who remain insulated from the worst of neoliberalism's destructive impact. Into this gaping hole step the writers of NN with their dark, seductive misrecognitions of the *Imaginary*, reluctant, or perhaps unable to join the dots in neoliberalism's deep generative context, but at least they are brave enough to alert their audience to the disquieting fact that the dots are there, and appearing in a thickening mass.

Meanwhile, in the Nordic hinterlands, rural cultures that once functioned as powerful and reliable tributaries feeding into social democratic electoral politics are either ignored, fantasized, or parodied as coy nostalgic metaphors. Worse, the liberal elite often portray them as the seedbeds of a regressive cultural atavism that threatens to drag culture back into a dark past and reverse the progress the liberal left prides itself as having made over recent decades on behalf of its officially approved victims. The metropolitan-centered liberal left, taught to be fearful of deep political intervention and immersed in the ideology of intersectional reconfiguration, issue-focused social movements, and autonomous 'grassroots' change overseen by a receptive and accommodating social management machine, are in the grip of a fundamental political problem. Their inexperience of the taciturn nuances that constitute rural and former proletarian cultural spaces, and their subsequent inability to make the crucial distinction between regressive, comfortable, progressive, and oppositional elements active in these spaces, have blunted their understanding of what really concerns the people who populate the 'grassroots'.

Inarticulate and articulate expressions of discontent emanating from the old heartlands but not expressed in approved politico-cultural terms are too often dismissed as regressive or dangerously populist. Again, the failure to distinguish between 'the regressive' and 'the oppositional' condemns popular discontent in the eyes of the metropolitan public, to whom it is heard only as a ghostly soundscape, a set of distant and rather chilling howls in the political wilderness. Across the mass media and social media landscape, constant attacks on traditional cultural institutions—work, nation, region, community, family, religion, masculinity, class identity, and so on—have tended to be rather indiscriminate, clumsily conflating them with genuinely regressive sentiments such as racism and sexism.[11] All this, of course, is manna to populist political organizations like the Sweden Democrats and the Norwegian Progress Party, who prosper simply by acknowledging the fact that, in an electoral democracy, traditional collective groups have an inalienable right to genuine political representation and have a role to play in defining nation states as unique, culturally specific places that can modify and improve yet endure as part of any progressive move into the future.

However, instead of acknowledging this in any meaningful way, what we are offered as the art of our time is a peculiar brand of Scandinavian political correctness where the *Real* can occasionally be sensed, but the sources of the external stimuli that activate its conflicting internal proto-symbolic drives can never be afforded full, honest, and contextualized explanations. It is for this reason that we can already discern an emerging new tendency within NN that exceeds even the 'retreatist' and 'sensationalist' tropes outlined previously. In the Swedish TV series *Jordskott* (2015–2017), for example, what starts out as a stock rural police drama quickly morphs into a tale of mystical forest people and spiritual themes linked to ecology. Unworldly tropes also feature in another Swedish crime drama, *Ängleby* (2015), while the recent Norwegian Netflix offering, *Ragnarok* (2020) plunges even deeper into the supernatural. Meanwhile, in literature, an emerging 'Nordic Fantasy Noir' is gaining traction, as works by the likes of Emil Hjörvar Petersen, Hildur Knútsdóttir, and Alexander Dan vie with more established forms of 'realist' NN fiction. These and other recent gratuitously escapist offerings clearly represent the endpoint of NN as originally conceived.[12] But perhaps this was to be expected. Like other crime genres before it, NN has regressed from realism *per se* to something better described as a 'realist aesthetic', and as such we can now see it for what it is. Put bluntly, in its current formulaic form NN, just like many other forms of contemporary popular culture, is simply offering a sublimated and highly stylized set of metaphors to aid neoliberalism in its fundamental politico-cultural task of obscuring and repressing the real contextual sources of insecurity, thus reproducing 'objectless anxiety' expressed as populist suspicion and cynicism.

Conclusion

In comfortable periods life follows art, but in times of disruption we always find the impulse to return to reality—not least because the institutionalized ideology that most art serves falls apart. In such times, art must follow life. Today, however, having lost its grip on the sense of reality that underpinned classic examples of the genre, NN can only mimic this return. Too much contemporary NN simply allows ever-more subjective *Imaginary* misrecognitions to take the place of the reality and the real political interventions the liberal left has sworn will never again be attempted. Therefore, what appears as a revived sensitivity amidst a new reality can be expressed in popular culture in a politically disembedded and safe way. This *Imaginary* field is not as irresponsible and dangerous as those offered by the far right, but its metaphorical vagaries, seductive melancholy, and nostalgic portal to a past that predates social democracy—and in some cases modernity—prolong misrecognition and delay any return to the construction of an efficient *Symbolic Order*.

In 1950, Ingmar Bergman directed the classic Swedish movie *High Tension* about spy rings on the Baltic coast. The original title of the film was to be *These Things Don't Happen Here*, but this idea was scrapped, perhaps because it may have been too literal for the great director. Commenting on the state of Swedish film in 2011, Daniel Brodên (2011:106), concluded that 'the thematic premise of Swedish crime films seems no longer to be "These Things Don't Happen Here", but rather "These Things Do Happen Here"'. In this chapter we have tried to show that Brodên's analysis was only partially correct. Today, as NN continues to drift away from realism towards fantasy, it might be more accurate to say that, while these things do indeed happen here, no one it seems is prepared to confront them in a meaningful, political way.

Notes

1 This chapter is an abridged and modified version of a journal article of the same name that appeared in *The British Journal of Criminology*, Volume 61, Issue 1, January 2021, Pages 1–21, https://doi.org/10.1093/bjc/azaa044.
2 Larsson's mode of feminism is controversial (Gallagher, 2013). For example, the writer NJ Cooper has expressed her concerns about both the graphic use of gendered violence in Larsson's writing and the 'unrealistic toughness' of the Salander character.
3 In contrast to the theme of 'melancholy' in art generally (Holly, 2013), 'Nordic melancholy' is more fundamentally preoccupied with light, climate, nature, and its relationship to emotions like longing, dreaming, and disconsolation (Waade, 2017:383).

4 The *Folkhemmet* ideal was enshrined in Swedish culture by a 1928 speech by then Prime Minister Per Albin Hansson. He declared that the basis for the Swedish people's home was 'togetherness and common feeling' and that under its protection no one would be either 'privileged or unappreciated'.

5 The phrase 'a nightmare that can make us happy' comes from Ken Tucker's *New York Times* review of Lars Kepler's NN potboiler *The Sandman* (2018).

6 Even though there has only ever been one recorded serial killer in Denmark, *Those Who Kill* follows a fictitious unit within the Copenhagen Police Department that specializes in the investigation of serial murders. Laughably, it is not uncommon for protagonists in the series to use the decline of the Danish welfare state as an explanatory mechanism for explaining a serial killer's behaviour.

7 This point is exemplified in the most recent series of *The Bridge*, where one of the detectives is forced to take in two teenage delinquents because neither the police nor the social services can adequately look after them.

8 Lacan's three orders of the psyche are force fields that permeate every mental act. Although each concept is subject to frequent reconfiguration across Lacan's work, for our purposes we can define each order as follows: *the Real*: the order which describes those areas of life that cannot be known. *The Real* defines and shapes our pre-symbolic subjective psychological experience, a milieu of conflicting and unexplained stimuli and drives. The word is capitalized to distinguish it from mere 'reality'; *the Imaginary*: the realm of narcissistic identification, where the ego splits and identifies with some spectral counterpart in the external world. It is a private space of susceptibility and self-deception where desires can easily be seduced and lured by external mediated images; *the Symbolic*: this order defines our psychological experience of everyday life and thus where we try to make sense of social reality. *The Symbolic Order* is therefore simply the social world of communication.

9 The political *Real* = the unexplained external stimuli created by socioeconomic disruption entering the psyche through experience, a process which then functions to activate drives.

10 In Kantian philosophy, the term 'noumenon' is used to describe a posited object or event that exists independently of human sense or perception. As such, it is often used in counterpoint to the term 'phenomenon', which typically refers to something that can be readily apprehended as an object of the senses.

11 It would be comforting to say that academic representations have been more careful and sophisticated, but the dismissal of categories such as class as a 'failed analytic' to be replaced by such crude and provocative stereotypes as 'whiteness' and 'toxic masculinity' would suggest otherwise.

12 Importantly, this is not to suggest that the region will no longer produce its share of outstanding cultural products. Far from it. Indeed, recent offerings such as the Swedish TV series *Caliphate* (2020–present) and the Danish movie *Go with Peace Jamil* (2008) suggest that, when freed from the constraints of the brooding/melancholic Noir aesthetic, art from this region can still be world-leading.

References

Arter, D. (2020). 'When a pariah party exploits its demonised status: The 2019 Finnish general election', *West European Politics*, 43(1):260–273.

Barry, E. and Anderson, C. (2018). 'Hand grenades and gang violence rattle Sweden's middle class', *New York Times*, 3rd March.

Barry, E. and Sorensen, M.S. (2018). 'In Denmark, harsh new laws for immigrant "Ghettos"', *New York Times*, 1 July.

Bergman, K. (2014). *Swedish crime fiction*, Rome: Mimesis.

Brodén, D. (2011). 'The dark ambivalences of the welfare state: Investigating the transformations of the Swedish crime film', *Northern Lights*, 9(1):995–109.

Clayton, J. and Hanrahan, C. (2018). 'Sweden's deadly problem with hand grenades', https://www.bbc.com/news/world-europe-43667367.

Creeber, G. (2015). 'Killing us softly: Investigating the aesthetics, philosophy and influences of *Nordic noir* television', *Journal of Popular Television*, 3(1):21–35.

Davidson, P. (2005). *The idea of north*. London: Reaktion Books.

Edling, N. (2019). *The changing meanings of the welfare state: Histories of a key concept in the Nordic countries*, New York: Berghahn.

Elgenius, G. and Rydgren, J. (2017). 'The Sweden democrats and the ethno-nationalist rhetoric of decay and betrayal', *Sociologisk Forskning*, 54(4):353–358.

Esping-Anderson, G. (1990). *The three worlds of welfare capitalism*, Princeton, NJ: Princeton University Press.

Esping-Anderson, G. and Korpi, W. (1987). 'From poor relief to institutional welfare states: The development of Scandinavian social policy', in: R. Erikson, R.J. Hansen and H. Uusitalo, eds. *The Scandinavian model*, New York: M.E. Sharpe, Inc.

Ferrell, J. (2007). 'For a ruthless critique of everything existing', *Crime, Media, Culture*, 3(1):91–100.

Ferrell, J., Hayward, K. and Young, J. (2015). *Cultural criminology*, London: Sage.

Forshaw, B. (2013a). *Nordic noir*, Harpenden: Pocket Essentials.

Frow, J. (2015). *Genre*, Abingdon: Routledge.

Gallagher, P. (2013). 'Nordic noir's sexual violence attacked by British crime writer', *The Guardian*, 28th September.

Garcia Avis, I. (2015). 'Adapting landscape and place in transcultural remakes: The case of *Bron/Broen*, *The Bridge* and *the Tunnel*', *International Journal of TV Series Narratives*, 1(2):127–138.

Hall, S. (2012a). 'The solicitation of the trap: On transcendence and transcendental materialism in advanced consumer-capitalism', *Human Studies: Special Issue on Transcendence and Transgression*, 35(3):365–338.

Hall, S. (2012b). *Theorizing crime and deviance*, London: Sage.

Hänninen, S., Lehtelä, K.-M. and Saikonnen, P. (2019). *The relational Nordic welfare state*, Cheltenham: Edward Elgar.

Hansen, K.T. and Waade, A.M. (2017). *Locating Nordic noir*, Cham, Switzerland: Palgrave.

Hague, H. (2003). *Post-danmark*, Copenhagen: Lindhardt og Ringhof.

Hayward, K. J. and Presdee, M. (2010). *Framing crime: Cultural criminology and the image*. Abingdon: Routledge.

Hayward, K. J. and Schuilenburg, M. (2014). 'To Resist=to Create?: Some thoughts on the concept of resistance in cultural criminology', *Tijdschrift over Cultuur and Criminaliteit*, 4:22–36.

Hayward, K. and Smith, O. (2017). 'Crime and consumer culture', in: A. Liebling, L. Macara and S. Maruna, eds. *The Oxford handbook of criminology*, Oxford: OUP, pp. 306–328.

Hayward, K. and Turner, T. (2019). '"Be more VIP": Deviant leisure and hedonistic excess in Ibiza's "Disneyized" party spaces', in: T. Raymen and O. Smith, eds. *Deviant Leisure*, New York: Springer, pp. 105–134.

Hedberg, A. (2017). 'The knife in the lemon: Nordic noir and the glocalization of crime fiction', in: L. Nilsson, D. Damrosch and T. D'haen, eds. *Crime fiction as world literature*, London: Bloomsbury, pp. 13–22.

Henley, J. (2019). 'Sweden bomb attacks reach unprecedented level as gangs feud', *The Guardian*, 4th November.

Hentilä, S. (1978). 'The origins of the *folkhem* ideology in Swedish social democracy', *Scandinavian Journal of History*, 3(1–4):323–345.

Hill, A. and Turnball, S. (2017). 'Nordic noir', *Oxford research encyclopedia of criminology and criminal justice*, www.criminology.oxfordre.com.

Holly, M.A. (2013). *The melancholy art*, Princeton, NJ: Princeton University Press.

Honkaphoja, S. (2009). *The 1990's financial crisis in the Nordic countries*, Helsinki: Bank of Finland.

James, C. (2020). 'Bleakness and tenacity: fin-de-siècle French literature and Nordic noir', in: G. Stacey and G. Guðmundsdóttir, eds. *Noir in the north*, London: Bloomsbury, pp. 183–198.

Johnston, A. (2008). *Žižek's ontology*, Evanston, IL: Northwestern University Press.

Kingsley, P. (2012). *How to be Danish*, London: Short Books.

Kølvraa, C. (2019). 'Embodying "the Nordic race": Imaginaries of Viking heritage in the online communications of the Nordic resistance movement', *Patterns of Prejudice*, 53(3):270–284.

Lacan, J. (1964). *The seminar book XI-the four fundamental concepts of psychoanalysis*. J.-A. Miller ed., New York: W.W. Norton.

Mäarklund, S. (1988). *Paradise lost?* Lund: Arkiv.

Nestingen, A. (2008). *Crime and fantasy in Scandinavia*, Seattle: Washington University Press.

Norman, K. (2018). *Sweden's dark soul*, London: Hurst.

Peacock, S. (2014). *Swedish crime fiction*, Manchester: Manchester University Press.

Pratt, J. (2008). 'Scandinavian exceptionalism in an era of penal excess: Part 2: Does scandinavian exceptionalism have a future?', *British Journal of Criminology*, 48:275–292.

Ravndal, J.A. (2018). 'Right-wing terrorism and militancy in the Nordic Countries: A comparative case study', *Terrorism and Political Violence*, 30(5):772–792.

Robbins, B. (2017). 'The detective is suspended: Nordic noir and the welfare state', in: L. Nilsson, D. Damrosch and T. D'haen, eds. *Crime fiction as world literature*, London: Bloomsbury, pp. 47–58.

Rydgren, J. (2004). 'Explaining the emergence of radical right-wing populist parties: The case of Denmark', *West European Politics*, 27: 474–502.

Sedgwick, M. (2013). 'Something varied in the state of Denmark: Neo-nationalism, anti-Islamic activism, and street-level thuggery', *Politics, Religion and Ideology*, 14(2):208–233.

Smith, O. and Raymen, T. (2018). 'Deviant leisure: A criminological perspective', *Theoretical Criminology*, 22:63–82.

Stougaard-Nielsen, J. (2017). *Scandinavian crime fiction*, London: Bloomsbury.

Tapper, M. (2011). 'Dirty Harry in the Swedish welfare state', in: A. Nestingen and P. Arvas, eds. *Scandinavian crime fiction*, Cardiff: University of Wales Press, pp. 21–33.

Teitelbaum, T.R. (2019). 'Tremors from afar: Negotiating the rise of Donald Trump on Sweden's populist right', *Patterns of Prejudice*, 53(5):534–553.

Waade, A.-M. (2011). 'Crime scenes: Conceptualizing Ystad as location in the Swedish and the British Wallander TV crime series', *Northern Lights*, 9(1):9–25.

Waade, A.-M. (2013). *Wallanderland*, Aalborg: Aalborg University Press.

Waade, A.-M. (2017). 'Melancholy in Nordic noir: Characters, landscapes, light and music', *Critical Studies in Television*, 12(4):380–394.

Waade, A.-M. and Jensen, P.M. (2013). 'Nordic noir production values', *Akademisk Kvarter*, 7(Fall):189–201.

Winlow, S., Hall, S. and Treadwell, J. (2017). *The rise of the right*, Bristol: Policy Press.

Žižek, S. (1999). *The Ticklish subject: The absent centre of political ontology*. London: Verso.

Žižek, S. (2003). 'Parallax', *London Review of Books*, 25. 22, 20th November.

Index